The M.   Letters in the Modern World

THE MAN OF LETTERS

IN THE MODERN WORLD

Selected Essays: 1928–1955

ALLEN TATE

Meridian Books
THE WORLD PUBLISHING COMPANY
CLEVELAND AND NEW YORK

Acknowledgments

The original periodical publication, American and foreign, of the essays in this volume was as follows:

The American Scholar: A Reading of Keats; *La Fiera Letteraria* (Rome): The Man of Letters in the Modern World; *Hound & Horn:* Hart Crane (in part); *The Hudson Review:* Longinus and the New Criticism; The Man of Letters in the Modern World; To Whom Is the Poet Responsible?; *The Kenyon Review:* The Angelic Imagination; The Symbolic Imagination; *The Nation:* Ezra Pound; *The New Republic:* Crane: The Poet As Hero; MacLeish's Conquistador; A Note on Donne; A Note on Elizabethan Satire; Edwin Arlington Robinson; *Partisan Review:* Ezra Pound and the Bollingen Prize; Is Literary Criticism Possible?; Our Cousin, Mr. Poe; *Poetry: A Magazine of Verse:* Hart Crane (in part); *Perspectives USA:* The Man of Letters in the Modern World; To Whom Is the Poet Responsible?; *The Sewanee Review:* The Hovering Fly; The Point of Dying; Techniques of Fiction; *The Southern Review:* John Peale Bishop; Literature as Knowledge; Tension in Poetry; Yeats' Romanticism; *The Symposium:* Emily Dickinson; *The Virginia Quarterly Review:* Narcissus as Narcissus; The New Provincialism; The Profession of Letters in the South; *The World Review* (London): The Man of Letters in the Modern World.

A MERIDIAN BOOK
Published by The World Publishing Company
2231 West 110th Street, Cleveland 2, Ohio
First Meridian printing September 1955.
Fifth printing April 1964.
Reprinted from *On the Limits of Poetry* and *The Forlorn Demon* by arrangement with Alan Swallow, Publisher, and Henry Regnery Company.
Library of Congress Catalog Card Number: 55-9689
Printed in the United States of America.   5WP464

Preface

This is the fourth preface that I have written for as many collections of my essays. Again I shrink from the task, which will be brief, and from the results, which I cannot foresee. It might have been more enlightening for myself, to write a review of an imaginary history of my literary opinions, and put it as a postscript at the back of the book, in the hope that few people would read it. On second thought, I could expect other persons to feel even less interest in my critical history than I myself feel. There was also the more ambitious possibility of a history of one's mind. But it is always a question whether one's egoism can be made to look unique, or anything but conventional and boring. To recover the secret motions of the heart, and then to testify, to bear witness, is a good thing for Christians to do; but it requires an innocence of which one can at most say that one may long ago have had it. To lay the heart bare is not at any rate the first obligation of the literary critic. As the particular virtue of the soldier is not statesmanship, and of the nuclear physicist not philosophizing, so the literary critic must not be expected to complete his nature in the public confession of mortal sin (in the French manner), or in the proclamation, rather than the exercise, of intellectual virtue. I suddenly find that I have been thinking of André Gide, who in book after book confessed and proclaimed little else.

The earliest of these essays appeared in a weekly journal twenty-seven years ago; it is nineteen years since some of them were collected in a book; the most recent book, from which I have included several essays, appeared in 1953. The present volume covers some twenty-five years of critical writing. It will be obvious to anybody who has done me the honor of reading my essays over a number of years, that I had to learn as I went along. But it was always necessary to move on, in the intervals between essays, and to think about something else, such as a room where one might write them, and whether the rent could be paid. Another matter for the mendicant poet to think about was poetry itself, and even how he might write some of it. I could echo without too much self-revelation Poe's famous (and humorless) excuse for having published so little verse: there is too much else that one must do—a distraction that frequently includes the prospect of not doing anything. I am not sure that I wanted to write more than three or four of these essays; the others I was asked to write; one can do what one does. I never knew what I thought about anything until I had written about it. To write an essay was to find out what I thought; for I did not know at the beginning how or where it would end.

Many of the opinions put forth in the early essays I no longer hold. I do not think that men can achieve salvation by painting pictures or writing poetry, or by cleaving to an historical or a social tradition; I believe I stopped short of thinking that the State could save us. Some of the early opinions that I still hold seem to be pompously or at least badly expressed. If I fail to cite examples of this fault, it is not merely because I feel responsible for my defects, and am willing to expose them; an imprecise phrase, or an illicit enthymeme, is usually implicated in a way of thinking that would be only superficially improved by a change of diction: small revisions may compound an old error with a new. I have supposed at times that I wanted to write a formal critical enquiry, on one subject, of book length, and I may write it yet (I have started one); but at present I am on record as a casual essayist of whom little consistency can be expected. I am not trying to excuse incoherence (a deeper fault than inconsistency) in the single essay or in the long development from the first essay to the latest. By development I do not mean growth, in the sense of improvement; one cannot know whether one has improved. I mean the gradual discovery of potentialities of the mind that must always have been there. Whether one is made better, or is only made aware of greater complexity, by this discovery, is a question that cannot be answered by the person who asks it about himself.

A critical skeptic cannot entirely imagine the use of a criticism in which the critic takes the deistic part of absentee expositor. To take this role is to pretend that a method can accomplish what the responsible intelligence is alone able to do. The act of criticism is analogous to the peripety of tragedy; it is a crisis of recognition always, and at times also of reversal, in which the whole person is involved. The literary critic is committed, like everybody else, to a particular stance, at a moment in time; he is governed by a point of view that method will not quite succeed in dispensing with. After the natural sciences began to influence literary criticism, scholars held that a point of view without method led inevitably to impressionism. This need not follow; it is obvious why I prefer to think that it need not. Impressionism—"what I like" —is never more intractable than when it is ordered to dine perpetually at the second table. The first table is usually an historical, or a philosophical "method"; but this is by no means the same as historical or philosophical criticism. I should like to think that criticism has been written, and may be again, from a mere point of view, such as I suppose myself to be possessed by. Of the range and direction of a point of view, and why a point of view exists in some persons, nobody can be certain. It seems to take what little life it may have from the object that it tries to see. There is surely little impropriety in describing it negatively, by what it cannot see. Whatever certainties one may cherish as a man—religious, or moral, or merely philosophical—it is almost certain that as literary critic one knows virtually nothing.

A. T.

March 9, 1955

Allen Tate

Allen Tate was born in Clarke County, Kentucky in 1899. Poet, critic, and editor, Mr. Tate is Professor of English at the University of Minnesota. In 1943–44 he held the Chair of Poetry in the Library of Congress, and in 1948 was given the award of the National Institute of Arts and Letters. His books include *The Forlorn Demon, On the Limits of Poetry, Poems: 1922–1947,* and *Stonewall Jackson: The Good Soldier*.

Contents

Contents

THE MAN OF LETTERS IN THE MODERN WORLD

To the question, What should the man of letters be in our time, we should have to find the answer in what we need him to do. He must do first what he has always done: he must recreate for his age the image of man, and he must propagate standards by which other men may test that image, and distinguish the false from the true. But at our own critical moment, when all languages are being debased by the techniques of mass-control, the man of letters might do well to conceive his responsibility more narrowly. He has an immediate responsibility, to other men no less than to himself, for the vitality of language. He must distinguish the difference between mere communication—of which I shall later have more to say—and the rediscovery of the human condition in the living arts. He must discriminate and defend the difference between mass communication, for the control of men, and the knowledge of man which literature offers us for human participation.

The invention of standards by which this difference may be known, and a sufficient minority of persons instructed, is a moral obligation of the literary man. But the actuality of the difference does not originate in the critical intelligence as such; it is exemplified in the specific forms of the literary arts, whose final purpose, the extrinsic end for which they exist, is not the control of other persons, but self-knowledge. By these arts, one means the arts without which men can live, but without which they cannot live well, or live as men. To keep alive the knowledge of ourselves with which the literary arts continue to enlighten the more ignorant portion of mankind (among whom one includes oneself), to separate them from other indispensable modes of knowledge, and to define

11

their limits, is the intellectual and thus the social function of the writer. Here the man of letters is the critic.

The edifying generality of these observations is not meant to screen the difficulties that they will presently encounter in their particular applications. A marked difference between communication and communion I shall be at some pains to try to discern in the remarks that follow. I shall try to explore the assertion: Men in a dehumanized society may communicate, but they cannot live in full communion. To explore this I must first pursue a digression.

What happens in one mind may happen as influence or coincidence in another; when the same idea spreads to two or more minds of considerable power, it may eventually explode, through chain reaction, in a whole society; it may dominate a period or an entire epoch.

When René Descartes isolated thought from man's total being he isolated him from nature, including his own nature; and he divided man against himself. (The demonology which attributes to a few persons the calamities of mankind is perhaps a necessary convention of economy in discourse.) It was not the first time that man had been at war with himself: there was that first famous occasion of immemorial antiquity: it is man's permanent war of internal nerves. Descartes was only the new strategist of our own phase of the war. Men after the seventeenth century would have been at war with themselves if Descartes had never lived. He chose the new field and forged the new weapons. The battle is now between the dehumanized society of secularism, which imitates Descartes' mechanized nature, and the eternal society of the communion of the human spirit. The war is real enough; but again one is conscious of an almost mythical exaggeration in one's description of the combatants. I shall not condescend to Descartes by trying to be fair to him. For the battle is being fought, it has always been fought by men few of whom have heard of Descartes or any other philosopher.

Consider the politician, who as a man may be as good as his quiet neighbor. If he acts upon the assumption (which he has never heard of) that society is a machine to be run efficiently by immoral—or, to him, amoral—methods, he is only exhibiting a defeat of the spirit that he is scarcely conscious of having suffered. Now consider his fellow-citizen, the knowing person, the trained man of letters, the cunning poet in the tradition of Poe and Mallarmé. If this person (who perhaps resembles ourselves) is aware of more, he is able to do less, than the politician, who does not know what he is doing. The man of letters sees that modern societies are machines, even if he thinks that they ought not to be: he is convinced that in its intractable Manicheeism, society cannot be redeemed. The shadowy political philosophy of modern literature, from Proust to Faulkner, is, in its moral origins, Jansenist: we are disciples of Pascal, the merits of whose Redeemer were privately available but could not affect the operation of the power-state. While the politician, in his cynical innocence, uses society, the man of letters disdainfully, or perhaps even absent-mindedly, withdraws from it: a withdrawal that few persons any longer observe, since withdrawal has become the social convention of the literary man, in which society, in so far as it is aware of him, expects him to conduct himself.

It is not improper, I think, at this point, to confess that I have drawn in outline the melancholy portrait of the man who stands before you. Before I condemn him I wish to examine another perspective, an alternative to the double retreat from the moral center, of the man of action and the man of letters, that we have completed in our time. The alternative has had at least the virtue of recommending the full participation of the man of letters in the action of society.

The phrase, "the action of society," is abstract enough to disarm us into supposing that perhaps here and there in the past, if not uniformly, men of letters were hourly participating in it: the supposition is not too deceptive a paralogism, provided we think of society as the City of Augustine and Dante, where it was possible for men to find in the temporal city the imperfect analogue to the City of God. (The Heavenly City was still visible, to Americans, in the political economy of Thomas Jefferson.) What we, as literary men, have been asked to support, and what we have rejected, is the action of society as *secularism,* or the society that substitutes means for ends. Although the idolatry of the means has been egregious enough in the West, we have not been willing to prefer the more advanced worship that prevails in Europe eastward of Berlin, and in Asia. If we can scarcely imagine a society like the Russian, deliberately committing itself to secularism, it is no doubt because we cannot easily believe that men will prefer barbarism to civilization. They come to prefer the senility (which resembles the adolescence) and the irresponsibility of the barbarous condition of man without quite foreseeing what else they will get out of it. Samuel Johnson said of chronic drunkenness: "He who makes a beast of himself gets rid of the pain of being a man." There is perhaps no anodyne for the pains of civilization but savagery. What men may get out of this may be seen in the western world today, in an intolerable psychic crisis expressing itself as a political crisis.

The internal crisis, whether it precede or follow the political, is inevitable in a society that multiplies means without ends. Man is a creature that in the long run has got to believe in order to know, and to know in order to do. For doing without knowing is machine behavior, illiberal and servile routine, the secularism with which man's specific destiny has no connection. I take it that we have sufficient evidence, generation after generation, that man will never be completely or permanently enslaved. He will rebel, as he is rebelling now, in a shocking variety of "existential" disorders, all over the world. If his *human* nature as such cannot participate in the action of society, he will not capitulate to it, if that action is inhuman: he will turn in upon himself, with the common gesture which throughout history has vindicated the rhetoric of liberty: "Give me liberty or give me death." Man may destroy himself but he will not at last tolerate anything less than his full human condition. Pascal said that the "sight of cats or rats is enough to unhinge the reason"—a morbid prediction of our contemporary existential philosophy, a modernized Dark Night of Sense. The impact of mere sensation, even of "cats and rats" (which enjoy the innocence of their perfection in the order of nature)—a simple sense-perception from a world no longer related to human beings —will nourish a paranoid philosophy of despair. Blake's "hapless soldier's sigh," Poe's "tell-tale heart," Rimbaud's nature careening in a "drunken boat," Eliot's woman "pulling her long black hair," are qualities of the life of Baudelaire's *fourmillante Cité,* the secularism of the swarm, of which we are the present citizens.

Is the man of letters alone doomed to inhabit that city? No, we are all in it—the butcher, the baker, the candlestick-maker, and the banker and the statesman. The special awareness of the man of letters, the source at once of his Gnostic arrogance and of his Augustinian humility, he brings to bear upon all men alike: his hell has not been "for those other people": he has reported his own. His report upon his own spiritual condition, in the last hundred years, has misled the banker and the statesman into the illusion that they have no hell because, as secularists, they have lacked the language to report it. What you are not able to name therefore does not exist—a barbarous disability, to which I have already alluded. There would be no hell for modern man if our men of letters were not calling attention to it.

But it is the business of the man of letters to call attention to whatever he is able to see: it is his function to create what has not been hitherto known and, as critic, to discern its modes. I repeat that it is his duty to render the image of man as he is in his time, which, without the man of letters, would not otherwise be known. What modern literature has taught us is not merely that the man of letters has not participated fully in the action of society; it has taught us that nobody else has either. It is a fearful lesson. The roll call of the noble and sinister characters, our ancestors and our brothers, who exemplify the lesson, must end in a shudder: Julien Sorel, Emma Bovary, Captain Ahab, Hepzibah Pyncheon, Roderick Usher, Lambert Strether, Baron de Charlus, Stephen Dedalus, Joe Christmas—all these and more, to say nothing of the precise probing of their, and our, sensibility, which is modern poetry since Baudelaire. Have men of letters perversely invented these horrors? They are rather the inevitable creations of a secularized society, the society of means without ends, in which nobody participates with the full substance of his humanity. It is the society in which everybody acts his part (even when he is most active) in the plotless drama of withdrawal.

I trust that nobody supposes that I see the vast populations of Europe and America scurrying, each man to his tree, penthouse, or cave, and refusing to communicate with other men. Humanity was never more gregarious, and never before heard so much of its own voice. Is not then the problem of communication for the man of letters very nearly solved? He may sit in a sound-proof room, in shirtsleeves, and talk at a metal object resembling a hornet's nest, throwing his voice, and perhaps also his face, at 587,000,000 people, more or less, whom he has never seen, and whom it may not occur to him that in order to love, he must have a medium even less palpable than air.

What I am about to say of communication will take it for granted that men cannot communicate by means of sound over either wire or air. They have got to communicate through love. Communication that is not also communion is incomplete. We *use* communication; we *participate* in communion. "All the certainty of our knowledge," says Coleridge, "depends [on this]; and this becomes intelligible to no man by the ministry of mere words from without. The medium, by which spirits understand each other, is not the surrounding air; but the *freedom* which they possess in common." (The italics are Coleridge's.) Neither the artist nor the statesman will communicate fully again until the rule of love, added to the rule of law, has liberated him. I am not suggesting that we all have an obligation of *personal* love towards one another. I regret that I must be explicit about this matter. No man, under any political dispensation known to us, has been able to avoid hating other men by deciding that it would be a "good thing" to love them; he loves his neighbor, as well as the man he has never seen, only through the love of God. "He that saith that he is in the light, and hateth his brother, is in darkness even until now."

I confess that to the otiose ear of the tradition of Poe and Mallarmé the simple-minded Evangelist may seem to offer something less than a solution to the problem of communication. I lay it down as a fact, that it is the only solution. "We must love one another or die," Mr. Auden wrote more than ten years ago. I cannot believe that Mr. Auden was telling us that a secularized society cannot exist; it obviously exists. He was telling us that a society which has once been religious cannot, without risk of spiritual death, preceded by the usual agonies, secularize itself. A society of means without ends, in the age of technology, so multiplies the means, in the lack of anything better to do, that it may have to scrap the machines as it makes them; until our descendants will have to dig themselves out of one rubbish heap after another and stand upon it, in order to make more rubbish to make more standing-room. The surface of nature will then be literally as well as morally concealed from the eyes of men.

Will congresses of men of letters, who expect from their conversations a little less than mutual admiration, and who achieve at best toleration of one another's personalities, mitigate the difficulties of communication? This may be doubted, though one feels that it is better to gather together in any other name than that of Satan, than not to gather at all. Yet one must assume that men of letters will not love one another personally any better than they have in the past. If there has been little communion among them, does the past teach them to expect, under perfect conditions (whatever these may be), to communicate their works to any large portion of mankind? We suffer, though we know better, from an ignorance which lets us entertain the illusion that in the past great works of literature were immediately consumed by entire populations. It has never been so; yet dazzled by this false belief, the modern man of letters is bemused by an unreal dilemma. Shall he persist in his rejection of the existential "cats and rats" of Pascal, the political disorder of the West that "unhinges the reason"; or shall he exploit the new media of mass "communication"—cheap print, radio, and television? For what purpose shall he exploit them?

The dilemma, like evil, is real to the extent that it exists as privative of good: it has an impressive "existential" actuality: men of letters on both sides of the Atlantic consider the possible adjustments of literature to a mass audience. The first question that we ought to ask ourselves is: *What* do we propose to communicate to *whom?*

I do not know whether there exists in Europe anything like the steady demand upon American writers to "communicate" quickly with the audience that Coleridge knew even in his time as the "multitudinous Public, shaped into personal unity by the magic of abstraction." The American is still able to think that he sees in Europe—in France, but also in England—a closer union, in the remains of a unified culture, between a sufficiently large public and the man of letters. That Alexis St.-Leger Leger, formerly Permanent Secretary of the French Foreign Office, could inhabit the same body with St.-John Perse, a great living French poet, points to the recent actuality of that closer union; while at the same time, the two names for the two natures of the one person suggest the completion of the Cartesian disaster, the fissure in the human spirit of our age; the inner division creating the outer, and the eventual loss of communion.

Another way of looking at the question, *What* do we propose to communicate to *whom?* would eliminate the dilemma, withdrawal *or* communication. It disappears if we understand that literature has never communicated, that it cannot *communicate:* from this point of view we see the work of literature as a participation in communion. Participation leads naturally to the idea of the common experience. Perhaps it is not too grandiose a conception to suggest that works of literature, from the short lyric to the long epic, are the recurrent discovery of the human communion *as experience,* in a definite place and at a definite time. Our unexamined theory of literature as communication could not have appeared in an age in which communion was still possible for any appreciable majority of persons. The word communication presupposes the victory of the secularized society of means without ends. The poet, on the one hand, shouts to the public, on the other (some distance away), not the rediscovery of the common experience, but a certain pitch of sound to which the well-conditioned adrenals of humanity obligingly respond.

The response is not the specifically human mode of behavior; it is the specifically animal mode, what is left of man after Occam's razor has cut away his humanity. It is a tragedy of contemporary society that so much of democratic social theory reaches us in the language of "drive," "stimulus," and "response." This is not the language of freemen, it is the language of slaves. The language of freemen substitutes for these words, respectively, *end, choice,* and *discrimination.* Here are two sets of analogies, the one sub-rational and servile, the other rational and free. (The analogies in which man conceives his nature at different historical moments are of greater significance than his political rhetoric.) When the poet is exhorted to communicate, he is being asked to speak within the orbit of an analogy that assumes that genuine communion is impossible: does not the metaphor hovering in the rear of the word "communication" isolate the poet before he can speak? The poet at a microphone desires to sway, affect, or otherwise influence a crowd (not a community) which is then addressed as if it were permanently over *there* —not *here,* where the poet himself would be a member of it; he is not a member, but a mere part. He stimulates his audience—which a few minutes later will be stimulated by a news-commentator, who reports the results of a "poll," as the Roman *pontifex* under Tiberius reported the color of the entrails of birds—the poet thus elicits a response, in the context of the preconditioned "drives" ready to be released in the audience. Something may be said to have been transmitted, or *communicated;* nothing has been shared, in a new and illuminating intensity of awareness.

One may well ask what these observations have to do with the man of letters in the modern world? They have nearly everything to do with him, since, unless I am wholly mistaken, his concern is with what has not been previously known about our present relation to an unchanging source of knowledge, and with our modes of apprehending it. In the triad of *end, choice,* and *discrimination,* his particular responsibility is for the last; for it is by means of discrimination, through choice, towards an end, that the general intelligence acts. The general intelligence is the intelligence of the man of letters: he must not be committed to the illiberal specializations that the nineteenth century has proliferated into the modern world: specializations in which means are divorced from ends, action from sensibility, matter from mind, society from the individual, religion from moral agency, love from lust, poetry from thought, communion from experience, and mankind in the community from men in the crowd. There is literally no end to this list of dissociations because there is no end yet in sight to the fragmenting of the western mind. The modern man of letters may, as a man, be as thoroughly the victim of it as his conditioned neighbor. I hope it is understood that I am not imputing to the man of letters a personal superiority; if he is luckier than his neighbors, his responsibility, and his capacity for the shattering peripeties of experience, are greater: he is placed at the precarious center of a certain liberal tradition, from which he is as strongly tempted as the next man to escape. This tradition has only incidental connections with political liberalism and it has none with the power-state; it means quite simply the freedom of the mind to discriminate the false from the true, the experienced knowledge from its verbal imitations. His critical responsibility is thus what it has always been—the recreation and the application of literary standards, which in order to be effectively literary, must be more than literary. His task is to preserve the integrity, the purity, and the reality of language wherever and for whatever purpose it may be used. He must approach his task through the letter—the letter of the poem, the letter of the politician's speech, the letter of the law; for the use of the letter is in the long run our one indispensable test of the actuality of our experience.

The letter then is the point to which the man of letters directs his first power, the power of discrimination. He will ask: Is there in this language genuine knowledge of our human community—or of our lack of it—that we have not had before? If there is, he will know that it is liberal language, the language of freemen, in which a choice has been made towards a probable end for man. If it is not language of this order, if it is the language of mere communication, of mechanical analogies in which the two natures of man are isolated and dehumanized, then he will know that it is the language of men who are, or who are waiting to be, slaves.

If the man of letters does not daily renew his dedication to this task, I do not know who else may be expected to undertake it. It is a task that cannot be performed today in a society that has not remained, in certain senses of the word that we sufficiently understand, democratic. We enjoy the privileges of democracy on the same terms as we enjoy other privileges: on the condition that we give something back. What the man of letters returns in exchange for his freedom is the difficult model of freedom for his brothers, Julien Sorel, Lambert Strether, and Joe Christmas, who are thus enjoined to be likewise free, and to sustain the freedom of the man of letters himself. What he gives back to society often enough carries with it something that a democratic society likes as little as any other: the courage to condemn the abuses of democracy, more particularly to *discriminate* the usurpations of democracy that are perpetrated in the name of democracy.

That he is permitted, even impelled by the democratic condition itself, to publish his discriminations of the staggering abuses of language, and thus of choices and ends, that vitiate the cultures of western nations, is in itself a consideration for the second thought of our friends in Europe. Might they not in the end ill prefer the upper millstone of Russia to the nether of the United States? Our formidable economic and military power—which like all secular power the man of letters must carry as his Cross; our bad manners in Europe; our ignorance of the plain fact that we can no more dispense with Europe than almighty Rome could have lived without a reduced Greece; our delusion that we are prepared to "educate" Europe in "democracy" by exporting dollars, gadgets, and sociology—to say nothing of the boorish jargon of the State Department—all this, and this is by no means all, may well tempt (in the words of Reinhold Niebuhr) "our European friends to a virtual Manicheeism and to consign the world of organization to the outer darkness of barbarism." But it should be pointed out, I think, to these same European brothers, that the darkness of this barbarism still shows forth at least one light which even the black slaves of the Old South were permitted to keep burning, but which the white slaves of Russia are not: I mean the inalienable right to talk back: of which I cite the present discourse as an imperfect example.

The man of letters has, then, in our time a small but critical service to render to man: a service that will be in the future more effective than it is now, when the cult of the literary man shall have ceased to be an idolatry. Men of letters and their followers, like the *parvenu* gods and their votaries of decaying Rome, compete in the dissemination of distraction and novelty. But the true province of the man of letters is nothing less (as it is nothing more) than culture itself. The state is the mere operation of society, but culture is the way society lives, the material medium through which men receive the one lost truth which must be perpetually recovered: the truth of what Jacques Maritain calls the "supra-temporal destiny" of man. It is the duty of the man of letters to supervise the culture of language, to which the rest of culture is subordinate, and to warn us when our language is ceasing to forward the ends proper to man. The end of social man is communion in time through love, which is beyond time.

1952

TO WHOM IS THE POET RESPONSIBLE?

And for what? The part of the question that I have used as the title has been widely asked in our generation. I have seldom heard anybody ask the second part: *For what?* I shall have to assume, without elucidating it, a certain moral attitude towards the idea of responsibility which is perhaps as little popular in our time as the accused poetry that has given rise to the controversy. Thus I take it for granted that nobody can be held generally responsible, for if our duties are not specific they do not exist. It was, I think, the failure to say what the modern poet was responsible *for* that made it easy to conclude, from the attacks ten years ago by Mr. MacLeish and Mr. Van Wyck Brooks, that in some grandiose sense the poet should be held responsible to society for everything that nobody else was paying any attention to. The poet was saddled with a total responsibility for the moral, political, and social well-being; it was pretty clearly indicated that had he behaved differently at some indefinite time in the near or remote past the international political order itself would not have been in jeopardy, and we should not perhaps be at international loggerheads today. We should not have had the Second World War, perhaps not even the First.

The historic political suspicion of poetry is one thing; but the attacks that I have alluded to were by men of letters, one of them a poet—and this is another thing altogether. I do not know to what extent the Marxist atmosphere of the thirties influenced the attacks. In trying to get to the bottom of them one may dismiss too quickly the Communist party-line as a perversion of the original Platonic rejection of poetry which holds that the arts of sensible imitation are a menace to the political order. One must dismiss it respectfully, because it contains a fundamental if one-eyed truth: that is to say, from Plato on there is in this tradition of thought the recognition that, however useful poetry may be as a civilizing virtue, it should not be allowed to govern the sensibility of persons who run the state. One may scarcely believe that Sophocles *as poet* was appointed *strategos* in the Samian war, even though that honorific office followed upon the great success of the *Antigone* in the Dionysia of 440 B.C. What I am getting at here is that, were we confronted with an unreal choice, it would be better to suppress poetry than to misuse it, to expect of it an order of action that it cannot provide. (Stalinist Russia seems to do both: it suppresses poetry and supports party verse.) In any literary history that I have read there is no record of a poet receiving and exercising competently high political authority. Milton wrote Cromwell's Latin correspondence, and tracts of his own; but he was never given power; and likewise his successor, Andrew Marvell. We have read some of Shelley's more heroic assertions, in "The Defense of Poetry," into the past, where we substitute what Shelley said ought to have been for what was. The claim that poets are "unacknowledged legislators" is beyond dispute, if we understand that as legislators they should remain unacknowledged and not given the direction of the state. This limit being set, we are ready to understand what Shelley really had to say—which is the true perception that there is always a reciprocal relation between life and art, at that point at which life imitates art.

If poetry makes us more conscious of the complexity and meaning of our experience, it may have an eventual effect upon action, even political action. The recognition of this truth is not an achievement of our own age; it is very old. Our contribution to it I take to be a deviation from its full meaning, an exaggeration and a loss of insight. Because poetry may influence politics we conclude that poetry is merely politics, or a kind of addlepated politics, and thus not good for anything. Why this has come about there is not time to say here, even if I knew. One may point out some of the ways in which it has affected our general views, and hence see how it works in us.

How does it happen that literary men themselves blame the poets first when society goes wrong? The argument we heard ten years ago runs somewhat as follows: The rise of Hitlerism (we were not then looking too narrowly at Stalinism) reflects the failure of our age to defend the principles of social and political democracy, a failure resulting from the apathy of responsible classes of society, those persons who have charge of the means of public influence that was formerly called language (but is now called "communications"). These persons are the writers, more particularly the poets or "makers," whose special charge is the purity of language and who represent the class of writers presumably at its highest. The makers, early in the nineteenth century, retired to a private world of their own invention, where they cultivated certain delusions—for example, their superiority to practical life, the belief in the autonomy of poetry, and the worship of the past. Some of them, like Baudelaire, actively disliked democracy. Their legacy to our tortured age turned out to be at once the wide diffusion and the intensification of these beliefs, with the result that we became politically impotent, and totalitarianism went unchecked.

This argument is impressive and we cannot wholly dismiss it; for directed somewhat differently it points to a true state of affairs: there was a moral and political apathy in the western countries, and there was no decisive stand against Nazism until it was too late to prevent war. Did the men of letters, the "clerks," have a monopoly upon this apathy? We may answer this question from two points of view. First, is there anything in the nature of poetry, as it has been sung or written in many different kinds of societies, which would justify putting so great a burden of *general* responsibility upon the man of imagination? Secondly, was there no other class of "intellectuals" in the modern world—scientists, philosophers, or statesmen—who might also be called into account?

If we address ourselves to the second question first, we shall have to observe that philosophers, scientists, and politicians have by and large assumed that they had no special responsibility for the chaos of the modern world. Mr. Einstein not long ago warned us that we now have the power to destroy ourselves. There was in his statement no reference to his own great and perhaps crucial share in the scientific progress which had made the holocaust possible. If it occurs, will Mr. Einstein be partly to blame, provided there is anybody left to blame him? Will God hold him responsible? I shall not try to answer that question. And I for one should not be willing to take the responsibility, if I had the capacity, of settling the ancient question of how much natural knowledge should be placed in the hands of men whose moral and spiritual education has not been impressive: by such men I mean the majority at all times and places, and more particularly the organized adolescents of all societies known as the military class.

Here we could meditate upon (or if we like better to do it, pray over) the spectacle, not military, widely reported in the newspapers, of the President of Harvard University congratulating his colleagues with evident delight when the first atom bomb was exploded in the desert. Among those present at Los Alamos on July 14, 1945, at five-thirty in the morning, were Mr. Conant and Mr. Bush. "On the instant that all was over," reported the *New York Times,* "these men leaped to their feet, the terrible tension ended, they shook hands, embraced each other and shouted in delight." We have no right to explore another man's feelings, or to say what should please him. Nobody then or since has said that Mr. Conant's emotions, whatever they may have been on that occasion, were irresponsible. Nor do I wish to use Mr. Conant or any other scientist, or administrator of the sciences, as a whipping-boy for his colleagues. Yet it is a fact that we cannot blink, that the Renaissance doctrine of the freedom of unlimited enquiry has had consequences for good and evil in the modern world. This doctrine has created our world; in so far as we are able to enjoy it we must credit unlimited enquiry with its material benefits. But its dangers are too notorious to need pointing out. An elusive *mystique* supports the general doctrine, which may be stated as follows: We must keep up the enquiry, come hell and high water.

One way to deal with this modern demi-religion is to say that a part of its "truth" must be suppressed. I am not ready to say that: I am only ready to point out that it is not suppression of *truth* to decline to commit wholesale slaughter even if we have the means of committing it beyond the reach of any known technique of the past. Is it suppression of truth to withhold from general use the means of exploiting a technique of slaughter? How might it be withheld, should we agree that it is both desirable and possible to do so? If we let government suppress it, government will in the long run suppress everything and everybody else—even democratic government. There is no just way of holding individuals and classes responsible for the moral temper of an entire civilization.

At this point the theologians and humanists, the men of God and the men of man, appear—or at any rate formerly appeared. The Christian religion, in its various sects, has been blamed for its historic conservatism in refusing to sanction the advances of science as they were made. It is my impression that this supposedly Christian skepticism is Arabic in origin. It was the followers of Averroës in Europe who upheld the secret cult of natural knowledge against the Thomists and the Scotists, who more than the disciples of Roger Bacon stood for the diffusion of scientific enquiry. It is significant that the one science of the ancient world that impinged directly upon the daily lives of men—medicine—was held to be esoteric; the school of Hippocrates hid the secrets of the "art" lest the uninitiate abuse them and pervert them to the uses of witchcraft. This is not the place, and I am not competent enough, to follow up this line of speculation. I have wished only to observe that before the Christian dispensation, and well into it, the professors of special knowledge tried to be responsible for the public use of their techniques. We have not, so far as I know, a record of any of their reasons for what we should consider an illiberal suppression of truth. But if we think of the Greek world of thought as having lasted about nine hundred years, down to the great pupils of Plotinus—Iamblichus and Porphyrius—we may see in it a sense of the whole of life which must not be too quickly disturbed for the prosecution of special scientific interests. Nature was investigated, but it was a nature whose destiny in relation to a transcendental order was already understood. The classical insight into this relation was, as usual, recorded very early in a myth—that of the brothers Prometheus and Epimetheus—which now gives signs of recovering the authority which in the modern world it had yielded to myths that science had created about itself.

The responsibility of the scientist has not, I am sure, been defined by this digression: I have merely suggested that if anybody have a specific responsibility it may be the scientist himself. His myth of omnipotent rationality has worked certain wonders; but perhaps a little too rapidly. In Shelley's "Defense of Poetry" there is a sentence that persons who press the poet to legislate for us seldom quote: "Our calculations have outrun conception; we have eaten more than we can digest." Shall we hold the scientists responsible for this? Have they made the child sick on green apples? I do not say that they have. But the child is sick. If the scientist is not responsible, are philosophers, statesmen, and poets, particularly poets, responsible?

Before I return to the poet's responsibility, I shall consider briefly the possible responsibility of other persons, excluding this time the scientists, about whom it has become evident that I know little; and I can scarcely do more than allude to the other intellectual classes whose special disciplines might conceivably implicate them in care for the public good. Of the philosophers I likewise speak with neither information nor knowledge. Like Mr. Santayana, I might somewhat presumptuously describe myself as "an ignorant man, almost a poet." But one gets strongly the impression that the classical metaphysical question—What is the nature of Being?—is semantically meaningless in our age, a mere historicism reserved for the frivolous occasions of lecture-room philosophy. Our going philosophy is reported to me as a curious, apostolic activity known as the "philosophy of science," an attempt to devise a language for all the sciences which through it would arrive at "unity." This is no doubt a laudable program, unity being usually better than disunity, unless the things to be joined do not like each other, or, again, unless the union take place at a level of abstraction at which certain things become excluded, such as human nature, of which the Nazi and the Stalinist unities for some reason took little account. But these are unities of the political order. What have the philosophers of unified science to do with them? They glanced at them, I believe, in resolutions passed at philosophical congresses, or in interviews for the press, where we were told that things will continue to go badly until men behave more rationally. Rationality usually turned out to be liberalism, or the doctrine that reason, conceived in instrumental terms, will eventually perfect us, even though our situation may be getting worse every day. This, it seems to me, was the contribution of certain philosophers to the recent war. Was the contribution responsible or irresponsible? Common sense ought to tell us that it was neither; and common sense tells us that not all philosophers talked this way. Everybody knows that modern philosophers, like their brother scientists, and not unlike their distant cousins the poets, are pursuing specialisms of various kinds; and from the point of view of these interests, the investigation of the nature of being, with the attendant pursuit of the love of wisdom, is no more within their purview than it is within mine. In his extra-laboratory pronouncements the merged philosopher-scientist sounds uncomfortably like his famous creation in allegorical fiction, the "man in the street"—the man without specialisms who used to sit on the cracker barrel, and who, in all ages since hats were invented, has talked through his hat. Perhaps it was neither responsible nor irresponsible: it was merely dull to use the prestige of the philosophy of science as the stump from which to deliver commonplaces that were already at your and my command and that were doing us so little good that they might be suspected of having caused a part of our trouble. Reason— in the sense of moderate unbelief in difficult truths about human nature—and belief in the perfectibility of man-in-the-gross, were the great liberal dogmas which underlay much of our present trouble. The men in charge of nature never told me that I ought to try to perfect myself; that would be done for me by my not believing that I could do anything about it, by relying upon history to do it, by the invocation of ideals that many of us thought were democratic, by the resolutions of committees, conventions, and associations; and not least by condescending affirmations of faith in the Common Man, a fictitious person with whom neither the philosopher-scientist nor I had even a speaking acquaintance. Will it not be borne in upon us in the next few years that Hitler and Stalin *are* the Common Man, and that one of the tasks of democracy is to allow as many men as possible to make themselves uncommon?

Thus it is my impression that belief in a false liberal democracy was not lacking among certain classes of "intellectuals" in the period between the wars: the period, in fact, in which Mr. MacLeish and Mr. Brooks said that we had staggered into a war that might have been prevented had the men of letters not given us such a grim view of modern man from their ivory towers, or simply refused to be concerned about him. If the more respectable "intellectuals" were not heeded in the call to democratic action, would the mere literary men have been heeded? Was the poet's prestige so great that his loss of democratic faith (assuming he had lost it) set so bad an example that it offset the testimony to the faith of even the statesman?

By the statesman one means, of course, the politician, though one would like to mean more, whether he carry the umbrella or the infectious smile, the swastika or the hammer-and-sickle. It would seem to have been the specific duty of the politician to have kept the faith and forestalled the rise of Nazism, though it was not generally supposed that it was up to him to do anything about Soviet Russia, which was tacitly assumed, if not by you and me, then by the leaves in Vallombrosa, to be on our side. My own disappointment in the politician is somewhat mitigated by the excuse which his failure provides for the poet: if he could not baulk the enemy, whom he directly confronted, what chance had the poet?—the poet, whose best weapon in history seems to have been Shelley's fleet of toy boats, each bearing a cargo of tracts, which he committed to the waters of Hyde Park.

I am sorry to sound frivolous; I confess that the political responsibility of poets bores me; I am discussing it because it irritates me more than it bores me. It irritates me because the poet has a great responsibility of his own: it is the responsibility to be a poet, to write poems, and not to gad about using the rumor of his verse, as I am now doing, as the excuse to appear on platforms and to view with alarm. I have a deep, unbecoming suspicion of such talking poets: whatever other desirable things they may believe in, they do not believe in poetry. They believe that poets should write tracts, or perhaps autobiographies, encourage the public, further this cause or that, good or bad, depending upon whose political ox is being gored.

My own political ox was at least driven into a fence-corner when Mr. Pound thumped his tub for the Axis; but what I cannot easily forgive him was thumping any tub at all—unless, as a private citizen, dissociated from the poet, he had decided to take political action at some modest level, such as giving his life for his country, where whatever he did would be as inconspicuous as his ejaculatory political philosophy demanded that it be. But on Radio Rome he appeared as Professor Ezra Pound, the great American Poet. Much the same can be said of Mr. MacLeish himself. It is irrelevant that I find his political principles (I distinguish his *principles* from his *views*), in so far as I understand them, more congenial than Mr. Pound's. The immediate *views* of these poets seem to me equally hortatory, quasi-lyrical, and ill-grounded. We might imagine for them a pleasant voyage in one of Percy Shelley's boats. If society indicted and condemned poets for the mixture and the misuse of two great modes of action, poetry and politics, we might have to indict Mr. Pound a second time, as it could conceivably be done in some Swiftian social order; and we should have in fairness to provide an adjoining cell for Mr. MacLeish.

The relation of poetry and of other high imaginative literature to social action was not sufficiently considered in the attacks and counter-attacks of the past ten years. No one knows precisely what the relation is; so I shall not try here to define it; though what I am about to say will imply certain assumptions. There is no doubt that poetry, even that of Mallarmé, has some effect upon conduct, in so far as it affects our emotions. To what extent is the poetry itself, even that of Mallarmé, an effect? The total complex of sensibility and thought, of belief and experience, in the society from which the poetry emerges, is the prime limiting factor that the poet must first of all be aware of; otherwise his language will lack primary reality, the nexus of thing and word. The failure to consider this primary reality produces willed poetry which usually ignores the human condition. The human condition must be faced and embodied in language before men in any age can envisage the possibility of action. To suggest that poets tell men in crisis what to do, to insist that *as poets* they acknowledge themselves as legislators of the social order, is to ask them to shirk their specific responsibility, which is quite simply the reality of man's experience, not what his experience ought to be, in any age. *To whom* is the poet responsible? He is responsible to his *conscience*, in the French sense of the word: the joint action of knowledge and judgment. This conscience has long known a severe tradition of propriety in discerning the poet's particular kind of actuality. No crisis, however dire, should be allowed to convince us that the relation of the poet to his permanent reality can ever change. And thus the poet is not responsible to society for a version of what it thinks it is or what it wants. *For what* is the poet responsible? He is responsible for the virtue proper to him as poet, for his special *arête:* for the mastery of a disciplined language which will not shun the full report of the reality conveyed to him by his awareness: he must hold, in Yeats' great phrase, "reality and justice in a single thought."

We have virtually turned the argument of the attack around upon itself. For it was an irresponsible demand to ask the poet to cease to be a poet and become the propagandist of a political ideal, even if he himself thought it a worthy ideal. If the report of the imagination on the realities of western culture in the past century was as depressing as the liberal mind said it was, would not the scientist, the philosopher, and the statesman have done well to study it? They might have got a clue to what was wrong. They were, I believe, studying graphs, charts, and "trends"—the indexes of power—but not human nature. The decay of modern society is nowhere more conspicuous than in the loss of the arts of reading on the part of men of action. It was said at the beginning of the war that the traditions of modern literature represented by Proust had powerfully contributed to the collapse of Europe. It was not supposed that the collapse of Europe might have affected those traditions. If the politicians had been able to read Proust, or Joyce, or even Kafka, might they not have discerned more sharply what the trouble was, and done something to avert the collapse? I doubt it; but it makes as much sense as the argument that literature can be a cause of social decay. If, for example, Mr. Churchill had been able to quote the passage about Ciacco from the *Inferno,* or the second part of *The Waste Land,* instead of Arthur Hugh Clough, might we have hoped that men would now be closer to the reality out of which sound political aspiration must arise?

I leave this subject with the observation that poetry had to be attacked for not having done all that men had expected of it at the end of the nineteenth century. "The future of poetry is immense," said Matthew Arnold. It had to be immense because, for men like Arnold, everything else had failed. It was the new religion that was destined to be lost more quickly than the old. Poetry was to have saved us; it not only hadn't saved us by the end of the fourth decade of this century; it had only continued to be poetry which was little read. It had to be rejected. The primitive Athenians, at the Thargelian festival of Apollo, killed two human beings, burnt them, and cast their ashes into the sea. The men sacrificed were called *pharmakoi:* medicines. We have seen in our time a powerful attempt to purify ourselves of the knowledge of evil in man. Poetry is one of the sources of that knowledge. It is believed by some classical scholars that the savage ritual of the *pharmakoi* was brought to Athens by Barbarians. In historical times effigies made of dough were substituted for human beings.

1951

LITERATURE AS KNOWLEDGE

Comment and Comparison

Matthew Arnold's war on the Philistines was fought, as everybody knows; but nobody thinks that it was won. Arnold conducted it in what he considered to be the scientific spirit. The Philistines had a passion for "acting and instituting," but they did not know "what we ought to act and to institute." This sort of knowledge must be founded upon "the scientific passion for knowing." But it must not stop there. Culture, which is the study of perfection and the constant effort to achieve it, is superior to the scientific spirit because it includes and passes beyond it. Arnold was, in short, looking for a principle of unity, but it must be a unity of experience. There was before him the accumulating body of the inert, descriptive facts of science, and something had to be done about it.

Yet if it is true, as T. S. Eliot said many years ago, that were Arnold to come back he would have his work to do over again, he would at any rate have to do it very differently. His program, culture added to science and perhaps correcting it, has been our program for nearly a century, and it has not worked. For the facts of science are not inert facts waiting for the poet, as emblematic guardian of culture, to bring to life in the nicely cooperative enterprise of scientist and poet which the nineteenth century puts its faith in. In this view the poet is merely the scientist who achieves completeness. "It is a result of no little culture," Arnold says, "to attain to a clear perception that science and religion are two wholly different things." Religion had yielded to the "fact" of science, but poetry on a positive scientific base could take over the work of religion, and its future was "immense."

34

The "fact" had undermined religion, but it could support poetry.

Although Arnold betrayed not a little uneasiness about this easy solution, it was his way of putting literature upon an equal footing with science. If Arnold failed, can we hope to succeed? Whether literature and science considered philosophically, as Coleridge would phrase it, are the same thing, or different but equal, or the one subordinate to the other, has become a private question. It does not concern the public at large. While Arnold's poet was extending the hand of fellowship to the scientist, the scientist did not return the greeting; for never for an instant did he see himself as the inert and useful partner in an enterprise of which he would not be permitted to define the entire scope. He was not, alas, confined to the inertia of fact; his procedure was dynamic all along; and it was animated by the confident spirit of positivism which has since captured the modern world.

Had he been what Arnold thought he was, how conveniently the partnership would have worked! For what was Arnold's scientist doing? He was giving us exact observation and description of the external world. The poet could give us that, and he could add to it exact observation and description of man's inner life, a realm that the positivist would never be so bold as to invade. But the poet's advantage was actually twofold. Not only did he have this inner field of experience denied to the scientist, he had a resource which was his peculiar and hereditary right—figurative language and the power of rhetoric.

If the inert fact alone could not move us, poetic diction could make it moving by heightening it; for poetry is "thought and art in one." This is an injustice to Arnold; he was a great critic of ideas, of currents of ideas, of the situation of the writer in his time; and from this point of view his theory of poetry is of secondary importance. But since I am now interested in the failure, ours as well as his, to understand the relation of poetry and science, it has been necessary to put his poetic theory in terms that will bring out its defects. On one side it is an eighteenth-century view of poetic language as the rhetorical vehicle of ideas; and it is connected with Arnold's famous definition of religion as "morality touched with emotion." Poetry is descriptive science or experience at that level, touched with emotion.

If Arnold had taste, he had very simple analytical powers, and we are never quite convinced by his fine quotations from the poets. Why is this so? Because he admires good things for bad reasons; or because at any rate his reasons invariably beg the question. In the famous passage on Dryden and Pope in "The Study of Poetry," these poets are not poetic because they are not *poetic*. (Arnold himself is responsible for the italics.) And he looks to us for immediate assent to a distinction between a "prose" classic and a "poetic" classic that has not been actually made. He cites his "touchstones" for the purpose of moving us, and the nice discrimination of feeling which awareness of the touchstones induces will permit us to judge other passages of verse in terms of feeling. The "high seriousness" is partly the elevated tone, a tone which is a quality of the poet's feeling about his subject: it is the poet's business to communicate it to the reader.

This attitude, this tone, centers in emotion. But its relation to what it is about, whether it is external to the subject or inherent in it, Arnold refuses to make clear. The high seriousness may be said to reflect the subject, which must have Aristotelian magnitude and completeness. Arnold had a shrewd sense of the disproportions of tone and subject which he developed into a principle in the Preface to the 1853 edition of his poems. He was suppressing the very fine "Empedocles on Aetna" because, he said, it has no action; it is all passive suffering; and passive suffering is not a proper subject for poetry. (A view that has been revived in our time by the late W. B. Yeats.) Action, then, is the subject of the greatest poetry. This conviction is so strong—who will question its rightness, *as far as it goes?*—that he actually puts into quotation marks words which are not quoted from anybody at all but which represent for him the consensus of the ancients on the importance of action: " 'All depends upon the subject; choose a fitting action, penetrate yourself with the feeling of its situations; this done, everything else will follow.' " But will everything else follow? Does a great style follow? To a gift for action Shakespeare "added a special one of his own; a gift, namely, of happy, abundant, and ingenious expression. . . ." I think we should attend closely here to the words "added" and "ingenious," for they reveal Arnold's view of the function of language. And suppose you have lyric poetry which may be, like Arnold's own fine lyrics, more meditative than dramatic, and more concerned with the futility of action than with action itself? It has never, I believe, been pointed out that the Preface of 1853 cuts all the props from under lyric poetry. The lyric at its best is "dramatic," but there is no evidence that Arnold thought it so; for the lyric, though it may be a moment of action, lacks magnitude and completeness; it may be the beginning, or the middle, or the end, but never all three. What, then, is the subject of the lyric? Is it all feeling, nothing but feeling? It is feeling about "ideas," not actions; and the feeling communicates "power and joy."

This gross summary of Arnold's poetics omits all the sensitive discriminations that he felt in reading the poets; it omits all but the framework of his thought. Yet the framework alone must concern us on this occasion. Arnold is still the great critical influence in the universities, and it is perhaps not an exaggeration of his influence to say that debased Arnold is the main stream of popular appreciation of poetry. It would be fairer to say that Arnold the critic was superior to his critical theory; yet at the distance of three generations we may look back upon his lack of a critical dialectic—he even had a certain contempt for it in other critics—as a calamity for that culture which it was his great desire to strengthen and pass on.

His critical theory was elementary, and if you compare him with Coleridge a generation earlier, he represents a loss. His position is nearer to the neo-classicism of Lessing, whom he praises in *Culture and Anarchy* for humanizing knowledge, a leveling-off of distinctions of which Lessing as a matter of fact was not guilty. He shares with Lessing the belief—but not its dialectical basis—that the language of poetry is of secondary importance to the subject, that it is less difficult than the medium of painting, and that, given the action, all else follows.

This remnant of neo-classicism in Arnold has been ably discerned by Mr. Cleanth Brooks in *Modern Poetry and the Tradition*. I go into it here not to deny that action is necessary to the long poem; for Arnold's view contains a fundamental truth. But it is not the whole truth; asserted in his terms, it may not be a truth at all. The important question goes further. It is: What is the relation of language to the "subject," to the dramatic and narrative subject as action, or to the lyrical subject as "idea"? The question may be pushed even further: Is it possible finally to distinguish the language from the subject? Are not subject and language one?

For Arnold the subject is what we commonly call the prose subject; that is to say, as much of the poetic subject as we can put into ordinary prose. The poet takes it up at the level at which the scientist—or Arnold's simulacrum of him—takes it: the level of observation and description. The poet now puts it into language that will bring the inert facts to life and move us. The language is strictly what Mr. Richards calls the "vehicle"—it does not embody the subject; it conveys it and remains external to it.

For what are action and subject? The positivists have their own notion of these terms; and their language of physical determinism suits that notion better than the poet's. The poet's language is useless.

II

Is it not easy to see how such a poetics gives the case for poetry away to the scientist? Not to Arnold's straw scientist, who politely kept to his descriptive place and left to literature man's evaluation of his experience; but to the scientist as he is: a remarkably ingenious and dynamic fellow whose simple fanaticism brooks no compromise with his special projects. Whatever these on occasion may be, he demands an exact one-to-one relevance of language to the objects and the events to which it refers. In this relevance lies the "meaning" of all terms and propositions in so far as they are used for the purpose of giving us valid knowledge. It is, of course, knowledge for action; and apart from this specific purpose, the problem of meaning is not even a real problem.

"Meaning" has been replaced by a concept of "operational validity"—that is to say, the "true" meaning of a term is not its definition; it is the number of statements containing it which can be referred to empirically observed events. Along with meaning and definition, universals also disappear; and with universals, cognition. A proposition does not represent an act of knowing by a knower—that is, a mind; it is, in a chemical metaphor, the expression of an interaction among certain elements of a "situation."

This advanced position in the philosophy of science has been set forth in the new *International Encyclopedia of Unified Science,* which is being published serially at the University of Chicago. Of great interest from the point of view of literary criticism are the brilliant studies of "semiosis," or the functioning of language as "signs." Mr. Charles W. Morris' "Foundations for the Theory of Signs," [1] is a model of exact exposition in a field of enormous complication. This field is popularly known as "semantics," but semantics in any exact sense is only one "dimension" of semiosis. In this brief glance at the aesthetic and critical implications of Mr. Morris' writings, his theory as a whole cannot be set forth.

Semiosis is the actual functioning of language in three dimensions which are located and described by means of the science of "semiotic." Semiotic, then, is the study of semiosis. The three dimensions in which all language, verbal, or mathematical, functions are: (1) the semantical, (2) the syntactical, and (3) the pragmatical; and the respective studies in these dimensions are semantics, syntactics, and pragmatics. It must be borne in mind that in semiosis the three dimensions are never separate; in semiotic they are distinguished abstractly for study. Semiotic looks towards the formation of rules which will govern the use of all language (signs), and it lays claim to an ultimate unification of all "knowledge."

That need not concern us here. Let us take a simple de-clarative sentence: "This county has an annual rainfall of fifty-one inches." From the semantical point of view the sen-tence designates certain conditions, or a situation: it is the "sign-vehicle" for that designation. If upon investigation we find that the situation actually exists, then it has not only been designated; it has also been *denoted*. From the syn-tactical point of view we are not concerned with what the sign-vehicle points to; for syntactics deals with the formal structure of the sentence, the relations of the words. From the pragmatical point of view the meaning of the sentence is the effect it has upon somebody who hears it or reads it. If I am about to buy a farm in this county, and learn that "this county has an annual rainfall of fifty-one inches," I may go elsewhere; at the moment I hear the sentence I may light a cigarette, or look the other way, or laugh, or swear. All this behavior would be the functioning of the sign in the pragmatic dimension.

The complex possibilities of semiotic may not be evident in this crude summary. Mr. Morris says: "The sign vehicle it-self is simply one object." It is an object that may function in other sign-vehicles; it may be designated, denoted, or re-acted to; and the process is infinite. The identification of signs and their relations is equally complex. There are, for example, a characterizing sign, a symbolic sign, an indexical sign, and an iconic sign; and any of these, in certain con-texts, may function as any other. I shall return to them pres-ently.

The only philosophic criticism of this system that I have seen is Howard D. Roelofs' article in the symposium on the "New Encyclopedists," published in the *Kenyon Review* (Spring 1939). Mr. Roelofs is concerned with Mr. Morris' rejection of the problem of universals and of cognition. It ought to be plain from my brief exposition of the pragmatic dimension of semiosis that the significant factor is what I *do,* not what I *think* leading to what I do; and that thus the bias of the science of semiotic is pragmatic in the ordinary sense, and even behavioristic. For Mr. Morris says: "A 'concept' [i.e., a universal] may be regarded as a semantical rule determining the use of characterizing signs." Mr. Roelofs' comment is interesting:

> *Morris has no trouble with this problem* [*i.e., the problem of universals*]. *It is simply a rule of our language that such a term as "man" can be used as often as the conditions stated in its definition are fulfilled. That makes the term a universal. If we then ask how it happens those conditions are in fact frequently fulfilled, we are informed, "It can only be said the world is such." And those who are tempted by this fact to believe that universals are somehow objective, functioning in nature, are silenced with a threat: to talk as if universals were entities in the world is "to utter pseudo-thing sentences of the quasi-semantical type."* . . . *the heart of the problem is dismissed with a phrase and a language rule offered as a solution.*

The bearing of Mr. Roelofs' criticism will be plainer in a moment. Now Mr. Morris, in discussing the syntactical dimension, says: "Syntactics, as the study of the syntactical relations of signs to one another *in abstraction* from the relations of signs to objects or to interpreters [persons], is the best developed of all the branches of semiotic." Exactly; because syntactics comes out of traditional formal logic and grammar, and because it "deliberately neglects what has here been called the semantical and the pragmatical dimensions of semiosis."

The role of syntactics in the semiotic science remains somewhat obscure; it seems to consist in a number of "transformation rules"—that is, in formulas by which given expressions in words, numbers, or symbols can be changed into equivalent but formally different expressions. What power of the mind there may be which enables us in the first place to form these expressions nowhere appears. (I daresay this statement is of the quasi-semantical type.) But Mr. Morris tells us how we are to think of the rules of the three dimensions of semiotic:

> *Syntactical rules determine the sign relations between sign vehicles; semantical rules correlate sign vehicles with other objects; pragmatical rules state the conditions in the interpreters under which the sign vehicle is a sign. Any rule when*

*actually in use operates as a type of behavior, and in this sense
there is a pragmatical component in all rules.*

If we imagine with Mr. Roelofs a situation in which semiosis is functioning, we shall see pretty clearly the behavioristic tendency of the science of semiotic; and we shall also see in what sense "there is a pragmatical component in all rules." A simplified process of semiosis, or the actual functioning of signs, is very easy to state. There is first of all the sign, which we get in terms of a sign-vehicle. It looks two ways; first, it points to something, designates something; and, secondly, what is designated elicits a response from persons who are present. The thing pointed to is thus the *designatum;* the response is the *interpretant.* By implication there is an interpreter, a person, a mind; but Mr. Morris is consistently vague about him: he is not a technical factor, he is a superfluous entity, in semiosis. That is to say, not only is he not needed in order to explain the functioning of signs; he would embarrass the explanation. Mr. Roelofs makes this clear, as follows:

*The innocent reader will take the analysis of the use of signs
to be the analysis of a cognitive process. The correctness of
the analysis as far as it goes conceals the fact that cognition
itself has been eliminated. Consider this illustration. A maid
enters the room and says to the three persons present, "The
doctor called." One person thereupon takes a pen and writes
a line in a diary; the second goes to a telephone and makes a
call; the third says, "Did he?" According to the analysis offered by Morris, the words uttered by the maid are the sign-
vehicle. The actual call of the doctor is the denotatum.[2] The
three persons are the interpreters, and their three different
actions are the interpretants, the responses of the interpreters
to the denotatum via the sign-vehicle. No one is likely to deny
these factors are present. It should be noted that the interpretants, to the extent that they are a sequence of physical actions,
can be perceived. It should also be noted that such sequences
of action are not cognitions . . . they are "interpretants," but
their being such depends upon the cognitions of the interpreters. These responses are not themselves knowledge. They do
depend upon knowledge, and that is precisely what Morris
leaves out. . . . Morris objects to the term "meaning." This is*

not surprising. His analysis leaves out meaning in the primary sense of meaning. This is not to say that meanings are "like marbles" [Morris' phrase]. Meanings, indeed, like knowledge in general, are a unique kind of thing. There is literally nothing like knowledge except knowledge itself.

I have quoted Mr. Roelofs at length because what he has to say about the problem of cognition bears directly upon the semiotic version of the aesthetic problem. He sums up his argument:

The procedure culminates in eliminating not only universals, but cognition itself. Just as the answer to the problem of universals is that they do not exist [that is, they are only a semantical rule], the answer to the problem of knowledge is that there is no such thing. There are responses, but no cognition; there is a language, but not knowledge. Knowledge cannot be reduced to exclusively perceptual terms. Therefore it does not exist. This is not empiricism. It is positivism. [Roman mine.]

In this positivist technique for the analysis of language, the interpreting mind, the cognizing intelligence, is lost in the perceptual account of its external behavior. Mr. Morris says: "In general, from the point of view of behavior, signs are 'true' in so far as they correctly determine the expectations of the users, and so release more fully the behavior which is implicitly aroused in the expectation or interpretation."

In Mr. Morris' aesthetics there is an aesthetic sign. Does it implicitly—or explicitly—arouse expectations in terms of behavior? Does it correctly determine our expectations? Is the aesthetic sign "true" in that it is a determinant of our behavior? Mr. Morris is not unequivocal in his answers to these questions.

III

No—and yes, replies Mr. Morris, in two essays[3] the cunning and scholastic ingenuity of which make even the beautiful essay on the general theory of signs look amateurish. No, he says, because the aesthetic sign is a special sort of sign: it is *iconic*. It does not correctly determine our behavior. Yes, because it bears the formidable responsibility of showing us what we ought to try to get out of our behavior. The function of the aesthetic sign is nothing less than the "vivid presentation" of *values,* a presentation that is not only vivid, but *immediate*—without mediation—for direct apprehension. The iconic sign, in other words, designates without denoting; or if it does denote anything its *denotatum* is already in its own "properties." "In certain kinds of insanity," writes Mr. Morris, "the distinction between the designatum and the denotatum vanishes; the troublesome world of existences is pushed aside, and the frustrated *interests* [italics mine] get what satisfaction they can in the domain of signs. . . ." Likewise *designata* and *denotata* become in aesthetics the same thing; but in this logical shuffle, worthy of a thirteenth-century *doctor subtilis,* the aesthetic sign is never confused "with the object it designates." It is that alone which saves it from the ignominy of insanity.

The difficulties of this theory must already be apparent. First, the difference between insanity and art is the hair's-breadth line, in the interpreter's response to the sign, between substituting the sign for reality and maintaining the distinction between sign and reality. The first question that one must ask, then, is this: With what does the interpreter make this distinction? If the distinction is not inherent in the nature of the sign, does the interpreter not perform an act of cognition? If the distinction is a mere interpretant, a behavioristic response, why do we not respond to a work of art uniformly; and why is that uniform response in every case not insane *unless we are capable of a primary act of knowledge,* of simply knowing the difference?

Secondly, if art is the realm of values—that is, if the peculiar nature of the aesthetic sign is that it shall convey values—the values must be inherent in the aesthetic sign, and must therefore compel in the interpreter the distinction between value and insanity; so that there is no possibility that the interpreter, who is incapable of cognition, will confuse the mere sign with reality. For the nature of the sign must determine the interpretant, or response.

There must therefore be a special "differentia" for the aesthetic sign that distinguishes it from all other signs whatever. "Lyric poetry," Mr. Morris says, "has a syntax and uses terms which designate things, but the syntax and the terms are so used that what stand out for the reader are values and evaluations." [4] Does not Mr. Morris confess his difficulty when he uses the vague metaphorical expression "stand out" and the even more vague "so used"? Just what is this use? It is significant that in Mr. Morris' two articles on aesthetics, in which the word poetry frequently appears, there is no actual analysis of a passage or even of a line of verse; and not even a quotation from any poem in any language. He contents himself with assertions that the future of semiotic in the field of poetry is immense, and that only the work has to be done.

Now, if the contradiction that I have pointed out in general terms exists, we may see its origin if we examine further Mr. Morris' idea of the aesthetic sign. It is a special variety of the iconic sign. To illustrate this it will be sufficient to relate the iconic to the characterizing sign, and to distinguish the icon from the symbol.

A characterizing sign [he says] characterizes that which it can denote. Such a sign may do this by exhibiting in itself the properties an object must have to be denoted by it, and in this case the characterizing sign is an icon; *if this is not so, the characterizing sign may be called a* symbol. *A photograph, a star chart, a model, a chemical diagram, are icons, while the word "photograph," the names of the stars and of chemical elements are symbols.*

The terminology is quite special. Icon is the Greek (εἰκών) for a sculptured figure. Ordinarily a symbol is what Mr. Morris claims for the icon: it exhibits in itself the qualities it stands for—like Christ on the Cross; or it represents by convention something other than itself, like πr^2 for the circumference of a circle. But here the terms are roughly equivalent, icon to image, symbol to concept; but only roughly, since in Mr. Morris' list of symbols "photograph" is not any particular photograph, while the name of a star must be the name of a particular star. There is a fundamental obscurity, that we shall have to pass over, in attributing to verbal language a thoroughly *iconic* property. In the list of icons, there are *a* photograph, *a* star chart, *a* model, *a* chemical diagram —all of them spatial and perceptual objects; but, while language is always used in a spatial setting, words appear in temporal sequence, and have only the spatial character of their occasion. We cannot *see* the properties of words in the words. We have simply got to know *what* the words convey. The phrase "a star chart" is not a star chart itself. Mr. Morris appears to have found in the term *icon,* at any rate so far as it pertains to aesthetics, merely a convenient evasion of the term *image;* for image would doubtless have held him to the old ontological aesthetics.

The essay "Esthetics and the Theory of Signs" deals with the specific problem "of stating the differentia of the esthetic sign." Mr. Morris is constantly reminding us that iconic signs appear in all discourse, and that all discourse is by no means aesthetic discourse. Yet the special function of the iconic sign makes it possible for us to use it as the aesthetic sign; and that function is stated in a "semantical rule":

The semantical rule for the use of an iconic sign is that it denotes any object which has the properties (in practice, a selection from the properties) which it itself has. Hence when an interpreter apprehends an iconic sign-vehicle he apprehends directly what is designated; here mediated and unmediated taking account of certain properties both occur;[5] put in still other terms, every iconic sign has its own sign-vehicle among its denotata.

This is a difficult conception; perhaps it can be illustrated with a few lines of verse:

> *That time of year thou mayst in me behold*
> *When yellow leaves, or none, or few do hang*
> *Upon those boughs which shake against the cold . . .*

According to Mr. Morris, the sign-vehicle here would be the leaves hanging on the boughs. This verbal sign-vehicle has the "properties" of the natural objects which it designates; and that which it denotes is in the designation itself. That is, leaves-bough does not point to a definite situation or condition beyond itself: we get "directly what is designated" because it is of the nature of the iconic sign to contain its own *denotatum*. (I have simplified this analysis by ignoring "That time of year," which I believe would make it impossible to apply Mr. Morris' terms coherently.)

The treatment of the iconic sign in semiotic is mysterious. If any generalization about it is legitimate, we may surmise that certain terms, which Mr. Morris calls "primary terms," are untranslatable; that is to say, they cannot be handled by any principle of reduction; they have a certain completeness and finality. They denote themselves; certain iconic signs seem to be such terms. They are sign-vehicles for images, and our apprehension of them is direct. For while the iconic sign may denote something beyond itself, its specific character as an iconic sign is that part of what it denotes is the sign itself. "These facts," says Mr. Morris, "taken alone, do not delimit the esthetic sign, for blueprints, photographs, and scientific models are all iconic signs—but seldom works of art." He continues in a passage of great interest:

If, however, the designatum of an iconic sign be a value [*roman mine*] (*and of course not all iconic signs designate values*), *the situation is changed: there is now not merely the designation of value properties (for such designation takes place even in science), nor merely the functioning of iconic signs (for these as such need not be esthetic signs), but there is the direct apprehension of value properties through the very presence of that which itself has the value it designates.*

There are thus three steps in the "delimitation" of the aesthetic sign: First, it is an iconic sign; secondly, it is an iconic sign which designates a value; thirdly, it is an iconic sign which designates a value in the sign itself, so that our "apprehension" of that value is unmediated, that is, *direct*.

The difficulties created by this aesthetic doctrine are slippery and ambiguous. We may, for convenience, see them in two ways. The first set of problems lies in the term "apprehension"; the second, in the term "value."

The primary meaning of apprehension is a grasping or a

taking hold of. What does Mr. Morris mean? If it means taking hold of by means of perception, we are asked to see ourselves *perceiving a value;* but a value cannot be an object of perception. If, however, apprehension means a direct, unmediated knowledge of a value, then there is an act of evaluation involved which implies the presence of a knowing mind. For the implied "semantical rule" for the aesthetic sign obviously forbids us to check the value wholly in terms of a situation external to the properties of the sign itself. We have got to *know* the value in itself; and only in an act of cognition can we know it. But if Mr. Morris means by apprehension the response, or mere "interpretant," of semiosis, it is difficult to see how a mere response can be semantically correct unless the sign-vehicle points to a situation outside itself in terms of which the response is relevant. If there is no such situation, is not the interpretant a piece of insanity?

I cannot see how there can be any direct apprehension unless there is an agency to do the apprehending; and the interpretant is not an agent, it is a response. "One additional point may be noted to confirm the sign status of the work of art: The artist often draws attention to the sign-vehicle in such a way as to prevent the interpreter from merely reacting to it as an object and not as a sign. . . ." Mr. Morris' phrases, "in such a way," "so used that," remain painfully evasive. What is that way? Now, if the preventive factor is inherent in the work of art, why did not the birds refrain from trying to eat the grapes in Zeuxis' picture? The citizens of Athens did not mistake the sign-vehicle for an object. Why? Because they *knew* the difference.

Mr. Morris' theory of value will further illuminate his difficulty. It is an "interest" theory of value for which he acknowledges an indebtedness to the pragmatic tradition of Mead and Dewey. Objects, according to this ancient theory, have value in relation to interests. "Values," says Mr. Morris, "are consummatory properties of objects or situations which answer to the consummation of interested acts." If I satisfy my hunger by eating a banana, the banana has value in relation to the specific interest, hunger. Does it follow that we have similar aesthetic interests, which we similarly satisfy?

No specific aesthetic interest appears in semiosis. The aesthetic satisfaction proceeds from the frustration of "real" interests, from the blockage of interests as they drive onward to real "consummations." The aesthetic sign is a value that has not been consummated. Art is the expression of what men desire but are not getting.

There are two passages in "Esthetics and the Theory of Signs" which reveal the fundamental ambiguity in Mr. Morris' conception of the aesthetic sign as a "value." We shall be struck, I believe, by the remarkable parallel between Mr. Morris' view of the aesthetic medium and the neo-classical view, which we saw in Matthew Arnold.

Even though the complexity of the total icon is so very great that no denotatum (other than the esthetic sign vehicle itself) can in actuality be found, the work of art can still be considered a sign—for there can be designation without denotation.

But can the aesthetic sign—and this is the center of the problem—designate an interest "value" if it does not point to an interest? It seems to me that it cannot be a value in any "interest" theory of value whatever. And when the aesthetic sign is so complex that it does not lead to denotation, is not this complexity a semantical failure so great that Mr. Morris actually ought to take it to an institution for the insane?

The traditional prestige of the arts is formidable; so, rather than commit himself to his logic of the aesthetic sign as a designation of a value which cannot be located and which thus cannot be an interest-value, he offers us the ordinary procedure of positivism; that is to say, he shows us how we may reduce the aesthetic sign to a *denotatum* after all.

Since a statement must say something about something, it must involve signs for locating what is referred to, and such signs are ultimately indexical signs [i.e., "pointing" signs]. An iconic sign in isolation cannot then be a statement, and a work of art, conceived as an iconic sign, cannot be true in the semantical sense of the term. Nevertheless, the statement that a work of art is "true" might under analysis turn out to be an elliptical form of syntactical, semantical, or pragmatical statements. Thus se-

mantically it might be intended to affirm that the work in question actually is iconic of the value structure of a certain object or situation. . . .

The work of art is elliptical and iconic; that is, it is an image from which the semantical dimension is omitted, or in which it remains vague. By translating the icon, by expanding it and filling it in with a *denotatum,* we construct a situation external to the work of art: a situation which replaces it. In the usual terms of literary criticism, this situation is the "subject" which exists outside the language of the poem. For the language is merely "iconic of" this ordinary prose subject.

So a neo-classical theory of poetic language not only gave the case for poetry away to the scientist; it has become the foundation of the scientists' theory of poetry. When Mr. Richards remarked, in *Science and Poetry,* that we were now getting on a large scale "genuine knowledge" which would soon reduce poetry to the level of the "pseudo-statement," we could not see how right he was—right from the point of view of neo-classical theory. So long as the scientific procedure was observation, description, and classification, it was not very different from the procedure of common sense and its feeling for the reality of ordinary experience. As late as the first edition (1892) of *The Grammar of Science,* Karl Pearson said: "The aesthetic judgment pronounces for or against the interpretation of the creative imagination according as that interpretation embodies or contradicts the phenomena of life, which we ourselves have observed." But from the point of view of Unified Science, this principle of common-sense observation will no longer serve; it does not go far enough. And so we have a dilemma. Since the language of poetry can be shown to be not strictly relevant to objects and situations as these are presented by the positivist techniques, poetry becomes either nonsense or hortatory rhetoric.

The semiotic approach to aesthetics "has the merit of concreteness"; yet we have seen that Mr. Morris never quite gets around to a specific work of art. In "Science, Art, and Technology," he distinguishes three primary forms of discourse and relates them to the three dimensions of semiosis:

1. Scientific discourse: semantical dimension.
2. Aesthetic discourse: syntactical dimension.
3. Technological discourse: pragmatical dimension.

We have seen that the iconic sign is semantically weak; so the aesthetic sign, a variety of iconic sign, must function primarily at the syntactical level; that is, if we look at it "indexically" it "points" first of all to itself. Looking at the aesthetic sign from this point of view, we are forced to see that it wholly lacks cognitive content, and it is subject to the operation of "transformation rules." Does the "concreteness" of the semiotic approach to art consist in this? Again, is the syntactical dimension that in which direct apprehension of the aesthetic sign is possible? Once more it must be said that this direct apprehension seems impossible unless there is an agency of apprehension—a knowing mind; without this we get only an "interpretant," which is conceivable only at the pragmatic level; and if the interpretant is intelligible, it is so in terms of semantical relevance, or of the scientific form of discourse. For Mr. Morris himself confesses: " . . . in so far as the knowledge of value which art gives is the more than the having of value [i.e., is the *knowing* of value] there is no reason to suppose that this knowledge is *other than scientific in character.*"

It is significant here that Mr. Morris conceives the character of poetry in the relation of pragmatics and semantics. What is our response to poetry and how do we behave when we read it: what, in a word, does it lead to? There is a certain uneasy piety in the extravagant claim that poetry is the realm of values; and there is no way, I think, to get around the conclusion that, since the values are not attached to reality, they are irresponsible feelings. They are, in fact, rhetoric. And it is also significant that for Mr. Morris the study of rhetoric is a branch of pragmatics; it is even a kind of technological instrument. For, in the essay "Science, Art, and Technology," poetry seems to acquire its main responsibility in the technological function of telling us what we *ought* to want and do. Here again neo-classical didacticism appears in terms of a rigorous instrumentalism.

Does the language of poetry mean what it says, or does it mean the "situation" that we get from it in a process of reduction? Although we have seen Mr. Morris' bias, we have also seen that he has not made up his mind: he would like to have it both ways. The origin of this dilemma is remote. But there is always "the sad ghost of Coleridge beckoning from the shades."

IV

The famous Chapter XIV of *Biographia Literaria* has been the background of the criticism of poetry for more than a hundred years. Its direct influence has been very great; its indirect influence, through Poe upon Baudelaire, and through the French Symbolists down to contemporary English and American poets, has perhaps been even greater. This chapter is the most influential statement on poetry ever formulated by an English critic: its insights, when we have them, are ours, and ours too its contradictions. Yet the remarkable "definition" of poetry, which I shall now quote, is not, as we shall presently see, the chief source of the aesthetic dilemma that we inherit today. (That source is another passage.) Here is the definition:

A poem is that species of composition, which is opposed to works of science, by proposing for its immediate *object pleasure, not truth; and from all other species—(having this object in common with it)—it is distinguished by proposing to itself such delight from the* whole, *as is compatible with a distinct gratification from each component part.*

Much of the annoyance and misunderstanding caused by this passage has not been Coleridge's fault; but is rather due to the failure of literary men to observe the accurate use of *species*. For Coleridge is giving us a strict Aristotelian definition of a *species* within a given *genus*. It is not a qualitative statement, and it does not answer the question: *What* is poetry? The *whatness* of poetry does not come within the definition; and I believe that nowhere else does Coleridge offer us an explicit qualitative distinction between poetry and other "species of composition" which may be "opposed" to it.

For what is Coleridge saying? (I have never seen a literal reading of the passage by any critic.) There is the generic division: composition. A poem is a species within the genus; but so is a work of science. How are the two species distinguished? By their immediate objects. It is curious that Coleridge phrases the passage as if a poem were a person "proposing" to himself a certain end, pleasure; so for *object* we have got to read *effect*. A poem, then, differs from a work of science in its immediate effect upon us; and that immediate effect is pleasure. But other species of composition may aim at the effect of pleasure. A poem differs from these in the relation of part to whole: the parts must give us a distinct pleasure, moment by moment, and they are not to be conceived as subordinate to the whole; they make up the whole.

If there is an objective relation of part to whole, Coleridge does not say what it is; nor does he distinguish that relation in terms of any specific poetic work. It is strictly a quantitative analogy taken, perhaps, from geometry. And the only purpose it serves is this: in the paragraph following the "definition" he goes on to say that "the philosophic critics of all ages coincide" in asserting that beautiful, isolated lines or distichs are not a poem, and that neither is "an unsustained composition" of uninteresting parts a *legitimate* poem." What we have here, then, is a sound but ordinary critical insight; but because it is merely an extension of the pleasure principle implicit in the "definition," we are not prepared by it to distinguish objectively a poem from any other form of expression. The distinction lies in the effect, and it is a psychological effect. In investigating the differentia of poetry—as Mr. Morris would put it—we are eventually led away from the poem into what has been known since Coleridge's time as the psychology of poetry.

The difficulties of this theory Coleridge seems not to have been aware of; yet he illustrates them perfectly. In the second paragraph after the famous definition he writes this remarkable passage:

The first chapter of Isaiah—(indeed a very large portion of the whole book)—is poetry in the most emphatic sense; yet it would be no less irrational than strange to assert, that pleasure, not truth, was the immediate object of the prophet. In short, whatever specific import we attach to the word, Poetry, there will be found involved in it, as a necessary consequence, that a poem of any length neither can be, nor ought to be, all poetry. Yet if an harmonious whole is to be produced, the remaining parts must be preserved in keeping with the poetry; and this can no otherwise be effected than by such a studied selection and artificial arrangement, as will partake of one, though not a peculiar property of poetry. And this again can be no other than the property of exciting a more continuous and equal attention than the language of prose aims at, whether colloquial or written.

This is probably the most confused statement ever uttered by a great critic, and it has probably done more damage to critical thought than anything else said by any critic. Isaiah is poetry in "the most emphatic sense," although his immediate object (effect) is truth. It will be observed that, whereas in the definition our attention is drawn to a species of composition, a poem, we are here confronted with the personage, Isaiah, who does have the power of proposing an object; and Isaiah's immediate object is truth. But are we to suppose that the effect of the poem and the object of the prophet are to be apprehended in the same way? Is our experience of truth the same as our experience of pleasure? If there is a difference between truth and pleasure, and if an immediate effect of pleasure is the specific "property" of poetry (how a property can be an effect it is difficult to see), how can the first chapter of Isaiah be poetry at all? It cannot be, looked at in these terms; and as a matter of fact Coleridge rather slyly withdraws his compliment to Isaiah when he goes on to say that a "poem of any length neither can be, nor ought to be, all poetry." Isaiah is not all poetry; he is partly truth, or even mostly truth. And the element of truth, while it is strictly speaking insubordinate and unassimilable, can be used by means of an artificial arrangement—meter. There is no doubt that meter does on the whole what Coleridge attributes to it: it demands a "continuous and equal attention." Does he mean to say that the insubordinate element of truth—insubordinate to the immediate effect of pleasure—should be given such conspicuous emphasis? Or does he perhaps mean that the attention will be fixed upon the metrical pattern, so that the nonpoetic element will be less conspicuous?

Coleridge's theory of meter is not quite pertinent here: in the later and more elaborate discussion of meter in *Biographia Literaria* there is the general conclusion that meter is indispensable to poetry. In Chapter XIV, now being examined, he speaks of meter as "an artificial arrangement . . . not a peculiar property of poetry."

There is, then, in Coleridge's poetic theory a persistent dilemma. *He cannot make up his mind whether the specifically poetic element is an objective feature of the poem, or is distinguishable only as a subjective effect.* He cannot, in short, choose between metaphysics and psychology. His general emphasis is psychological, with metaphysical ambiguities.

The distinction between Fancy and Imagination is ultimately a psychological one: he discusses the problem in terms of separate faculties, and the objective poetical properties, presumably resulting from the use of these faculties, are never defined, but are given only occasional illustration. (I have in mind his magnificent analysis of "Venus and Adonis," the value of which lies less perhaps in the critical principles he supposes he is illustrating, than in the perfect taste with which he selects the good passages for admiration.) When Coleridge speaks of the "esemplastic power" of the Imagination, it is always a "faculty" of the mind, not an objective poetic order. When he says that a poem gives us "a more than usual state of emotion with more than usual order," we acknowledge the fact, without being able to discern in the merely comparative degree of the adjective the fundamental difference between the poetic and the philosophic powers which Coleridge frequently asserts, but which he nowhere objectively establishes. The psychological bias of his "system" is perfectly revealed in this summary passage of Chapter XIV:

My own conclusions on the nature of poetry, in the strictest use of the word, have been in part anticipated in some of the remarks on the Fancy and Imagination in the early part of this work. What is poetry?—is so nearly the same question with, what is a poet?—that the answer to the one is involved in the solution to the other. For it is a distinction resulting from the poetic genius itself, which sustains and modifies the images, thoughts, and emotions of the poet's own mind.

There can be little doubt that Coleridge's failure to get out of the dilemma of Intellect-or-Feeling has been passed on to us as a fatal legacy. If the first object of poetry is an effect, and if that effect is pleasure, does it not necessarily follow that truth and knowledge may be better set forth in some other order altogether? It is true that Coleridge made extravagant claims for a poetic order of truth, and it is upon these claims that Mr. I. A. Richards has based his fine book, *Coleridge on Imagination:* Mr. Richards' own testimony is that the claims were not coherent. The coherent part of Coleridge's theory is the fatal dilemma that I have described. Truth is only the secondary consideration of the poet, and from the point of view of positivism the knowledge, or truth, that poetry gives us is immature and inadequate. What of the primary consideration of the poet—pleasure?

Pleasure is the single qualitative feature of Coleridge's famous definition; but it is not *in* the definition objectively. And with the development of modern psychology it has ceased to be qualitative, even subjectively. It is a *response*. The fate of Coleridge's system, then, has been its gradual extinction in the terminology of experimental psychology. The poetry has been extinguished in the poet. The poetic "effect" is a "response" to a "stimulus"; and in the early works of Mr. Richards we get for the first time the questions, rigorously applied: Is the poetic response relevant to the real world? Is it relevant to action? Poetry has come under the general idea of "operational validity." So we must turn briefly to Mr. Richards.

v

In *Science and Poetry,* Mr. Richards condensed in untechnical language the position that he had set forth in detail earlier, in *The Principles of Literary Criticism.* The positivist side of Mr. Richards' thought at that time is plainly revealed in a passage like this:

You contrive not to laugh [*in church*]*; but there is no doubt about the activity of the impulses in their restricted form. The much more subtle and elaborate impulses which a poem excites are not different in principle.* They do not show themselves as a rule, they do not come out into the open, largely because they are so complex. [*Roman mine.*] *When they have adjusted themselves to one another and become organized into a coherent whole, the needs concerned may be satisfied.* In a fully developed man a state of readiness for action will take the place of action when the full appropriate situation for action is not present.[6] [*Mr. Richards' roman.*]

The mere state of readiness for action is the poetic experience in terms of value and relevance. The readiness points to the "direct apprehension" of an interest-value in Mr. Morris' sense; but the failure of the action to come off, the lack of the "full appropriate situation for action," indicates the absence of a *denotatum.* We receive the designation of a value without being provided with a situation in which we can act upon it. The remarkable parallel between Mr. Richards' early theories of poetry and the recent theories of Mr. Morris need not detain us. It is enough to point out that Mr. Richards anticipated fifteen years ago everything that Mr. Morris' science of semiotic has to say about the language of poetry.

I have romanized a sentence, in the quotation from Mr. Richards, for two reasons: first, the vagueness of the language is significant; secondly, the idea of the coherent whole into which the "impulses" are organized has no experimental basis in terms of impulses. Mr. John Crowe Ransom remarks that Mr. Richards never shows us *how* this ordering act of poetry upon our minds takes place, and then proceeds to discern the reason for Mr. Richards' vague statements about the conduct of poetic stimulation and response:

Most readers will retort, of course, that in the very large majority of cases the spiritual happenings are the only happenings we have observed, and the neural happenings are simply what the behaviorists would like to observe. [*Roman mine.*] *At present the mental datum is the fact and the neural datum is the inference.*[7]

In throwing out the mental fact Mr. Richards in his early writings preceded Mr. Morris in his rejection of the cognitive powers of the mind. I do not suggest any direct influence from Mr. Richards upon Mr. Morris, although Mr. Morris has acknowledged the work of his predecessor: it is easier to relate these men to a much wider movement. That movement is positivism, and it is more than a strict scientific method.

It is a general attitude towards experience. If it is not, why should Mr. Richards have attempted in his early criticism to represent the total poetic experience and even the structure of poetry in one of the positivist languages—experimental psychology? It was representation by analogy. The experimental basis for such a representation was wholly lacking. Mr. Richards, had we listened hard enough, was saying in *The Principles of Literary Criticism* and *Science and Poetry* that here at last is what poetry would be if we could only reduce it to the same laboratory technique that we use in psychology; and without warning to the unwary reader, whose credulity was already prepared by his own positivist *Zeitgeist,* Mr. Richards went on to state "results" that looked like the results of an experiment; but the experiment had never been made. It had been inferred. The "impulses" that we feel in response to a poem, says Mr. Richards, "do not show themselves as a rule." There is no scientific evidence that they have ever shown themselves to Mr. Richards or to anybody else. Mr. Richards, like a good positivist, was the victim of a deep-seated compulsive analogy, an elusive but all-engrossing assumption that all experience can be reduced to what is actually the very limited frame of reference supplied by a doctrine of correlation, or of the relevance of stimulus to response. This early procedure of Mr. Richards' was not even empiricism, for in empiricism the cognitive intelligence is not eliminated in the pursuit of verifiable facts. Mr. Richards, like Mr. Morris after him, eliminated cognition without demonstrating experimentally the *data* of his behavioristic poetics. So this doctrine was not empiricism: it came out of the demireligion of positivism. The poetry had been absorbed into a pseudo-scientific jargon, no more "relevant" to poetry than the poetic pseudo-statement was relevant to the world: the net result was zero from both points of view.

I have put this brief commentary on Mr. Richards' early poetics in the past tense because it is no longer his poetics. From 1926, the year of *Science and Poetry,* he has come a long way. It is perhaps not an extravagant claim to make for Mr. Richards' intellectual history, that it will probably turn out to be the most instructive, among critics, of our age. His great intellectual powers, his learning, his devotion to poetry—a devotion somewhat frustrated but as marked fifteen years ago as now—are qualities of an intellectual honesty rare in any age. In exactly ten years, from 1926, he arrived, in *The Philosophy of Rhetoric* (1936), at such a statement as this:

So far from verbal language being a "compromise for a language of intuition"—a thin, but better-than-nothing, substitute for real experience—language, well used, is a completion *and does what the intuitions of sensation by themselves cannot do. Words are the meeting points at which regions of experience which can never combine in sensation or intuition, come together. They are the occasion and means of that growth which is the mind's endless endeavor to order itself. That is why we have language. It is no mere signalling system. [Roman mine.] It is the instrument of all our distinctively human development, of everything in which we go beyond the animals. [Pp. 130-131.]*

These words should be read and re-read with the greatest care by critics who still cite the early Richards as the continuing head of a positivist tradition in criticism. There is,

in this passage, first of all, an implicit repudiation of the
leading doctrine of *The Principles of Literary Criticism*. The
early doctrine did look upon poetic language as a "substitute
for real experience," if by experience is meant responses
relevant to scientifically ascertained facts and situations: this
early doctrine, as I have indicated, anticipated in psychological terms Mr. Morris' poetic doctrine of designation without
denotatum, of value without consummation of value, of interpretant without an interpreter. Mr. Richards' more familiar equivalents of the semiotic terms were: pseudo-statement
without referents; poetry as the orderer of our minds, as the
valuer, although the ordering mysteriously operated in fictions irrelevant to the real world; a response, a behavioristic
"readiness for action," without a knowing mind.

Language, says Mr. Richards, "is no mere signalling system." With that sentence the early psychological doctrine is
discreetly put away. Is it too much to assume that the adjective "signalling" may indicate the relation of Mr. Richards' present views to the pragmatic bias of Mr. Morris'
aesthetics? He speaks of the inadequacy of "sensation" and
"intuition," and of the equal inadequacy of "intuitions of
sensation." Is not the mere sensation Mr. Morris' interpretant, the intuition of sensation his iconic sign? What is the
"completion" which language "well used" can achieve beyond
sensation and intuition?

It is doubtless knowledge of a kind that we can discuss
only if we assume the action of a knowing mind. Of what
is it the completion? In the paragraph following the passage
that I have just quoted, Mr. Richards cites Coleridge:

*Are not words parts and germinations of the plant? And what
is the law of their growth? In something of this sort I would
destroy the old antithesis of Words and Things: elevating, as
it were, Words into Things and living things too.*

This attribution to the language of poetry of a special
kind of "life" goes back to Mr. Richards' *Coleridge on Imagination* (1935), the most ambitious attempt of a modern
critic to force into unity the antithesis of language and subject, of pleasure and truth. It is an antithesis which, as we

have seen, has harassed critical theory since the time of
Coleridge. Mr. Richards' book may be looked upon as an
effort to finish Coleridge's own uncompleted struggle with
this neo-classical dilemma. This is not the place to describe
the entire nature and scope of his effort, or to estimate it.
A single chapter of the book, "The Wind Harp," contains
the clearest presentation of the antithesis that I have seen by
a modern critic.

There are "two doctrines," he says, which have tended to
flourish independently—"And yet, neither is intelligible, apart
from Imagination." He continues:

The two doctrines can be stated as follows:
*1. The mind of the poet at moments . . . gains an insight
into reality, reads Nature as a symbol of something behind or
within Nature not ordinarily perceived.*
*2. The mind of the poet creates a Nature into which his
own feelings, his aspirations and apprehensions, are projected.*

Now the positivist sciences have denied all validity to the
first doctrine: as a proposition, in the many forms in which
it may be stated, it is strictly meaningless. For the sole
effective procedure towards nature is the positivist. The
second doctrine is the standard poetics of our time: projection of feeling. The confusion and contradiction that we saw
in Mr. Morris and in the early Richards came of trying to
square a theory of interest-value with a theory of emotional
projection which was not firmly based upon positivist knowledge. That contradiction is the clue to the "unintelligibility"
of the doctrines if held separately. If you take the first
alone, eliminating the second, you eliminate the "mind," and
you get pure positivism: in thus eliminating cognition you
lose "everything in which we go beyond the animals." If you
take the second alone, and eliminate the external world in
any of the four meanings[8] that Mr. Richards gives to the
phrase, you have a knowing mind without anything that it
can know.

Before the development of the positivist procedures towards nature, the pressure of this dilemma was not seriously
felt. We have seen in Matthew Arnold (the determined

anti-dialectician) the belief that the subject is external to the language—a merely common-sense view inherited from neo-classical theory. The poetic subject was the world of ordinary experience; but as soon as the subject—Nature—became the field of positivism, the language of poetry ceased to represent it; ceased, in fact, to have any validity, or to set forth anything real. (The world of positivism is a world without minds to know the world; and yet Mr. Morris does not hesitate to assert that his Unified Science will save the world. For whom will it be saved?)

What is this Imagination which Mr. Richards says will make the two doctrines intelligible? No doubt it becomes in his hands something different from Coleridge's conception of it: it closely resembles an Hegelian synthesis, which joins the opposites in a new proposition in which their truths, no longer contradictory, are preserved.

They are [says Mr. Richards of the two doctrines] neither consequences of a priori *decisions, nor verifiable as the empirical statements of science are verifiable; and all verifiable statements are independent of them. But this does not diminish in the least their interest, or that of the other senses in which they may be true.*

With that we are almost ready to leave Mr. Richards, who offers no final solution of the problem of the unified imagination. "It is the privilege of poetry," he says finely, "to preserve us from mistaking our notions either for things or for ourselves. *Poetry is the completest mode of utterance.*" [9] It is neither the world of verifiable science nor a projection of ourselves; yet it is *complete*. And because it is complete knowledge we may, I think, claim for it a unique kind of responsibility, and see in it at times an irresponsibility equally distinct. The order of completeness that it achieves in the great works of the imagination is not the order of experimental completeness aimed at by the positivist sciences, whose responsibility is directed towards the verification of limited techniques. The completeness of science is an abstraction covering an ideal of cooperation among specialized methods. No one can have an experience of science, or of a single science. For the completeness of *Hamlet* is not of the experimental order, but of the experienced order: it is, in short, of the mythical order. And here Mr. Richards can give us a final insight. Myths, he says,

> . . . *are no amusement or diversion to be sought as a relaxation and an escape from the hard realities of life. They are these hard realities in projection, their symbolic recognition, co-ordination and acceptance. . . . The opposite and discordant qualities in things in them acquire a form. . . . Without his mythologies man is only a cruel animal without a soul . . . a congeries of possibilities without order and aim.*[10]

Man, without his mythologies, is an interpretant. Mr. Richards' books may be seen together as a parable, as a mythical and dramatic projection, of the failure of the modern mind to understand poetry on the assumptions underlying the demi-religion of positivism. We do not need to reject the positive and rational mode of inquiry into poetry; yet even from Mr. Morris we get the warning lest we substitute the criticism for the poem, and thus commit ourselves to a "learned ignorance." We must return to, we must never leave, the poem itself. Its "interest" value is a cognitive one; it is sufficient that here, in the poem, we get knowledge of a whole object. If rational inquiry is the only mode of criticism, we must yet remember that the way we employ that mode must always powerfully affect our experience of the poem. I have been concerned in this commentary with the compulsive, almost obsessed, application of an all-engrossing principle of pragmatic reduction to a formed realm of our experience, the distinction of which is its complete knowledge, the full body of the experience that it offers us. However we may see the completeness of poetry, it is a problem less to be solved than, in its full import, to be preserved.

1941

TENSION IN POETRY

Many poems that we ordinarily think of as good poetry—and some, besides, that we neglect—have certain common features that will allow us to invent, for their sharper apprehension, the name of a single quality. I shall call that quality tension. In abstract language, a poetic work has distinct quality as the ultimate effect of the whole, and that whole is the "result" of a configuration of meaning which it is the duty of the critic to examine and evaluate. In setting forth this duty as my present procedure I am trying to amplify a critical approach that I have used on other occasions, without wholly giving up the earlier method, which I should describe as the isolation of the general ideas implicit in the poetic work.

Towards the end of this essay I shall cite examples of "tension," but I shall not say that they exemplify tension only, or that other qualities must be ignored. There are all kinds of poetry, as many as there are good poets, as many even as there are good poems, for poets may be expected to write more than one kind of poetry; and no single critical insight may impute an exclusive validity to any one kind. In all ages there are schools demanding that one sort only be written—their sort: political poetry for the sake of the cause; picturesque poetry for the sake of the home town; didactic poetry for the sake of the parish; even a generalized personal poetry for the sake of the reassurance and safety of numbers. This last I suppose is the most common variety, the anonymous lyricism in which the common personality exhibits its commonness, its obscure yet standard eccentricity, in a language that seems always to be deteriorating; so that today many poets are driven to inventing private languages, or very narrow ones, because public speech has become heavily tainted with mass feeling.

Mass language is the medium of "communication," and its users are less interested in bringing to formal order what is sometimes called the "affective state" than in arousing that state.

Once you have said that everything is One it is obvious that literature is the same as propaganda; once you have said that no truth can be known apart from the immediate dialectical process of history it is obvious that all contemporary artists must prepare the same fashionplate. It is clear too that the One is limited in space as well as time, and the no less Hegelian Fascists are right in saying that all art is patriotic.

What Mr. William Empson calls patriotic poetry sings not merely in behalf of the State; you will find it equally in a ladylike lyric and in much of the political poetry of our time. It is the poetry of the mass language, very different from the "language of the people" which interested the late W. B. Yeats. For example:

> *What from the splendid dead*
> *We have inherited—*
> *Furrows sweet to the grain, and the weed subdued—*
> *See now the slug and the mildew plunder.*
> *Evil does overwhelm*
> *The larkspur and the corn;*
> *We have seen them go under.*

From this stanza by Miss Millay we infer that her splendid ancestors made the earth a good place that has somehow gone bad—and you get the reason from the title: "Justice Denied in Massachusetts." How Massachusetts could cause a general desiccation, why (as we are told in a footnote to the poem) the execution of Sacco and Vanzetti should have anything to to with the rotting of the crops, it is never made clear. These lines are mass language: they arouse an affective state in one set of terms, and suddenly an object quite unrelated to those terms gets the benefit of it; and this effect, which is usually achieved, as I think it is here, without conscious effort, is sentimentality. Miss Millay's poem was admired when it first appeared about ten years ago, and is no doubt still admired, by persons to whom it communicates certain feelings about social justice, by persons for whom the lines are the occasion of feelings shared by them and the poet. But if you do not share those feelings, as I happen not to share them in the images of desiccated nature, the lines and even the entire poem are impenetrably obscure.

I am attacking here the fallacy of communication in poetry. (I am not attacking social justice.) It is no less a fallacy in the writing of poetry than of critical theory. The critical doctrine fares ill the further back you apply it; I suppose one may say—if one wants a landmark—that it began to prosper after 1798; for, on the whole, nineteenth-century English verse is a poetry of communication. The poets were trying to use verse to convey ideas and feelings that they secretly thought could be better conveyed by science (consult Shelley's *Defense*), or by what today we call, in a significantly bad poetic phrase, the Social Sciences. Yet possibly because the poets believed the scientists to be tough, and the poets joined the scientists in thinking the poets tender, the poets stuck to verse. It may scarcely be said that we change this tradition of poetic futility by giving it a new name, Social Poetry. May a poet hope to deal more adequately with sociology than with physics? If he seizes upon either at the level of scientific procedure, has he not abdicated his position as poet?

At a level of lower historical awareness than that exhibited by Mr. Edmund Wilson's later heroes of the Symbolist school, we find the kind of verse that I have been quoting, verse long ago intimidated by the pseudo-rationalism of the Social Sciences. This sentimental intimidation has been so complete that, however easy the verse looked on the page, it gave up all claim to sense. (I assume here what I cannot now demonstrate, that Miss Millay's poem is obscure but that Donne's "Second Anniversarie" is not.) As another example of this brand of obscurity I have selected at random a nineteenth-century lyric, "The Vine," by James Thomson:

> *The wine of love is music,*
> *And the feast of love is song:*

> *When love sits down to banquet,*
> *Love sits long:*
>
> *Sits long and rises drunken,*
>   *But not with the feast and the wine;*
> *He reeleth with his own heart,*
>   *That great rich Vine.*

The language here appeals to an existing affective state; it has no coherent meaning either literally or in terms of ambiguity or implication; it may be wholly replaced by any of its several paraphrases, which are already latent in our minds. One of these is the confused image of a self-intoxicating man-about-town. Now good poetry can bear the closest literal examination of every phrase, and is its own safeguard against our irony. But the more closely we examine this lyric, the more obscure it becomes; the more we trace the implications of the imagery, the denser the confusion. The imagery adds nothing to the general idea that it tries to sustain; it even deprives that idea of the dignity it has won at the hands of a long succession of better poets going back, I suppose, to Guinizelli:

> *Al cor gentil ripara sempre Amore*
> *Come alla selva augello in la verdura . . .*

What I want to make clear is the particular kind of failure, not the degree, in a certain kind of poetry. Were we interested in degrees, we might give comfort to the nineteenth century by citing lines from John Cleveland or Abraham Cowley, bad lyric verse no better than "The Vine," written in an age that produced some of the greatest English poetry. Here are some lines from Cowley's "Hymn: to light," a hundred-line inventory of some of the offices performed by the subject in a universe that still seems to be on the whole Ptolemaic; I should not care to guess the length the poem might have reached under the Copernican system. Here is one of the interesting duties of light:

> *Nor amidst all these Triumphs does thou scorn*
>   *The humble glow-worm to adorn,*
>   *And with those living spangles gild,*
> *(O Greatness without Pride!) the Bushes of the Field.*

Again:

> *The Violet, springs little Infant, stands,*
> *Girt in thy purple Swadling-bands:*
> *On the fair Tulip thou dost dote;*
> *Thou cloath'st it in a gay and party-colour'd Coat.*

This, doubtless, is metaphysical poetry; however bad the lines
may be—they are pretty bad—they have no qualities, bad or
good, in common with "The Vine." Mr. Ransom has given
us, in a remarkable essay, "Shakespeare at Sonnets" [1] (*The
World's Body*, 1938), an excellent description of this kind of
poetry: "The impulse to metaphysical poetry . . . consists
in committing the feelings in the case . . . to their determi-
nation within the elected figure." That is to say, in metaphysical poetry the logical order is explicit; it must be coherent;
the imagery by which it is sensuously embodied must have
at least the appearance of logical determinism: perhaps the
appearance only, because the varieties of ambiguity and contradiction possible beneath the logical surface are endless, as
Mr. Empson has demonstrated in his elucidation of Marvell's
"The Garden." Here it is enough to say that the development of imagery by extension, its logical determinants being
an Ariadne's thread that the poet will not permit us to lose,
is the leading feature of the poetry called metaphysical.

But to recognize it is not to evaluate it; and I take it that
Mr. Ransom was giving us a true Aristotelian definition of a
genus, in which the identification of a type does not compel
us to discern the implied values. Logical extension of imagery is no doubt the key to the meaning of Donne's "Valediction: forbidding mourning"; it may equally initiate inquiry
into the ludicrous failure of "Hymn: to light," to which I now
return.

Although "The Vine" and "Hymn: to light" seem to me
equally bad poetry, Cowley's failure is somewhat to be preferred; its negative superiority lies in a firmer use of the language. There is no appeal to an affective state; the leading
statement can be made perfectly explicit: God is light, and
light is life. The poem is an analytical proposition exhibiting
the properties inherent in the major term; that is, exhibiting

as much of the universe as Cowley could get around to before he wearied of logical extension. But I think it is possible to infer that good poetry could have been written in Cowley's language; and we know that it was. Every term, even the verbs converted into nouns, denotes an object, and, in the hands of a good poet, would be amenable to controlled distortions of literal representation. But here the distortions are uncontrolled. Everything is in this language that a poet needs except the poetry, or the imagination, or what I shall presently illustrate under the idea of tension.

I have called "Hymn: to light" an analytical proposition. That is the form in which the theme must have appeared to Cowley's mind; that is to say, simple analysis of the term *God* gave him, as it gave everybody else in Christendom, the proposition: God is light. (Perhaps, under neo-Platonic influence, the prime Christian symbol, as Professor Fletcher and others have shown in reducing to their sources the powers of the Three Blessed Ladies of *The Divine Comedy*.) But in order to write his poem Cowley had to develop the symbol by synthetic accretion, by adding to light properties not inherent in its simple analysis:

> *The Violet, springs little Infant, stands,*
> *Girt in thy purple Swadling-bands . . .*

The image, such as it is, is an addition to the central figure of light, an assertion of a hitherto undetected relation among the objects, light, diapers, and violets—a miscellany that I recommend to the consideration of Mr. E. E. Cummings, who could get something out of it that Cowley did not intend us to get. If you will think again of "The Vine," you will observe that Thomson permits, in the opposite direction, an equal license with the objects *de*noted by his imagery, with the unhappy results that we have already seen.

"The Vine" is a failure in denotation. "Hymn: to light" is a failure in connotation. The language of "The Vine" lacks objective content. Take "music" and "song" in the first two lines; the context does not allow us to apprehend the terms in extension; that is, there is no reference to objects that we may distinguish as "music" and "song"; the wine of love could have as well been song, its feast music. In "Hymn: to light," a reduction to their connotations of the terms *violet, swadling-bands,* and *light* (the last being represented by the pronoun *thou*) yields a clutter of images that may be unified only if we forget the firm denotations of the terms. If we are going to receive as valid the infancy of the violet, we must ignore the metaphor that conveys it, for the metaphor renders the violet absurd; by ignoring the diaper, and the two terms associated with it, we cease to read the passage, and begin for ourselves the building up of acceptable denotations for the terms of the metaphor.

Absurd: but on what final ground I call these poems absurd I cannot state as a principle. I appeal to the reader's experience, and invite him to form a judgment of my own. It is easy enough to say, as I shall say in detail in a moment, that good poetry is a unity of all the meanings from the furthest extremes of intension and extension. Yet our recognition of the action of this unified meaning is the gift of experience, of culture, of, if you will, our humanism. Our powers of discrimination are not deductive powers, though they may be aided by them; they wait rather upon the cultivation of our total human powers, and they represent a special application of those powers to a single medium of experience—poetry.

I have referred to a certain kind of poetry as the embodiment of the fallacy of communication: it is a poetry that communicates the affective state, which (in terms of language) results from the irresponsible denotations of words. There is a vague grasp of the "real" world. The history of this fallacy, which is as old as poetry but which towards the end of the eighteenth century began to dominate not only poetry, but other arts as well—its history would probably show that the poets gave up the language of denotation to the scientists, and kept for themselves a continually thinning flux of peripheral connotations. The companion fallacy, to which I can give only the literal name, the fallacy of mere denotation, I have also illustrated from Cowley: this is the poetry which contradicts our most developed human insights in so far as it fails to use and direct the rich connotation with which language has been informed by experience.

II

We return to the inquiry set for this discussion: to find out whether there is not a more central achievement in poetry than that represented by either of the extreme examples that we have been considering. I proposed, as descriptive of that achievement, the term *tension*. I am using the term not as a general metaphor, but as a special one, derived from lopping the prefixes off the logical terms *ex*tension and *in*tension. What I am saying, of course, is that the meaning of poetry is its "tension," the full organized body of all the extension and intension that we can find in it. The remotest figurative significance that we can derive does not invalidate the extensions of the literal statement. Or we may begin with the literal statement and by stages develop the complications of metaphor: at every stage we may pause to state the meaning so far apprehended, and at every stage the meaning will be coherent.

The meanings that we select at different points along the infinite line between extreme intension and extreme extension will vary with our personal "drive," or "interest," or "approach": the Platonist will tend to stay pretty close to the end of the line where extension, and simple abstraction of the object into a universal, is easiest, for he will be a fanatic in morals or some kind of works, and will insist upon the shortest way with what will ever appear to him the dissenting ambiguities at the intensive end of the scale. The Platonist (I do not say that his opponent is the Aristotelian) might decide that Marvell's "To His Coy Mistress" recommends immoral behavior to the young men in whose behalf he would try to suppress the poem. That, of course, would be one "true" meaning of "To His Coy Mistress," but it is a meaning that the full tension of the poem will not allow us to entertain exclusively. For we are compelled, since it is there, to give equal weight to an intensive meaning so rich that, without contradicting the literal statement of the lover-mistress convention, it lifts that convention into an insight into one phase of the human predicament—the conflict of sensuality and asceticism.

I should like to quote now, not from Marvell, but a stanza from Donne that I hope will reinforce a little what I have just said and connect it with some earlier remarks.

> *Our two soules therefore, which are one,*
> *Though I must goe, endure not yet*
> *A breach, but an expansion,*
> *Like gold to aiery thinnesse beate.*

Here Donne brings together the developing imagery of twenty lines under the implicit proposition: the unity of two lovers' souls is a nonspatial entity, and is therefore indivisible. That, I believe, is what Mr. John Crowe Ransom would call the logic of the passage; it is the abstract form of its extensive meaning. Now the interesting feature here is the logical contradiction of embodying the unitary, non-spatial soul in a spatial image: the malleable gold is a plane whose surface can always be extended mathematically by one-half towards infinity; the souls are this infinity. The finite image of the gold, in extension, logically contradicts the intensive meaning (infinity) which it conveys; but it does not invalidate that meaning. We have seen that Cowley compelled us to ignore the denoted diaper in order that we might take seriously the violet which it pretended to swathe. But in Donne's "Valediction: forbidding mourning" the clear denotation of the gold contains, by intension, the full meaning of the passage. If we reject the gold, we reject the meaning, for the meaning is wholly absorbed into the image of the gold. Intension and extension are here one, and they enrich each other.

Before I leave this beautiful object, I should like to notice two incidental features in further proof of Donne's mastery. "Expansion"—a term denoting an abstract property common to many objects, perhaps here one property of a gas: it expands visibly the quality of the beaten gold.

> . . . *endure not yet*
> *a breach* . . .

But if the lovers' souls are the formidable, inhuman entity that we have seen, are they not superior to the contingency of a breach? Yes and no: both answers are true answers; for by means of the sly "yet" Donne subtly guards himself against our irony, which would otherwise be quick to scrutinize the extreme metaphor. The lovers have not endured a breach, but they are simple, miserable human beings, and they may quarrel tomorrow.[2]

Now all this meaning and more, and it is all one meaning, is embedded in that stanza: I say "more" because I have not exhausted the small fraction of significance that my limited powers have permitted me to see. For example, I have not discussed the rhythm, which is of the essential meaning; I have violently isolated four lines from the meaning of the whole poem. Yet, fine as it is, I do not think the poem the greatest poetry; perhaps only very little of Donne makes that grade, or of anybody else. Donne offers many examples of tension in imagery, easier for the expositor than greater passages in Shakespeare.

But convenience of elucidation is not a canon of criticism. I wish now to introduce other kinds of instance, and to let them stand for us as sort of Arnoldish touchstones to the perfection that poetic statement has occasionally reached. I do not know what bearing my comment has had, or my touchstones may have, upon the larger effects of poetry or upon long poems. The long poem is partly a different problem. I have of necessity confined both commentary and illustration to the slighter effects that seemed to me commensurate with certain immediate qualities of language. For, in the long run, whatever the poet's "philosophy," however wide may be the extension of his meaning—like Milton's Ptolemaic universe in which he didn't believe—by his language shall you know him; the quality of his language is the valid limit of what he has to say.

I have not searched out the quotations that follow: they at once form the documentation and imply the personal bias from which this inquiry has grown. Only a few of the lines will be identified with the metaphysical technique, or, in Mr. Ransom's fine phrase, the metaphysical strategy. Strategy

would here indicate the point on the intensive-extensive
scale at which the poet deploys his resources of meaning. The
metaphysical poet as a rationalist begins at or near the extensive or denoting end of the line; the romantic or Symbolist poet at the other, intensive end; and each by a straining
feat of the imagination tries to push his meanings as far as he
can towards the opposite end, so as to occupy the entire scale.
I have offered one good and one bad example of the metaphysical strategy, but only defective examples of the Symbolist, which I cited as fallacies of mass language: Thomson
was using language at its mass level, unhappily ignorant of
the need to embody his connotations in a rational order of
thought. (I allude here also, and in a quite literal sense, to
Thomson's personal unhappiness, as well as to the excessive
pessimism and excessive optimism of other poets of his time.)
The great Symbolist poets, from Rimbaud to Yeats, have
heeded this necessity of reason. It would be a hard task to
choose between the two strategies, the Symbolist and the
metaphysical; both at their best are great, and both are
incomplete.

These touchstones, I believe, are not poetry of the extremes, but poetry of the center: poetry of tension, in which
the "strategy" is diffused into the unitary effect.

> Ask me no more whither doth hast
> The Nightingale when May is past:
> For in your sweet dividing throat
> She winters, and keeps warm her note.
>
> *   *   *
>
> O thou Steeled Cognizance whose leap commits
> The agile precincts of the lark's return . . .
>
> *   *   *
>
> That time of year thou mayst in me behold
> When yellow leaves, or none, or few do hang
> Upon those boughs which shake against the cold,
> Bare ruined choirs where late the sweet birds sang.
>
> *   *   *
>
> Beauty is but a flower
> Which wrinkles will devour;
> Brightness falls from the air,
> Queens have died young and fair,

Dust hath closed Helen's eye.
I am sick, I must die.
   Lord, have mercy upon us!
                *   *   *

And then may chance thee to repent
The time that thou hast lost and spent
   To cause thy lovers sigh and swoon;
Then shalt thou know beauty but lent,
   And wish and want as I have done.
                *   *   *

We have lingered in the chambers of the sea
By seagirls wreathed with seaweed red and brown
Till human voices wake us and we drown.
                *   *   *

I am of Ireland
And the Holy Land of Ireland
And time runs on, cried she.
Come out of charity
And dance with me in Ireland.
                *   *   *

And my poor fool is hanged! No, no, no life!
Why should a dog, a horse, a rat, have life
And thou no breath at all? Thou'lt come no mo...
Never, never, never, never, never!—
Pray you undo this button; thank you, sir.—
Do you see this? Look on her,—look,—her lips,—
Look there, look there!
                *   *   *

'Tis madness to resist or blame
The force of angry heavens flame:
   And, if we would speak true,
   Much to the Man is due,
Who, from his private Gardens, where
He liv'd reserved and austere,
   As if his highest plot
   To plant the Bergamot,
Could by industrious Valour climbe
To ruin the great Work of Time,
   And cast the Kingdome old
   Into another Mold.
                *   *   *

Cover her face; mine eyes dazzle; she die.! .oung.

III

There are three more lines that I wish to look at: a tercet from *The Divine Comedy*. I know little of either Dante or his language; yet I have chosen as my final instance of tension —the instance itself will relieve me of the responsibility of the term—not a great and difficult passage, but only a slight and perfect one. It is from a scene that has always been the delight of the amateur reader of Dante; we can know more about it with less knowledge than about any other, perhaps, in the poem. The damned of the Second Circle are equivocally damned: Paolo and Francesca were illicit lovers but their crime was incontinence, neither adultery nor pandering, the two crimes of sex for which Dante seems to find any real theological reprobation, for they are committed with the intent of injury.

You will remember that when Dante first sees the lovers they are whirling in a high wind, the symbol here of lust. When Francesca's conversation with the poet begins, the wind dies down, and she tells him where she was born, in these lines:

> *Siede la terra dove nata fui*
> *Sulla marina dove il Po discende*
> *Per aver pace co' seguaci sui.*

Courtney Landon renders the tercet:

> *The town where I was born sits on the shore,*
> *Whither the Po descends to be at peace*
> *Together with the streams that follow him.*

But it misses a good deal; it misses the force of *seguaci* by rendering it as a verb. Professor Grandgent translates the third line: "To have peace with its pursuers," and comments: "The tributaries are conceived as chasing the Po down to the sea." Precisely; for if the *seguaci* are merely followers, and not pursuers also, the wonderfully ordered density of this simple passage is sacrificed. For although Francesca has told Dante where she lives, in the most directly descriptive language possible, she has told him more than that. Without the least imposition of strain upon the firmly denoted natural setting, she fuses herself with the river Po near which she was born. By a subtle shift of focus we see the pursued river as Francesca in Hell: the pursuing tributaries are a new visual image for the pursuing winds of lust. A further glance yields even more: as the winds, so the tributaries at once pursue and become one with the pursued; that is to say, Francesca has completely absorbed the substance of her sin— she is the sin; as, I believe it is said, the damned of the *Inferno* are plenary incarnations of the sin that has put them there. The tributaries of the Po are not only the winds of lust by analogy of visual images; they become identified by means of sound:

> . . . *discende*
> *Per aver pace co' seguaci sui.*

The sibilants dominate the line; they are the hissing of the wind. But in the last line of the preceding tercet Francesca has been grateful that the wind has subsided so that she can be heard—

> *Mentre che il vento, come fa, si tace.*

After the wind has abated, then, we hear in the silence, for the first time, its hiss, in the susurration to the descending Po. The river is thus both a visual and an auditory image, and since Francesca is her sin and her sin is embodied in this image, we are entitled to say that it is a sin that we can both hear and see.

1938

TECHNIQUES OF FICTION

There must be many techniques of fiction, but how many? I suppose a great many more than there are techniques of poetry. Why this should be so, if it is, nobody quite knows, and if we knew, I do not know what use the knowledge would have. For the great disadvantage of all literary criticism is its practical ignorance, which in the very nature of its aims must be incurable. Even the aims of criticism are unknown, beyond very short views; for example, in the criticism of the novel, Mr. Percy Lubbock tells us that the secret of the art is the strategy of "point of view"; Mr. E. M. Forster, that the novelist must simply give us "life," or the illusion of "bouncing" us through it—which looks like a broader view than Mr. Lubbock's, until we pause to examine it, when it turns out to be worse than narrow, since to look at everything is to see nothing; or, again, Mr. Edwin Muir holds that "structure" is the key to the novelist's success or failure. There is no need here to explain what these critics mean by "point of view," or "life," or "structure"; but they all mean something useful—in a short view, beyond which (I repeat) critics seem to know little or nothing.

What the novelists know may be another thing altogether, and it is that knowledge which ought to be our deepest concern. You will have to allow me the paradox of presuming to know what the novelists know—or some of them at any rate—while as a critic I profess to know nothing. The presumption might encourage us to predict from the very nature of the critic's ignorance the nature and quality of the knowledge possible to good writers of fiction. The novelist keeps before him constantly the structure and substance of his fiction as a whole, to a degree to which the critic can never apprehend it. For the first cause of critical ignorance is, of course, the limitations of our minds, about which we can do little, work at them as we will. It is the special ignorance by which we, as critics, are limited in the act of reading any extended work of the imagination. The imaginative work must always differ to such a great degree as almost to differ in kind from philosophical works, which our minds apprehend and retain almost as wholes through the logical and deductive structures which powerfully aid the memory. Who can remember, well enough to pronounce upon it critically, all of *War and Peace,* or *The Wings of the Dove,* or even *Death in Venice,* the small enclosed world of which ought at least to do something to aid our memories? I have re-read all three of these books in the past year; yet for the life of me I could not pretend to know them as wholes, and without that knowledge I lack the materials of criticism.

Because Mr. Lubbock seems to know more than anybody else about this necessary ignorance of the critic, and for other important reasons, I believe him to be the best critic who has ever written about the novel. His book, *The Craft of Fiction,* is very nearly a model of critical procedure. Even in so fine a study as Albert Thibaudet's *Gustave Flaubert* there is nothing like the actual, as opposed to the merely professed, critical modesty of numerous statements like this by Lubbock: "Our critical faculty may be admirable; we may be thoroughly capable of judging a book justly, if only we could watch it at ease. But fine taste and keen perception are of no use to us if we cannot retain the image of the book; and the image escapes and evades us like a cloud." Where, then, does Lubbock get the material of his criticism? He gets as much of it as any critic ever gets by means of a bias which he constantly pushes in the direction of extreme simplification of the novel in terms of "form," or "point of view" (after James' more famous phrase, the "post of observation"), or more generally in terms of the controlling intelligence which determines the range and quality of the scene and the action. It is the only book on fiction which has earned unanimous dislike among other critics (I do not know three novelists who have read it), and the reason, I think, is that it is, in its limited terms, wholly successful; or, if that is too great praise, it is successful in the same sense, and to no less degree than the

famous lecture notes on the Greek drama taken down by an
anonymous student at the Lyceum in the fourth century
B.C. The lecture notes and *The Craft of Fiction* are studies
of their respective arts in terms of form; and I think that
Lubbock had incomparably the more difficult job to do. The
novel has at no time enjoyed anything like the number and
the intensity of objective conventions which the drama, even
in its comparatively formless periods, has offered to the critic.
The number of techniques possible in the novel are probably
as many as its conventions are few.

Having said so much in praise of Mr. Lubbock, I shall not,
I hope, seem to take it back if I say that even his intense
awareness of what the novelist knows fails somehow, or perhaps inevitably, to get into his criticism. Anybody who has
just read his account of *Madame Bovary* comes away with a
sense of loss, which is the more intense if he has also just read
that novel; though what the loss is he no more than Mr.
Lubbock will be able to say. Yet no critic has ever turned so
many different lights, from so many different directions,
upon any other novel (except perhaps the lights that are
called today the social and the historical); and yet what we
get is not properly a revelation of the techniques of *Madame
Bovary* but rather what I should call a marvelously astute
chart of the operations of the central intelligence which
binds all the little pieces of drama together into the pictorial
biography of a silly, sad, and hysterical little woman, Emma
Bovary. It is this single interest, this undeviating pursuit of
one great clue, this sticking to the "short view" till the last
horn blows and night settles upon the hunting field, which
largely explains both the greatness of Mr. Lubbock's book
and the necessary and radical ignorance of criticism. We
cannot be both broad and critical, except in so far as knowledge of the world, of ideas, and of man generally is broaden-
ing; but then that knowledge has nothing to do specifically
with the critical job; it only keeps it from being inhuman.
That is something; but it is not criticism. To be critical is to
be narrow in the crucial act or process of judgment.

But after we gather up all the short views of good critics,
and have set the limits to their various ignorances, we are
confronted with what is left out or, if you will, left over: I

have a strong suspicion that this residue of the novel or the story is what the author knew as he wrote it. It is what makes the little scenes, or even the big ones, "come off." And while we no doubt learn a great deal about them when, with Mr. Muir, we study the general structure, or the relation of scenes, or, with Mr. Lubbock, follow the godlike control of the mind of Flaubert or of James through all the scenes to the climax—while this knowledge is indispensable, I should, myself, like to know more about the making of the single scene, and all the techniques that contribute to it; and I suspect that I am not asking the impossible, for this kind of knowledge is very likely the only kind that is actually within our range. It alone can be got at, definitely and at particular moments, even after we have failed, with Mr. Lubbock (honorable failure indeed), to "retain the image of the book."

It sounds very simple, as no doubt it is essentially a simple task to take a scene from a novel apart, and to see what makes it tick; but how to do it must baffle our best intentions. Suppose you want to understand by what arts Tolstoy, near the beginning of *War and Peace,* before the ground is laid, brings Peter, the bastard son of old Count Bezuhov, into the old Count's dying presence, and makes, of the atmosphere of the house and of the young man and the old man, both hitherto unknown to us, one of the great scenes of fiction; you would scarcely know better than I where to take hold of it, and I have only the merest clue. Suppose you feel, as I do, that after Rawdon Crawley comes home (I believe from jail—it is hard to remember Thackeray) and finds Becky supping alone with Lord Steyne—suppose you feel that Thackeray should not have rung down the curtain the very moment Becky's exposure was achieved, but should have faced up to the tougher job of showing us Becky and Rawdon alone after Lord Steyne had departed: Is this a failure in a great novelist? If it is, why? The negative question, addressed to ourselves as persons interested in the techniques of an art, may also lead us to what the novelists know, or to much the same thing, what they should have known. And, to come nearer home, what is the matter with Ty Ty Walden's philosophical meditations, towards the end of *God's Little Acre,* which freezes up our credulity and provokes our fiercest denial? It is surely not that Ty Ty is merely expressing as well as he can the doctrine of the innate goodness of man in the midst of depravity. That doctrine will do as well as any other in the mouth of a fictional character provided his scene and his experience within the scene entitle him to utter it; but before we can believe that Ty Ty is actually thinking anything whatever, we have got in the first place to believe that Ty Ty is a man—which is precisely what Mr. Caldwell evidently did not think it important to make us do.

How shall we learn what to say about particular effects of the story, without which the great over-all structure and movement of the human experience which is the entire novel cannot be made credible to us? The professional critics pause only at intervals to descend to these minor effects which are of course the problems without which the other, more portentous problems which engage criticism could not exist. The fine artists of fiction, I repeat, because they produce these effects must understand them. And having produced them, they are silent about the ways they took to produce them, or paradoxical and mysterious like Flaubert, who told Maupassant to go to the station and look at the cab-drivers until he understood the typical cab-driver, and then to find the language to distinguish one cab-driver from all others in the world. It is the sort of *obiter dicta* which can found schools and movements, and the schools and movements often come to some good, even though the slogan, like this one, means little.

I suppose only the better novelists, like Defoe, Madame de La Fayette, Turgenev, Dickens, Flaubert, many others as great as these, some greater, like Tolstoy and Dostoevsky, knew the special secrets which I am trying, outside criticism, so to speak, to bring before you. There is almost a masonic tradition in the rise of any major art, from its undifferentiated social beginnings to the conscious aptitude which is the sign of a developed art form. Doubtless I ought to repeat once more that for some reason the moment the secrets of this aptitude come within the *provenance* of formal criticism, they vanish. They survive in the works themselves, and in the living confraternity of men of letters, who pass on by personal instruction to their successors the "tricks of the trade " The only man I have known in some twenty years of literary experience who was at once a great novelist and a great teacher, in this special sense, was the late Ford Madox Ford. His influence was immense, even upon writers who did not know him, even upon other writers, today, who have not read him. For it was through him more than any other man writing in English in our time that the great traditions of the novel came down to us. Joyce, a greater writer than Ford, represents by comparison a more restricted practice of the same literary tradition, a tradition that goes back to Stendhal in France, and to Jane Austen in England, coming down to us through Flaubert, James, Conrad, Joyce, Virginia Woolf, and Ernest Hemingway.

It is a tradition which has its own secrets to offer; yet in saying that I am not claiming for it greater novelists than some other school can produce or novelists greater than those who just happen. There is Meredith (for those who, like Ramon Fernandez, can read him); there is Thomas Hardy; there is even the early H. G. Wells. But there is not Arnold Bennett; there is not John Galsworthy; not Hugh Walpole nor Frank Swinnerton. This is prejudice, not criticism. And these are all Britons, not Americans. I have no desire to play 'possum on the American question. Yet I am convinced that among American novelists who have had large publics since the last war, only Dreiser, Faulkner, and Hemingway are of major importance. There are "good" popular novelists who have done much to make us at home physically in our own country; they have given us our scenes, our people, and above all our history; and these were necessary to the preliminary knowledge of ourselves which we have been a little late in getting and which must be got and assimilated if we are going to be a mature people. Possibly the American novel had to accomplish the task that in Europe had been done by primitive chronicle, mémoire, ballad, strolling player. The American novel has had to find a new experience, and only in our time has it been able to pause for the difficult task of finding out how to get itself written. That is an old story with us, yet beneath it lies a complexity of feeling that from Hawthorne down to our time has baffled our best understanding. The illustration is infinite in its variety. At this moment I think of my two favorite historians, Herodotus and Joinville, and I am embarrassed from time to time because Herodotus, the pagan, seems nearer to my experience than Joinville, the Christian chronicler of St. Louis. It is perhaps easier for us to feel comfortable with the remote and relatively neutral elements of our culture. Those experiences of Europe which just precede or overlap the American experience bemuse us, and introduce a sort of chemical ambivalence into our judgment. Joinville is both nearer to me than Herodotus, and less immediate. What American could not be brought to confess a similar paradox? To our European friends who are now beginning to know us, and who in all innocence may subscribe to the popular convention of The Simple American Mind, I would say, if it is not too impolite: Beware.

But the American novel is not my present subject, nor, thank heaven, the American mind. My subject is merely the technique of fiction which now at last I feel that I am ready to talk about, not critically, you understand, but as a member of a guild. Ford used to say that he wrote his novels in the tone of one English gentleman whispering into the ear of another English gentleman: how much irony he intended I never knew; I hope a great deal. I intend none at all when I say that these remarks are set down by an artisan for other artisans.

Gustave Flaubert created the modern novel. Gustave Flaubert created the modern short story. He created both because he created modern fiction. I am not prepared to say that he created all our fictional forms and structures, the phases of the art of fiction that interest Mr. Lubbock and Mr. Muir. He did not originate all those features of the short story which interest historians and anthologists. These are other matters altogether. And I do not like to think that Flaubert created modern fiction, because I do not like Flaubert. It was the fashion in France, I believe, until the Fall, to put Stendhal above Flaubert. I am not sure but I suspect that a very tired generation felt more at ease with a great writer whose typical heroes are persons of mere energy and whose books achieve whatever clarity and form that they do achieve as an accident of the moral ferocity of the author. But without *Le Rouge et*

Le Noir, or without what it put into circulation in French literary *milieux* after 1830, Flaubert could not have written *Madame Bovary.* I do not like to think that Stendhal did this because I do not like Stendhal. Both Stendhal and Flaubert had the single dedication to art which makes the disagreeable man. Doubtless it would be pleasanter if the great literary discoveries could be made by gentlemen like Henry James, who did make his share, and who, of course, was a greater novelist than either of these Frenchmen; or by English squires; but we have got to take them, as Henry James would not do in the instance of Flaubert, as they come, and they often come a little rough.

A moment ago I introduced certain aspersions upon a few English novelists of the recent past, but it was with a purpose, for their limitations, sharply perceived by the late Virginia Woolf in her famous essay *Mr. Bennett and Mrs. Brown,* will make quite clear the difference between the novelist who, with Mr. Forster, merely bounces us along and the novelist who tries to do the whole job, the job that Flaubert first taught him to do. Mrs. Woolf is discussing Hilda Lessways, Arnold Bennett's heroine, and she says:

But we cannot hear her mother's voice, or Hilda's voice; we can only hear Mr. Bennett's voice telling us facts about rents and freeholds and copyholds and fines. What can Mr. Bennett be about? I have formed my own opinion of what Mr. Bennett is about—he is trying to make us imagine for him. . . .

"Trying to make us imagine for him"—the phrase erects a Chinese wall between all that is easy, pleasant, and perhaps merely socially useful in modern fiction, and all that is rigorous, sober, and self-contained. Mrs. Woolf, again, in speaking of the novels of Galsworthy, Bennett, and Wells, says: "Yet what odd books they are! Sometimes I wonder if we are right to call them books at all. For they leave one with a strange feeling of incompleteness and dissatisfaction. In order to complete them it seems necessary to do something—to join a society, or, more desperately, to write a cheque."

That is very nearly the whole story: the novelist who tries to make us imagine for him is perhaps trying to make us write a check—a very good thing to do, and I am not sure that even the socially unconscious Flaubert was deeply opposed to it, though I shall not attempt to speak for him on the question of joining societies. Let us see this matter as reasonably as we can. All literature has a social or moral or religious purpose: the writer has something that he has got to say to the largest public possible. In spite of Flaubert's belief that he wrote only for himself, this is as true of Madame Bovary as of *Uncle Tom's Cabin*. Is there a real difference between these books that might justify us in setting apart two orders of literature? Perhaps; for the difference is very great between getting it all inside the book and leaving some of it irresponsibly outside. For even though the check be written in a good cause it is the result of an irresponsible demand upon the part of the novelist. But the distinction is not, I think, absolute, nor should it be. And I am sure that Sainte-Beuve was right when he wrote in his review of *Madame Bovary* that not all young married women in Normandy were like Emma: was there not the case of the childless young matron of central France who, instead of taking lovers and then taking arsenic, "adopted children about her . . . and instructed them in moral culture"? Very good; for it is obvious that persons who join societies and write checks for moral culture are proper characters of fiction, as indeed all human beings of all degrees of charity or misanthropy are. But that is not the point at issue.

That point is quite simply that Flaubert, for the first time consciously and systematically, but not for the first time in the history of fiction, and not certainly of poetry—Flaubert taught us how to put this overworked and allegorical check *into* the novel, into its complex texture of scene, character, and action: which, of course, is one way of saying that he did the complete imaginative job himself, and did not merely point to what was going on, leaving the imaginative specification to our good will or to our intellectual vanity. (I pause here to remark the existence of a perpetual type of critic who prefers inferior literature, because it permits him to complete it. Flaubert understood the critics who, committed to the public function of teacher, resent being taught.) This completeness of presentation in the art of fiction was not, I repeat, something new, but I gather that it had previously appeared only here and there, by the sheer accident of genius: I think of Petronius; a few incidents in Boccaccio; half a dozen scenes by the Duke of Saint-Simon (the memorialists shade imperceptibly into the novelists); the great scene in which the Prince de Clèves tells his wife that he has refrained from expressing his love for her because he wished to avoid conduct improper to a husband; Emma Woodhouse with Mr. Knightly at the parlor table looking at the picture-album; countless other moments in early prose literature; but most of all that great forerunner, *Moll Flanders,* which is so much all of a piece in the Flaubertian canon that sometimes I think that Flaubert wrote it; or that nobody wrote either Defoe or Flaubert. For when literature reaches this stage of maturity, it is anonymous, and it matters little who writes it.

This is extravagant language. Or is it? It is no more than we are accustomed to when we talk about poetry, or music, or, most of all, the classical drama. The fourth-century lecture notes, to which I have already referred, some time ago licensed the most pretentious claims for the stage, and for poetry generally. I am only saying that fiction can be, has been, and *is* an art, as the various poetries are arts. Is this an extravagant claim? Only, I am convinced, in the minds of the more relaxed practitioners of this art, who excuse something less than the utmost talent and effort, and in the minds of critics who find the critical task more exacting than historical reporting, which reduces the novel to a news supplement. Was, as a matter of fact, Emma typical of young Norman womanhood? Are the Okies and Arkies just as Steinbeck represents them? What a triumph for the historians when it was found that there had actually been a young man whose end was like Julien Sorel's! And is it true what Mr. Faulkner says about Dixie? If it is, is what Mr. Stark Young says also true? This, I submit, is the temper of American criticism of fiction, with rare exceptions of little influence.

It is time now, towards the end of this *causerie,* to produce an image, an *exemplum,* something out of the art of fiction that underlies all the major problems of "picture and drama," symmetry, foreshortening, narrative pattern, pace, and language—all those complexities of the novelist's art which

Henry James, alone of the great fictionists, tried to explain (how much he coyly evaded!) in his famous Prefaces: problems that laid the ground for Mr. Lubbock's beautiful study. I am looking for something very simple and, in its direct impact, conclusive; a scene or an incident that achieves fullness of realization in terms of what it gives us to see and to hear. It must offer us fullness of rendition, not mere direction or statement. Don't state, says James, time and again— render! Don't tell us what is happening, let it happen! So I would translate James. For our purposes here it cannot be too great a scene, if we would see all round it: it must be a scene that will give us the most elementary instruction in that branch of the art of which the critics tell us little. What shall it be? Shall it be Prince André lying wounded under the wide heavens? Shall it be Moll Flanders peeping out of the upstairs window of the inn at her vanishing fourth (or is it fifth?) and undivorced husband, slyly avoiding him because she is in the room with her fifth or is it sixth? I could find perfect *exempla* in James himself. What could be better than Milly Theale's last *soirée* before she becomes too ill to appear again? Then there are James' fine "sitting-room scenes," the man and the woman talking out the destiny of one or both of them: Lambert Strether and Maria Gostrey, John Marcher and May Bartram, Merton Densher and Milly Theale. Or there is Strether looking down upon the boat in which Chad Newsome and Madame de Vionnet, unaware of Strether's scrutiny, betray that air of intimacy which discloses them for the first time to Strether as lovers.

Yet about these excellent scenes there is something outside our purpose, a clue that would sidetrack us into the terms of form and structure which I have virtually promised to neglect. Let us select an easy and perhaps even quite vulgar scene, a stock scene, in fact, that we should expect to find in a common romantic novel, or even in a Gothic story provided the setting were reduced to the bourgeois scale. Let the situation be something like this: A pretty young married woman, bored with her husband, a small-town doctor, has had an affair of sentiment with a young man, who has by this time left town. Growing more desperate, she permits herself to be seduced by a neighboring landowner, a coarse Lothario, who soon tires of her. Our scene opens with the receipt of his letter of desertion. He is going away and will not see her again. The young woman receives the letter with agitation and runs upstairs to the attic, where, having read the letter, she gives way to hysteria. She looks out the window down into the street, and decides to jump and end it all. But she grows dizzy and recoils. After a moment she hears her husband's voice; the servant touches her arm; she comes to and recovers.

It is distinctly unpromising: James would not have touched it; Balzac, going the whole hog, might have let her jump, or perhaps left her poised for the jump while he resumed the adventures of Vautrin. But, in any case, there she stands, and, as I have reported the scene, you have got to take my word for it that she is there at all: you do not see her, you do not hear the rapid breathing and the beating heart, and you have, again, only my word for it that she is dizzy. What I have done here, in fact, is precisely what Mrs. Woolf accused the Georgian novelists of doing: I am trying to make you imagine for me, perhaps even covertly trying to make you write a check for the Society for the Improvement of Provincial Culture, or the Society for the Relief of Small Town Boredom, or for a subscription to the Book-of-the-Month Club which would no doubt keep the young woman at improving her mind, and her mind off undesirable lovers. I hope that we shall do all these good things. But you must bear in mind that the Book-of-the-Month Club would probably send her the kind of literature that I have just written for you, so that she too might take to writing checks. Is there any guarantee that they would be good checks? The question brings us up short against certain permanent disabilities of human nature, which we should do well to see as objectively as possible, in the language of a greater artist; which is just what we shall now proceed to do:

Charles was there; she saw him; he spoke to her; she heard nothing, and she went on quickly up the stairs, breathless, distraught, dumb, and ever holding this horrible piece of paper, that crackled between her fingers like a plate of sheet-iron. On the second floor she stopped before the attic-door, that was closed.

Then she tried to calm herself; she recalled the letter; she must finish it; she did not dare to. And where? How? She would be seen! "Ah, no! here," she thought, "I shall be all right."

Emma pushed open the door and went in.

The slates threw straight down a heavy heat that gripped her temples, stifled her; she dragged herself to the closed garret-window. She drew back the bolt, and the dazzling light burst in with a leap.

Opposite, beyond the roofs, stretched the open country till it was lost to sight. Down below, underneath her, the village square was empty; the stones of the pavement glittered, the weathercocks on the houses were motionless. At the corner of the street from a lower story, rose a kind of humming with strident modulations. It was Binet turning.

She leant against the embrasure of the window, and re-read the letter with angry sneers. But the more she fixed her attention upon it, the more confused were her ideas. She saw him again, heard him, encircled him with her arms, and the throbs of her heart, that beat against her breast like blows of a sledge-hammer, grew faster and faster, with uneven intervals. She looked about her with the wish that the earth might crumble into pieces. Why not end it all? What restrained her? She was free. She advanced, looked at the paving-stones, saying to herself, "Come! Come!"

The luminous ray that came straight up from below drew the weight of her body towards the abyss. It seemed to her that the floor dipped on end like a tossing boat. She was right at the edge, almost hanging, surrounded by vast space. The blue of the heavens suffused her, the air was whirling in her hollow head; she had but to yield, to let herself be taken; and the humming of the lathe never ceased, like an angry voice calling her.

"Emma! Emma!" cried Charles.

She stopped.

"Wherever are you? Come!"

The thought that she had just escaped from death made her faint with terror. She closed her eyes; then she shivered at the touch of a hand on her sleeve; it was Félicité.

"Master is waiting for you, madame; the soup is on the table."
And she had to go down to sit at table.

The English translation is not good; its failure to convey the very slight elevation of tone is a fundamental failure. It is not a rhetorical elevation, but rather one of perfect formality and sobriety. We are not looking at this scene through Emma's eyes. We occupy a position slightly above and to one side, where we see her against the full setting; yet observe that at the same time we see nothing that she does not see, hear nothing that she does not hear. It is one of the amazing paradoxes of the modern novel, whose great subject is a man alone in society or even against society, almost never with society, that out of this view of man isolated we see developed to the highest possible point of virtuosity and power a technique of putting man wholly into his physical setting. The action is not stated from the point of view of the author; it is rendered in terms of situation and scene. To have made this the viable property of the art of fiction was to have virtually made the art of fiction. And that, I think, is our debt to Flaubert.

But we should linger over this scene if only to try our hands at what I shall now, for the first time, call sub-criticism, or the animal tact which permits us occasionally to see connections and correspondences which our rational powers, unaided, cannot detect. What capital feature of the scene seems (if it does) to render the actuality more than any other? The great fact, I think, is the actuality, and your sense of it is all that is necessary. Yet I like to linger over the whirring lathe of old Binet, a lay figure or "flat character" who has done little in the novel and will never do much, and whose lathe we merely noted from the beginning as a common feature of a small town like Yonville. I should like to know when Flaubert gave him the lathe, whether just to tag him for us; whether, writing the present scene, he went back and gave it to him as a "plant" for use here later; or whether, having given him the lathe, he decided it would be useful in this scene.

What is its use? James said that the work of fiction must be "a direct impression of life," a very general requirement; but in the perspective of nearly ninety years since the publication of *Madame Bovary* and the rise of the Impressionist novel through Henry James, James Joyce, and Virginia Woolf, the phrase takes on a more specific sense. Mind you the phrase is not "direct representation," which only the stage can give us. But here, using this mechanic's tool, Flaubert gives us a direct *impression* of Emma's sensation at a particular moment (which not even the drama could accomplish), and thus by rendering audible to us what Emma alone could hear he charged the entire scene with actuality. As Emma goes to the window she merely notes that Binet's lathe is turning— *C'était Binet qui tournait.* Then she looks down at the street which seems to rise towards her—*Allons! Allons!* she whispers, because she cannot find the will to jump. We have had rendered to us visually the shock of violent suicide. Now comes the subtle fusion of the reaction and of the pull toward self-destruction, which is the humming in her head: how can Flaubert *render* it for us? Shall we not have to take his word for it? Shall we not have to imagine for him? No: *l'air circulait dans sa tête creuse,* he says; and then: *le ronflement du tour ne discontinuait pas, comme une voix furieuse qui l'appelait*—"the whirring of the lathe never stopped, like a voice of fury calling her." The humming vertigo that draws the street towards her is rendered audible to us by the correlative sound of the lathe.

That is all, or nearly all, there is to it; but I think it is enough to set up our image, our *exemplum*. I leave to you, as I constantly reserve for myself, the inexhaustible pleasure of tracing out the infinite strands of interconnection in this and other novels, complexities as deep as life itself but ordered, fixed, and dramatized into arrested action. If I have made too much of Flaubert, or too much of too little of Flaubert, I can only say that I have not willfully ignored men as great, or greater. It is proper to honor France, and to honor the *trouvère*, the discoverer; for it has been through Flaubert that the novel has at last caught up with poetry.

1944

THE SYMBOLIC IMAGINATION

The Mirrors of Dante

It is right even if it is not quite proper to observe at the beginning of a discourse on Dante, that no writer has held in mind at one time the whole of *The Divine Comedy:* not even Dante, perhaps least of all Dante himself. If Dante and his Dantisti have not been equal to the view of the whole, a view shorter than theirs must be expected of the amateur who, as a writer of verses, vainly seeks absolution from the mortal sin of using poets for what he can get out of them. I expect to look at a single image in the *Paradiso,* and to glance at some of its configurations with other images. I mean the imagery of light, but I mean chiefly its reflections. It was scarcely necessary for Dante to have read, though he did read, the *De Anima,* to learn that sight is the king of the senses and that the human body, which like other organisms lives by *touch,* may be made actual in language only through the imitation of *sight.* And sight in language is imitated not by means of "description"—*ut pictura poesis*—but by doubling the image: our confidence in its spatial reality is won quite simply by casting the image upon a glass, or otherwise by the insinuation of space between.

I cannot undertake to examine here Dante's double imagery in all its detail, for his light alone could lead us into complexities as rich as life itself. I had almost said richer than life, if by life we mean (as we must mean) what we ourselves are able daily to see, or even what certain writers have seen, with the exception of Shakespeare, and possibly of Sophocles and Henry James. A secondary purpose that I shall have in view will be to consider the dramatic implications of the light imagery as they emerge at the resolution of the poem, in Canto XXXIII of the *Paradiso*. These implications suggest, to my mind, a radical change in the interpretation of *The Divine Comedy,* and impel me to ask again: What kind of poem is it? In asking this question I shall not be concerned with what we ordinarily consider to be literary criticism; I shall be only incidentally judging, for my main purpose is to describe.

In *Purgatorio* XXX Beatrice appears to Dante first as a voice (what she says need not detain us here), then as light; but not yet the purest light. She is the light of a pair of eyes in which is reflected the image of the gryphon, a symbol of the hypostatic union, of which she herself is a "type." But before Dante perceives this image in her eyes, he says: "A thousand desires hotter than flame held my eyes bound to the shining eyes. . . ." [1] I see no reason to suppose that Dante does not mean what he says. *Mille disiri più che fiamma caldi* I take to be the desires, however interfused by this time with courtly and mystical associations, of a man for a woman: the desires that the boy Dante felt for the girl Beatrice in 1274 after he had passed her in a street of Florence. She is the same Beatrice, Dante the same Dante, with differences which do not reject but rather include their sameness. Three dancing girls appear: Dante's allegory, formidable as it is, intensifies rather than impoverishes the reality of the dancers as girls. Their dance is a real dance, their song, in which they make a charming request of Beatrice, is a real song. If Dante expected us to be interested in the dancers only as the Theological Virtues, I see no good reason why he made them girls at all. They are sufficiently convincing as the Three Graces, and I cannot feel in the pun a serious violation of Dante's confidence. The request of the girls is sufficiently remarkable: *Volgi, Beatrice, volgi gli occhi santi*—"Turn, Beatrice, turn those holy eyes." Let Dante see your holy eyes; look into his eyes. Is it extravagant to substitute for the image of the gryphon the image of Dante in Beatrice's eyes? I think not. *He is in her eyes*—as later, in *Paradiso* XXXIII, he will be "in" God. Then a startling second request by the dancers: "Of thy grace do us the favor that thou unveil thy mouth to him"—*disvele/a lui la bocca tua* . . . "that he may discern the second beauty which thou hidest"—*la seconda bel-*

leza che tu cele. At this point we get one of the innumerable proofs of Dante's greatness as a poet. We are not shown *la seconda belleza,* the smiling mouth; we are shown, instead, in the first four *terzine* of the next canto, the effect on Dante. For neither Dante nor Homer *describes* his heroine. As Beatrice's mouth is revealed, all Dante's senses but the sense of sight are *tutti spenti;* and sight itself is caught in *l'antica rete*—"the ancient net"—a variation of *l'antica fiamma*—"the ancient flame"—that he had felt again when he had first seen Beatrice in the Earthly Paradise.

What the net is doing here seems now to me plain, after some ten years of obtuseness about it. The general meaning is, as Charles Williams holds, that Dante, having chosen the Way of Affirmation through the physical image, feels here in the Earthly Paradise all that he had *felt* before, along with what he now *knows.* Why did he put the worldly emotion of his youthful life into the figure of the net? It is not demanded by the moment; we should not have the sense of missing something if it were not there. If it is a simple metaphor for the obfuscation of sensuality, it is not a powerful metaphor; we must remember that Dante uses very few linguistic metaphors, as distinguished from analogical or symbolic objects; when he uses them they are simple and powerful. The net, as I see it, is not simply a metaphor for the "catching" of Dante by Beatrice in 1274, though it is partly *that* ancient net; it is also a net of even more famous antiquity, that in which Venus caught Mars; and it is thus a symbolic object. Moreover, if Beatrice's eyes are univocally divine, why do the three Theological Dancers reproach him with gazing at her "too fixedly"—*troppo fiso*—as if he or anybody else could get too much of the divine light? He is, of course, not yet ready for the full Beatific Vision. But an astonishing feature of the great scene of the divine pageant is that, as a trope, a subjective effect, the smile of Beatrice simultaneously revives his human love (Eros) and directs his will to the anticipation of the Beatific Vision (Agapé): both equally, by means of the action indicated by the blinding effect of both; he is blinded by the net and by the light, not alternately but at one instant.[2]

To bring together various meanings at a single moment of action is to exercise what I shall speak of here as the symbolic imagination; but the line of *action* must be unmistakable, we must never be in doubt about what is happening; for at a given stage of his progress the hero does one simple thing, and one only. The symbolic imagination conducts an action through analogy, of the human to the divine, of the natural to the supernatural, of the low to the high, of time to eternity. My literary generation was deeply impressed by Baudelaire's sonnet *Correspondances,* which restated the doctrines of medieval symbolism by way of Swedenborg; we were impressed because we had lost the historical perspective leading back to the original source. But the statement of a doctrine is very different from its possession as experience in poetry. Analogical symbolism need not move towards an act of imagination. It may see in active experience the qualities necessary for static symbolism; for example, the Grave of Jesus, which for the theologian may be a symbol to be expounded in the Illuminative Way, or for the mystic may be an object of contemplation in the Unitive Way. Despite the timeless orders of both rational discourse and intuitive contemplation, it is the business of the symbolic poet to return to the order of temporal sequence—to *action*. His purpose is to show men experiencing whatever they may be capable of, with as much meaning as he may be able to see in it; but the action comes first. Shall we call this the Poetic Way? It is at any rate the way of the poet, who has got to do his work with the body of this world, whatever that body may look like to him, in his time and place—the whirling atoms, the body of a beautiful woman, or a deformed body, or the body of Christ, or even the body of this death. If the poet is able to put into this moving body, or to find in it, a coherent chain of analogies, he will inform an intuitive act with symbolism; his will be in one degree or another the symbolic imagination.

Before I try to illustrate these general reflections, I must make a digression, for my own guidance, which I am not competent to develop as searchingly as my subject demands. The symbolic imagination takes rise from a definite limitation of human rationality which was recognized in the West until the seventeenth century; in this view the intellect cannot have direct knowledge of essences. The only created mind that has this knowledge is the angelic mind.[3] If we do not believe in angels we shall have to invent them in order to explain by parable the remarkable appearance, in Europe, at about the end of the sixteenth century, of a mentality which denied man's commitment to the physical world, and set itself up in quasi-divine independence. This mind has intellect and will without feeling; and it is through feeling alone that we witness the glory of our servitude to the natural world, to St. Thomas' accidents, or, if you will, to Locke's secondary qualities; it is our tie with the world of sense. The angelic mind suffers none of the limitations of sense; it has immediate knowledge of essences; and this knowledge moves through the perfect will to divine love, with which it is at one. Imagination in an angel is thus inconceivable, for the angelic mind transcends the mediation of both image and discourse. I call that human imagination angelic which tries to disintegrate or to circumvent the image in the illusory pursuit of essense. When human beings undertake this ambitious program, divine love becomes so rarefied that it loses its human paradigm, and is dissolved in the worship of intellectual power, the surrogate of divinity that worships itself. It professes to know nature as essence at the same time that it has become alienated from nature in the rejection of its material forms.

It was, however high the phrases [writes Charles Williams], *the common thing from which Dante always started, as it was certainly the greatest and most common to which he came. His images were the natural inevitable images—the girl in the street, the people he knew, the language he learned as a child. In them the great diagrams were perceived; from them the great myths open; by them he understands the final end.*[4]

This is the simple secret of Dante, but it is a secret which is not necessarily available to the Christian poet today. The Catholic faith has not changed since Dante's time. But the

Catholic sensibility, as we see it in modern Catholic poetry, from Thompson to Lowell, has become angelic, and is not distinguishable (doctrinal differences aside) from poetry by Anglicans, Methodists, Presbyterians, and atheists. I take it that more than doctrine, even if the doctrine be true, is necessary for a great poetry of action. Catholic poets have lost, along with their heretical friends, the power to start with the "common thing": they have lost the gift for concrete experience. The abstraction of the modern mind has obscured their way into the natural order. Nature offers to the symbolic poet clearly denotable objects in depth and in the round, which yield the analogies to the higher syntheses. The modern poet rejects the higher synthesis, or tosses it in a vacuum of abstraction.[5] If he looks at nature he spreads the clear visual image in a complex of metaphor, from one catachresis to another through Aristotle's permutations of genus and species. He cannot sustain the prolonged analogy, the second and superior kind of figure that Aristotle doubtless had in mind when he spoke of metaphor as the key to the resemblances of things, and the mark of genius.

That the gift of analogy was not Dante's alone every medievalist knows. The most striking proof of its diffusion and the most useful example for my purpose that I know, is the letter of St. Catherine of Siena to Brother Raimondo of Capua. A young Sienese, Niccolo Tuldo, had been unjustly convicted of treason and condemned to death. Catherine became his angel of mercy, giving him daily solace—the meaning of the Cross, the healing powers of the Blood; and so reconciled him to the faith that he accepted his last end. Now I have difficulty believing people who say that they live in the Blood of Christ, for I take them to mean that they have the faith and hope some day to live in it. The evidence of the Blood is one's power to produce it, the power to show it as a "common thing" and to make it real, literally, in action. For the report of the Blood is very different from its reality. St. Catherine does not report it; she recreates it, so that its analogical meaning is confirmed again in blood that she has seen. This is how she does it:

Then [the condemned man] came, like a gentle lamb; and see-
ing me he began to smile, and wanted me to make the sign of
the Cross. When he had received the sign, I said, "Down! To
the bridal, my sweetest brother. For soon shalt thou be in the
enduring life." He prostrated himself with great gentleness,
and I stretched out his neck; and bowed me down, and recalled
to him the Blood of the Lamb. His lips said naught save Jesus!
and Catherine! And so saying, I received his head in my hands,
closing my eyes in the divine goodness and saying, "I will."

When he was at rest my soul rested in peace and quiet, and in
so great fragrance of blood that I could not bear to remove the
blood which had fallen on me from him.

It is deeply shocking, as all proximate incarnations of the
Word are shocking, whether in Christ and the Saints, or in
Dostoevsky, James Joyce, or Henry James. I believe it was
T. S. Eliot who made accessible again to an ignorant generation a common Christian insight, when he said that people
cannot bear very much reality. I take this to mean that only
persons of extraordinary courage, and perhaps even genius,
can face the spiritual truth in its physical body. Flaubert
said that the artist, the soldier, and the priest face death
every day; so do we all; yet it is perhaps nearer to them
than to other men; it is their particular responsibility. When
St. Catherine "rests in so great fragrance of blood," it is no
doubt the Blood of the Offertory which the celebrant offers
to God *cum odore suavitatis,* but with the literal odor of the
species of wine, not of blood. St. Catherine had the courage
of genius which permitted her to *smell* the Blood of Christ
in Niccolo Tuldo's blood clotted on her dress: she smelled
the two bloods *not alternately but at one instant,* in a single
act compounded of spiritual insight and physical perception.

Chekhov said that a gun hanging on the wall at the beginning of a story has got to be fired off before the story
ends: everything in potency awaits its completed purpose
in act. If this is a metaphysical principle, it is also the prime
necessity of the creative imagination. Is not St. Catherine
telling us that the Blood of Christ must be perpetually re-

created as a brute fact? If the gun has got to be fired, the Blood has got to be shed, if only because that is the first condition of its appearance; it must move towards the condition of human action, where we may smell it, touch it, and taste it again.

When ecclesiastical censorship of this deep insight in the laity exceeds a just critical prudence, the result is not merely obscurantism in the arts; it is perhaps a covert rejection of the daily renewal of the religious life. Twenty-five years ago the late W. B. Yeats had a controversy with the Irish bishops about the famous medieval Cherry Tree Carol, which the hierarchy wished to suppress as blasphemous. The Blessed Virgin is resting under a cherry tree, too tired to reach up and pluck a cherry. Since Christ lives from the foundations of the world, He is omnipotent in the womb, and He commands the tree to lower a bough for His Mother's convenience; which it obligingly does, since it cannot do otherwise. Here again the gun is fired and the Blood is shed. If the modern Church has lost the historic experience of this kind of symbolism, which is more tolerable, I believe, in the Latin countries than with us, it is at least partial evidence that the Church has lost the great culture that it created, and that at intervals has created the life of the Church.

I return from this digression to repeat that Dante was the great master of the symbolism, the meaning of which I have been trying to suggest. But the symbolic "problem" of *The Divine Comedy* we must not suppose Dante to have undertaken analytically; it is our problem, not his. Dr. Flanders Dunbar has stated it with great penetration:

As with his progress he perceives more and more of ultimate reality through the symbol [Beatrice], at the same time the symbol occupies less and less of his attention, until ultimately it takes its place among all created things on a petal of the rose, while he gazes beyond it into the full glory of the sun.[6]

The symbolic problem, then, is: How shall Dante move step by step (literally and allegorically) from the Dark Wood, the negation of light, to the "three circles, of three colors and one magnitude," God Himself, or pure light, where there are no sensible forms to reflect it? There can be no symbol for God, for that which has itself informed step by step the symbolic progress. Vision, giving us clear visual objects, through physical sight, moving steadily upward towards its anagogical transfiguration, is the first matrix of the vast analogical structure. As Dante sees more he sees less: as he sees more light the nearer he comes to its source, the less he sees of what it had previously lit up. In the Empyrean, at the climax of the Illuminative Way, Beatrice leaves Dante and takes her place in the Rose; St. Bernard now guides him into the Intuitive Way.

For the Illuminative Way is the way to knowledge through the senses, by means of aided reason, but here the "distance" between us and what we see is always the distance between a concept and its object, between the human situation in which the concept arises and the realization of its full meaning. Put otherwise, with the beginning of the *Vita Nuova* in mind, it is the distance between the knowledge of love, which resulted from the earthly love of Dante for Beatrice, and the distant "object," or God, that had made the love in the first place possible: the distance between Beatrice and the light which had made it possible for him to see her. The Kantian synthetic proposition of the entire poem, as we enter it through the symbolism of light, is: Light is Beatrice. Here the eye is still on the human image; it is still on it up to the moment when she takes her place with the other saints in the Rose, where she is only one of many who turn their eyes to the "eternal fountain." Light is Beatrice; light is her *smile;* her final smile, which Dante sees as she enters the Rose, is no longer the mere predicate of a sentence, for there is now no distance between the smile and what had lit it. Although, in so far as it is a smile at all, it is still the smile at the unveiling of the mouth, it is now the smile without the mouth, the smile of light. And thus we arrive at the converse of the proposition: Beatrice is light. Now Dante's eye is on the light itself, but he cannot see it because Beatrice, through whose image he had progressively seen more light, has disappeared; and he can see nothing. There is nothing to *see.* For that which enables sight is not

an object of vision. What has been seen is, in what is surely
one of the greatest passages of all poetry, "the shadowy
prefaces of their truth." Illumination, or intellect guided by
divine grace, powerful as it is, halts at the "prefaces." But
the Unitive Way leads to the Presence, where both sight and
discursive thought cease.

Whether Dante should have tried to give us an image of
God, of that which is without image and invisible, is an unanswerable question. Is it possible that we have here a break
in the symbolic structure, which up to the end of the poem
has been committed to the visible? At the end we are with
Love, whose unpredicated attribute is the entire universe.
Has Dante given us, in the "three circles, of three colors
and one magnitude," merely the trinitarian and doctrinal
equivalent of the ultimate experience, instead of an objective
symbol of the experience itself? In the terms of Dante's
given structure, such a symbol was perhaps not possible; and
strictly speaking it is never possible. If he was going to give
us anything he doubtless had to give us just what he gave;
he gave it in an act of great artistic heroism. For in the
center of the circles he sees the image of man. This is the
risk, magnified almost beyond conception, of St. Catherine:
the return of the supra-rational and supra-sensible to the
"common thing." It is the courage to see again, even in its
ultimate cause, the Incarnation.

If we will look closely at the last four lines of the *Paradiso*,
and double back on our tracks, I believe that we will see that
there is no break in the *dramatic* structure—the structure of
the action.[7] For the poem is an action: a man is acting and
going somewhere, and things are happening both to him
and around him; otherwise the poem would be—what I
may have given the impression of its being—a symbolic
machine. In the space of an essay I cannot prepare properly the background of the suggestion that I am about to
offer. For one thing, we should have to decide who "Dante"
is, and where he is in the action that he has depicted—questions that nobody seems to know much about. For what it
may be worth, I suggest that the poet has undertaken to involve a fictional character named Dante—at once the poet

and not the poet of that name—in a certain action of the greatest possible magnitude, the issue of which is nothing less, perhaps something greater, than life or death. In this action the hero fails. He fails in the sense that he will have to start over again when he steps out of the "poem," as he surely must do if he is going to write it.

Thus I see *The Divine Comedy* as essentially dramatic and, in one of its modes, tragic. Are we to suppose that the hero actually attained to the Beatific Vision? No; for nobody who had would be so foolish as to write a poem about it, if in that spiritual perfection it could even occur to him to do so. The poem is a vast paradigm of the possibility of the Beatific Vision. No more than its possibility for the individual person, for "Dante" himself, is here entertained. What shall we make of his failure of memory, the slipping away of the final image, which he calls *tanto oltraggio*—"so great an outrage?" It would be a nice question to decide whether something had slipped away, or whether it had ever been fully there. The vision is imagined, it is *imaged;* its essence is not possessed. I confess that it is not an argument from the poem to say that had Dante claimed its possession, he would have lost that "good of the intellect" which we forfeit when we presume to angelic knowledge; and it was through the good of the intellect that he was able to write the poem. But it is an external argument that I believe cannot be entirely ignored.

The last *terzina* of the last canto tells us: *All' alta fantasia qui mancò possa*—"To the high fantasy here power failed." What power failed? The power to write the poem, or the power to possess as experience the divine essence? Is it a literary or a religious failure? It is obviously and honorably both. It makes no more sense to say Dante achieved his final vision as direct experience than to say that Sophocles married his mother and put out his own eyes; that the experience of the *Oedipus Rex* represents the personal experience of Sophocles. What Dante achieved is an *actual* insight into the great dilemma, eternal life or eternal death, but he has not hedged the dilemma like a bet to warrant himself a favorable issue. As the poem closes, he still faces it, like the rest of us. Like Oedipus, the fictional Dante learns in humility a certain discipline of the will: we may equate up to a point the dark-blindness of Oedipus and the final light-blindness of Dante; both men have succeeded through suffering in blinding themselves to knowledge-through-sense, in the submission of *hybris* to a higher will.[8] The fictional Dante at the end steps out of the frame and becomes again the historical Dante; Oedipus steps out of his frame, his fictional plot is done, he is back in the world of unformed action, blind and, like Dante, an exile. Shall Oedipus be saved? Shall Dante? We do not know, but to ask the question is to point to a primary consideration in the interpretation of *The Divine Comedy,* particularly if we are disposed, as some commentators have been, to believe that Dante the man used his poem arrogantly to predict his own salvation.

If Dante does not wholly succeed in giving us in the "three circles, of three colors and one magnitude," an image of the Godhead, I think we are ready to see that it was not necessary; it was not a part of his purpose. Such an image is not the "final cause" of the poem. The poem is an action; it is an action to the end. For the image that Dante gives us of the Godhead is not an image to be received by the reader as essential knowledge in his own "angelic" intelligence, as an absolute apart from the action. It is a dramatic image; the image is of the action and the action is Dante's. To read Canto XXXIII in any other way would be perhaps to commit the blunder that M. Gilson warns us against: the blunder of thinking that Dante was writing a super-philosophical tract, or a pious embellishment of the doctrines of Thomas Aquinas, instead of a poem. The question, then, is not what is the right anagogical symbol for God; it is rather what symbol for God will serve tropologically (that is, morally and dramatically) for the tragic insight of the poet who knows, through the stages of the Three Ways, that the Beatific Vision is possible but uncertain of realization. Dante sees himself, Man, in the Triune Circles, and he is in the Seraphic Heaven of Love. But at the end desire and will are like a "wheel moving equally"; motion imparted to it at one point turns it as a whole, but it has to be moved, as the wheel of our own desire and will must be moved, by a force outside it. The wheel is Dante's last symbol of the great failure. Since it must be moved, it is not yet at one, not yet in unity, with the divine will; it obeys it, as those other wheels, the sun and stars, moved by love, obey.

I take it that the wheel is the final geometrical projection of the *visual* matrix of analogy; it is what the eye sees, the material form, and what in its anagoge it eventually aspires to become. We must remember that Beatrice's eyes are spheres, no less than the physical universe itself, which is composed of concentric spheres. The first circles that Dante shows us are in Canto III of the *Inferno,* Charon's—"for round his eyes were wheels of flame." The last, the Triune Circles, are the anagoge of the visual circle, and are without extension; they are pure light, the abstraction or sublimation of flame. Flame burning in a circle and light lighting up a circle, and what it encloses, are the prime sensible symbols of the poem. Only Satan, at the geometrical center of the world, occupies a point that cannot be located on any existing arc of the cosmos. This is the spherical (or circular) expression of Satan's absolute privation of light-as-love which in the Empyrean turns the will-wheel of Dante with the cosmic spheres. These are the will of God as love; and if we ignore the dramatic structure, and fail to look closely at the symbolic, we shall conclude that Dante is at one with the purpose of the universe. But, as we have seen, the symbolic structure is complicated by the action, and in the end the action prevails. That is to say, Dante is *still moving.* Everything that moves, says Dante the Thomist in his letter to Can Grande, has some imperfection in it because it is, in the inverse degree of its rate of motion, removed from the Unmoved Mover, the Triune Circles, God. By a twist of this argument, which, of course, as I shall presently indicate, is specious, Satan himself has no imperfection: he too lies immobile—except for the fanning wings that freeze the immobile damned in Giudecca—as the Still Point in the Triune Circles is immobile. If Dante's will is turning like a wheel, he is neither damned nor saved; he is morally active in the universal human predicament. His participation in the love imparted as motion to the universe draws him towards the Triune Circles and to the immobility of peace at the center, as it draws all creatures; but a defection of the will could plunge him into the other "center."

Now Dante is astonished when he sees in the Primum Mobile a reversal of the ratio of speed of the spheres as he had observed it on earth, through the senses. "But in the universe of sense," he says to Beatrice, "we may see the circlings more divine as from the center they are more removed." In the spiritual universe the circlings are more divine the nearer they are to the center. It is a matter of perspective; from the earth outward the revolutions of the spheres are increasingly rapid up to the ninth, the Primum Mobile, whose speed is just short of infinite; the Primum Mobile is trying to achieve with all points of its surface a simultaneous contact with the Still Point of the Empyrean. What he sees in the Primum Mobile is this perspective visually reversed; instead of being the outer "crust" of the universe, the Primum Mobile is actually next to the central Still Point, whirling with inconceivable speed. God, the Still Point, is a non-spatial entity which is *everywhere* and *nowhere*. The Ptolemaic cosmos, which had been Christianized by the imposition of the angelic hierarchy of Dionysius, has been, in a way not to be completely visualized, turned inside out. The spheres, which began their career as an astronomical hypothesis, are now no longer necessary; they are replaced in the ultimate reality by nine non-spatial gradations of angelic intelligence, in three triads, the last and ninth circle of "fire" being that of the simple angels, the "farthest" removed in the non-spatial continuum from the Divine Love.

Where then is the earth, with Satan at its exact center? I think we must answer: Where it has always been. But "where" that is we had better not try to say. At any rate neither Satan nor the earth is at the spiritual center. His immobility thus has no perfection. In the full spiritual reality of which the center of the material universe becomes an outermost "rind," beyond space, Satan does not exist: he exists in the world of sense and in the human will. The darkness of hell, from the point of view of God (if I may be allowed the expression), is not an inner darkness, but an outer. So, in the progress from hell to the Empyrean, Dante has come from the inner darkness of man to the inner light of God; from the outer darkness of God to the outer light of man.

This anagogical conversion of symbol that I have been trying to follow in one of its threads is nowhere by Dante merely *asserted;* it is constantly moving, rendered moment by moment as *action.* Like most good poets, great or minor, Dante wrote better than he had meant to do; for if we took him at his word, in the letter to Can Grande, we should conclude that the *Paradiso* is a work of rhetoric calculated "to remove those living in this life from a state of misery and to guide them to a state of happiness." It seems probable that persons now enrolled among the Blessed got there without being compelled to see on the way all that Dante saw. Were we reading the poem for that kind of instruction, and knew not where else to find it, we might conclude that Dante's *luce intellectual,* with its transformations in the fourfold system of interpretation, is too great a price to pay even for salvation; or, at any rate, for most of us, the wrong price. It would perhaps be a mistake for a man to decide that he has become a Christian at the instance of Dante, unless he is prepared to see all that Dante saw—which is one thing, but always seen in at least two ways.

A clue to two of the ways is the mirror symbol. As we approach it, the kind of warning that Dante at intervals pauses to give us is not out of place. For if the way up to now has been rough, we may expect it from now on to be even rougher. The number of persons, objects, and places in *The Divine Comedy* that are reflections, replicas, or manifestations of things more remote is beyond calculation. The entire natural world is a replica *in reverse* of the supernatural world. That, I believe, we have seen so far only on the dubious authority of my own assertion. But if Dante is a poet (I agree with M. Gilson that he is) he will not be satisfied with assertion as such, even with the authority of the Church to support it. The single authority of poetry is a difficult criterion of actuality that must always remain beyond our reach. And in some sense of this actuality Dante has got to place his vast two-way analogy (heaven like the world, the world like heaven) on the scene of action, and make it move. Let us take the stance of Dante at the beginning of *Paradiso* XXVIII, and try to suggest some of the ways in which he moves it:

> *as in the mirror a taper's flame, kindled behind a man, is seen by him before it be in his sight or thought,*
> *as he turns back to see whether the glass speak truth to him, and sees that it accords with it as song-words to the music;*
> *so my memory recalls that I did turn, gazing upon the lovely eyes whence love had made the noose to capture me;*
> *and when I turned, and my own eyes were struck by what appears in that orb whenever upon its circling the eye is well fixed,*
> *a point I saw which rayed forth light so keen that all the vision that it flames upon must close because of its sharp point.*

(One observes in passing that even in the Primum Mobile Beatrice bears the net-noose dimension of meaning.) Beatrice's eyes are a mirror in which is reflected that "sharp point," to which Dante, still at a distance from it, now turns his direct gaze. As he looks at it he sees for the first time what its reflection in Beatrice's eyes could not convey: that it is the sensible world turned inside out. For the sensible world as well as her eyes is only a reflection of the light from the sharp point. Now he is looking at the thing-in-itself. *He has at last turned away from the mirror which is the world.* What happens when we turn away from a mirror to look directly at the object which we saw reflected? I must anticipate Beatrice's famous experiment with one of my own. If you will place upon a table a box open at one end, the open end towards a mirror, and then look into the mirror, you will see the open end. Turn from the mirror and look at the box itself. You still see the open end, and thus you see the object *reversed*. If the box were reproduced, in the sense of being continued or moved *into* the mirror, the actual box would present, when we turn to it, a closed end; for the box and its reflection would show their respectively corresponding sides in congruent projection. Quantitative visualization of the cosmic reversal is not completely possible. But through the mirror analogy Dante performs a stupendous feat of the imagination that in kind has probably not been rivalled by any other poet. And it is an analogy that has been firmly grounded in action.

In conclusion I shall try to point to its literal base; for we have seen it, in *Paradiso* XXVIII, only as a simile; and if we had not had it laid down earlier as a physical fact to which we must assent, a self-contained phenomenon of the natural order, it would no doubt lack at the end that fullness of actuality which we do not wholly understand, but which we require of poetry. The self-contained fact of the natural order is established in Canto II of the *Paradiso,* where Beatrice performs a physical experiment. Some scholars have been moved by it to admire Dante for this single ray of positivistic enlightenment feebly glowing in the mind of a medieval poet. So far as I know, our critics have not considered it necessary to be sufficiently unenlightened to see that Beatrice's experiment is merely poetry.

Before I reproduce it I shall exhibit a few more examples of the mirror symbol that appear at intervals in the five last cantos. In Canto XXIX, 25-27, form permeates matter "as in glass . . . a ray so glows that from its coming to its pervading all, there is no interval." Still in XXIX, 142-145, at the end: "See now the height and breadth of the eternal worth, since it has made itself so many mirrors in which it is reflected, remaining in itself one as before." At line 37 of Canto XXX we enter the Empyrean where Dante sees the great River of Light "issuing its living sparks"; it too is a mirror, for Beatrice explains: "The river and the topaz gems that enter and go forth, and the smiling grasses are prefaces of their truth" (i.e., of what they reflect). In Canto XXX, 85-87, Dante bends down to the waves "to make mirrors of my eyes"; and again in XXX he sees the Rose of Paradise, another mirror, in one of his great similes:

And as a hillside reflects itself in water at its foot, as if to look upon its own adornment, when it is rich in grasses and in flowers,

so, mounting in the light, around, around, casting reflection
  in more than a thousand ranks I saw all that of us have
  won return up yonder.

And finally the climactic reflection, the "telic principle" and
the archetype of them all, in Canto XXX, 127-132:

The circling that in thee [in the Triune God] appeared to be
  conceived as a reflected light, by my eyes scanned a little,
in itself, of its own color, seemed to be painted with our
  effigy, and thereat my sight was all committed to it.

Where have these mirrors, which do their poetic work, the
work of making the supra-sensible visible—one of the tasks
of all poetry—where have they come from? The remote
frame is doubtless the circular or spherical shape of the
Ptolemaic cosmos;[9] but if there is glass in the circular frame,
it reflects nothing until Virgil has left Dante to Beatrice's
guidance in the Earthly Paradise (*Purgatorio* XXXI); where
we have already glanced at the unveiling of mouth and eyes.
I suggest that Beatrice's eyes in *Purgatorio* XXXI are the
first mirror. But the image is not, at this early stage of Beatrice, sufficiently developed to bear all the strain of analogical
weight that Dante intends to put upon it. For that purpose
the mirror must be established as a literal mirror, a plain
mirror, a "common thing."

He not only begins with the common thing; he continues
with it, until at the end we come by disarming stages to a
scene that no man has ever looked upon before. Every detail
of Paradise is a common thing; it is the cumulative combination and recombination of natural objects beyond their "natural" relations, which staggers the imagination. "Not," says
Beatrice to Dante, "that such things are in themselves harsh;
but on your side is the defect, in that your sight is not yet
raised so high."

A mirror is an artifact of the practical intellect, and as
such can be explained by natural law: but there is no natural law which explains man as a mirror reflecting the image
of God. The great leap is made in the interval between Canto
II and Canto XXXIII of the *Paradiso*.

Dante, in Canto II, is baffled by the spots on the moon,

supposing them to be due to alternating density and rarity of matter. No, says Beatrice in effect, this would be monism, a materialistic explanation of the diffusion of the divine light. The true explanation is very different: all saved souls are equally saved, and all the heavenly spheres are equally in heaven; but the divine light reaches the remoter spheres and souls according to the spiritual gifts of which they were capable in the natural world. "This is the formal principle," Beatrice says, summing up, "which produces, in conformity to the excellence of the object, the turbid and the clear."

Meanwhile she has asked Dante to consider a physical experiment to illustrate the unequal reception of the divine substance. Take three mirrors, she says, and set two of them side by side, and a third in the middle but farther back. Place a candle behind you, and observe its image reflected in each of the three mirrors. The middle reflection will be smaller but not less bright than the two others: "smaller" stands quantitatively for unequal reception of a quality, spiritual insight; "not less bright" likewise for equality of salvation. But what concerns us is a certain value of the experiment that Dante, I surmise, with the cunning of a great poet, slyly refuses to consider: the dramatic value of the experiment.

There are *three*[10] mirrors each reflecting the *one* light. In the heart of the Empyrean, as we have seen, Dante says:

In the profound and shining being of the deep light appeared to me three *circles, of* three *colors and one magnitude.*

In the middle is the effigy of man. The physical image of Dante had necessarily been reflected in each of the three mirrors of Canto II; but he had not seen it. I suggest that he was not then ready to see it; his dramatic (i.e., tropological) development fell short of the final self-knowledge. Self-knowledge comes to him, as an Aristotelian Recognition and Reversal, when he turns the cosmos inside out by turning away from the "real" mirrors to the one light which has cast the three separate images. For the first time he sees the "one magnitude," the candle itself. And it is all done with the simple apparatus and in conditions laid down in Canto II;

he achieves the final anagoge and the dramatic recognition by turning around, as if he were still in Canto II, and by looking at the candle that has been burning all the time behind his back.

I have described some motions of the symbolic imagination in Dante, and tried to develop a larger motion in one of its narrower aspects. What I have left out of this discussion is very nearly the entire poem. In the long run the light-imagery is not the body, it is what permits us to *see* the body, of the poem. The rash suggestion that *The Divine Comedy* has a tragic mode—among other modes—I shall no doubt be made to regret; I cannot defend it further here. Perhaps the symbolic imagination is tragic in sentiment, if not always in form, in the degree of its development. Its every gain beyond the simple realism of experience imposes so great a strain upon any actuality of form as to set the ultimate limit of the gain as a defeat. The high order of the poetic insight that the final insight must elude us, is dramatic in the sense that its fullest image is an action in the shapes of this world: it does not reject, it includes; it sees not only with but through the natural world, to what may lie beyond it. Its humility is witnessed by its modesty. It never begins at the top; it carries the bottom along with it, however high it may climb.

1951

THE ANGELIC IMAGINATION

Poe as God

With some embarrassment I assume the part of amateur theologian and turn to a little-known figure, Edgar Allan Poe, another theologian only less ignorant than myself. How seriously one must take either Poe or his present critic in this new role I prefer not to be qualified to say. Poe will remain a man of letters—I had almost said a poet—whose interest for us is in the best sense historical. He represents that part of our experience which we are least able to face up to: the Dark Night of Sense, the cloud hovering over that edge of the eye which is turned to receive the effluvia of France, whence the literary power of his influence reaches us today. In France, the literary power has been closely studied; I shall not try to estimate it here. Poe's other power, that of the melancholy, heroic life, one must likewise leave to others, those of one's own compatriots who are not interested in literature. All readers of Poe, of the work or of the life, and the rare reader of both, are peculiarly liable to the vanity of discovery. I shall be concerned in the ensuing remarks with what I think I have seen in Poe that nobody else has seen: this undetected quality, or its remote source in Poe's feeling and thought, I believe partly explains an engagement with him that men on both sides of the Atlantic have acknowledged for more than a century.

It was recently acknowledged, with reservations, by Mr. T. S. Eliot, whose estimate must be reckoned with: Poe, he tells us, won a great reputation in Europe because the continental critics habitually view an author's work as a whole; whereas English and American critics view each work separately and, in the case of Poe, have been stopped by its defects. Mr. Eliot's essay[1] is the first attempt by an English-

113

speaking critic to bring to Poe the continental approach and to form a general estimate. I quote from what I take to be Mr. Eliot's summary; Poe, he says,

appears to yield himself completely to the idea of the moment: the effect is, that all his ideas seem to be entertained rather than believed. What is lacking is not brain-power, but that maturity of intellect which comes only with the maturing of the man as a whole, the development and coordination of the various emotions.

What I shall say towards the end of this essay I believe will show that Mr. Eliot is partly wrong, but that on the whole his estimate of Poe's immaturity is right. Does Poe merely "entertain" *all* his ideas? Perhaps all but one; but that one makes all the difference. Its special difference consists in his failure to see what the idea really was, so that he had perpetually to shift his ground—to "entertain," one after another, shabby rhetorics and fantasies that could never quite contain the one great idea. He was a religious man whose Christianity, for reasons that nobody knows anything about, had got short-circuited; he lived among fragments of provincial theologies, in the midst of which "coordination," for a man of his intensity, was difficult if not impossible. There is no evidence that Poe used the word coordination in the sense in which Mr. Eliot finds him deficient in it; but it is justly applied. I am nevertheless surprised that Mr. Eliot seems to assume that *coordination* of the "various emotions" is ever possible: the word gives the case away to Poe. It is a morally neutral term that Poe himself might have used, in his lifelong effort to impose upon experience a mechanical logic; possibly it came into modern literary psychology from analytic geometry. I take it that the word was not used, if in Mr. Eliot's sense it was known, when considerable numbers of persons were able to experience coordination. I suppose Mr. Eliot means by it a harmony of faculties among different orders of experience; and Poe's failure to harmonize himself cannot be denied.

The failure resulted in a hypertrophy of the three classical faculties: feeling, will, and intellect. The first I have discussed elsewhere.[2] It is the incapacity to represent the human condition in the central tradition of natural feeling. A nightmare of paranoia, schizophrenia, necrophilism, and vampirism supervenes, in which the natural affections are perverted by the will to destroy. Poe's heroines—Berenice, Ligeia, Madeline, Morella, with the curious exception of the abstemious Eleanora—are ill-disguised vampires; his heroes become necromancers (in the root meaning of the word) whose wills, like the heroines' wills, defy the term of life to keep them equivocally "alive." This primary failure in human feeling results in the loss of the entire natural order of experience.

The second hypertrophy is the thrust of the will beyond the human scale of action. The evidence of this is on nearly every page of Poe's serious prose fiction. Poe's readers, especially the young, like the quotation from Glanvill that appears as the epigraph to "Ligeia": "Man does not yield himself to the angels, nor unto Death utterly, save only through the weakness of his feeble will." It is the theme of the major stories. The hero professes an impossibly high love of the heroine that circumvents the body and moves in upon her spiritual essence. All this sounds high and noble, until we begin to look at it more narrowly, when we perceive that the ordinary carnal relationship between man and woman, however sinful, would be preferable to the mutual destruction of soul to which Poe's characters are committed. The carnal act, in which none of them seems to be interested, would witness a commitment to the order of nature, without which the higher knowledge is not possible to man. The Poe hero tries in self-love to turn the soul of the heroine into something like a physical object which he can know in direct cognition and then possess.

Thus we get the third hypertrophy of a human faculty: the intellect moving in isolation from both love and the moral will, whereby it declares itself independent of the human situation in the quest of essential knowledge.

The three perversions necessarily act together, the action of one implying a deflection of the others. But the actual emphases that Poe gives the perversions are richer in philosophical implication than his psychoanalytic critics have been prepared to see. To these ingenious persons, Poe's works have almost no intrinsic meaning; taken together they make up a *dossier* for the analyst to peruse before Mr. Poe steps into his office for an analysis. It is important at this point to observe that Poe takes for granted the old facultative psychology of intellect, will, and feeling. If we do not observe this scheme, and let it point our enquiry, we shall fail to understand two crucial elements in Poe: first, that Poe's symbols refer to a known tradition of thought, an intelligible order, apart from what he was as a man, and are not merely the index to a compulsive neurosis; and, secondly, that the symbols, cast into the framework of the three faculties, point towards this larger philosophical dimension, implicit in the serious stories, but very much at the surface in certain of Poe's works that have been almost completely ignored.

I shall discuss here these neglected works: *The Conversation of Eiros and Charmion, The Colloquy of Monos and Una, The Power of Words,* and *Eureka.* The three first are dialogues between spirits in heaven, after the destruction of the earth; all four set forth a cataclysmic end of the world, modelled on the Christian eschatology. We shall see that *Eureka* goes further, and offers us a semi-rational vision of the final disappearance of the material world into the first spiritual Unity, or God.

It would be folly to try to see in these works the action of a first-rate philosophical mind; there is ingenuity rather than complex thinking. What concerns us is the relation of the semi-philosophical works to Poe's imaginative fiction; that is, a particular relation of the speculative intellect to the work of imagination. I shall have to show that Poe, as a critical mind, had only a distant if impressive insight into the disintegration of the modern personality; and that this insight was not available to him as an imaginative writer, when he had to confront the human situation as a whole man. He was the victim of a disintegration that he seems only intermittently to have understood. Poe is thus a man we must return to: a figure of transition, who retains a traditional insight into a disorder that has since become typical, without being able himself to control it.

Before we examine this insight it will be necessary to fix more clearly in mind than I have yet done the character of Poe as a transitional man. Madame Raïssa Maritain, in a valuable essay, *Magie, Poésie, et Mystique,*[3] says:

Je ne vois guère de place dans la cosmologie d'Edgar Poe pour des recherches de recettes magiques. Et moins encore dans sa poésie, qui a toujours été parfaitement libre de toute anxiété de ce genre, et dont il n'aurait jamais voulu faire un instrument de pouvoir.

[*I see little place in the cosmology of Edgar Poe for the pursuit of magic recipes. And still less in his poetry, which was always perfectly free of all anxiety of this kind, and of which he never wished to make an instrument of power.*]

I am not sure that Madame Maritain is entirely right about the absence of magic, but there is no doubt that Poe *as poet* accepted certain limitations of language. He accepted them in practice. The obscurity of Poe's poetic diction is rather vagueness than the obscurity of complexity; it reflects his uncertain grasp of the relation of language to feeling, and of feeling to nature. But it is never that idolatrous dissolution of language from the grammar of a possible world, which results from the belief that language itself can be reality, or by incantation can create a reality: a superstition that comes down in French from Lautréamont, Rimbaud, and Mallarmé to the Surrealists, and in English to Hart Crane, Wallace Stevens, and Dylan Thomas. (I do not wish it to be understood that I am in any sense "rejecting" these poets, least of all under the rubric "superstition." When men find themselves cut off from reality they will frequently resort to magic rites to recover it—a critical moment of history that has its own relation to reality, from which poetry of great power may emerge.)

Poe, then, accepted his genre *in practice.* If the disorganized, synaesthetic sensibility arrives in the long run at a corresponding disintegration of the forms of grammar and rhetoric, it must be admitted that Poe stopped short at the mere *doctrine* of synaesthesia. In *The Colloquy of Monos and Una,* the angel Monos describes his passage into the after-life: "The senses were unusually active, although eccentrically so—assuming each other's functions at random. The taste and the smell were inextricably confounded, and became one sentiment, abnormal and intense." [4] But this is not the experience of synaesthesia rendered to our consciousness; to put it as Poe puts it is merely to consider it as a possibility of experience. Eighty years later we find its actuality in the language of an American poet:

> *How much I would have bartered! the black gorge*
> *And all the singular nestings in the hills*
> *Where beavers learn stitch and tooth.*
> *The pond I entered once and quickly fled—*
> *I remember now its singing willow rim.*

Rimbaud's "derangement of the senses" is realized. Why did not Poe take the next step and realize it himself? The question is unanswerable, for every writer is who he is, and not somebody else. The discoverer of a new sensibility seldom pushes it as far as language will take it; it largely remains a premonition of something yet to come. Another phase of Poe's disproportion of language and feeling appears in the variations of his prose style, which range from the sobriety and formal elegance of much of his critical writing, to the bathos of stories like *Ligeia* and *Berenice.* When Poe is not involved directly in his own feeling he can be a master of the *ordonnance* of eighteenth century prose; there are passages in *The Narrative of Arthur Gordon Pym* that have the lucidity and intensity of Swift. But when he approaches the full human situation the traditional rhetoric fails him. It becomes in his hands a humorless, insensitive machine whose elaborate motions conceal what it pretends to convey; for without the superimposed order of rhetoric the disorder hidden beneath would explode to the surface, where he would not be able to manage it. Poe is the transitional figure in modern literature because he discovered our great subject, the disintegration of personality, but kept it in a language that had developed in a tradition of unity and order. Madame Maritain is right in saying that he does not *use* language as magic. But he considers its possibility, and he thinks of lan·· guage as a potential source of quasi-divine power. He is at the parting of the ways; the two terms of his conflict are thus more prominent than they would appear to be in a writer, or in an age, fully committed to either extreme. "When all are bound for disorder," says Pascal, "none seems to go that way."

Of the three dialogues that I shall discuss here, the first, *The Conversation of Eiros and Charmion,* published in 1839, was the earliest written. It is Poe's first essay at a catastrophic version of the disappearance of the earth: a comet passes over the earth, extracting the nitrogen from the atmosphere and replacing it with oxygen, so that the accelerated oxidation ends in world-wide combustion. But in treating the most unpromising materials Poe means what he says, although the occasions of journalism may not allow him to say all that he means. He *means* the destruction of the world. It is not only a serious possibility, it is a moral and logical necessity of the condition to which man has perversely brought himself.

Man's destruction of his relation to nature is the subject of the next dialogue, *The Colloquy of Monos and Una* (1841). From the perversion of man's nature it follows by a kind of Manichean logic that external nature itself must be destroyed: man's surrender to evil is projected symbolically into the world.

This dialogue, the sequel to *The Conversation of Eiros and Charmion,* is a theological fantasy of the destruction of the earth by fire. I call the vision "theological" because the destruction is not, as it was in the preceding dialogue, merely the result of an interstellar collision. Monos says, "That man, as a race, should not become extinct, I saw that he must be *'born again.'* " Rebirth into the after-life is the mystery that Monos undertakes to explain to Una; but first he makes this long digression:

> *One word first, my Una, in regard to man's general condition at this epoch. You will remember that one or two of the wise men among our forefathers . . . had ventured to doubt*

the propriety of the term "improvement" as applied to the progress of our civilization. [They uttered] principles which should have taught our race to submit to the guidance of the natural laws, rather than attempt their control. Occasionally the poetic intellect—that intellect which we now feel to have been the most exalted of all—since those truths to us were of the most enduring importance and could only be reached by that analogy *which speaks in proof-tones to the imagination alone, and to the unaided reason bears no weight—occasionally did this poetic intellect proceed a step farther in the evolving of the vaguely philosophic, and find in the mystic parable that tells of the tree of knowledge . . . death-producing, a distinct intimation that knowledge was not meet for man in the infant condition of his soul. . . .*

Yet these noble exceptions from the general misrule served but to strengthen it by opposition. The great "movement"— that was the cant term—went on: a diseased commotion, moral and physical. Art—the Arts—rose supreme, and, once enthroned, cast chains upon the intellect which had elevated them to power. Even while he stalked a God in his own fancy, an infantine imbecility came over him. As might be supposed from the origin of his disorder, he grew infected with system, and with abstraction. He enwrapped himself in generalities. Among other odd ideas, that of universal equality gained ground; and in the face of analogy and of God—in spite of the laws of graduation so visibly pervading all things . . . — wild attempts at an omnipresent Democracy were made. Yet this evil sprang necessarily from the leading evil—knowledge. . . . Meanwhile huge smoking cities arose, innumerable. Green leaves shrank before the hot breath of furnaces . . . now it appears that we had worked out our own destruction in the perversion of our taste [roman mine] *or rather in the blind neglect of its culture in the schools. For in truth it was at this crisis that taste alone—that faculty which,* holding a middle position between the pure intellect and the moral sense [roman mine], *could never safely have been disregarded—it was now that taste alone could have led us gently back to Beauty, to Nature, and to Life.*

. . . it is not impossible that the sentiment of the natural, had time permitted it, would have regained its old ascendancy over the harsh mathematical reasoning of the schools. . . . This the mass of mankind saw not, or, living lustily although unhappily, affected not to see.

I have quoted the passage at great length in the hope that a certain number of persons at a certain place and time will have read it. Poe's critics (if he have any critics) have not read it. When they refer to it, it is to inform us that Poe was a reactionary Southerner who disliked democracy and industrialism. It would not be wholly to the purpose but it would be edifying to comment on the passage in detail, for it adumbrates a philosophy of impressive extent and depth. When we remember that it was written in the United States in the early 1840's, an era of the American experiment that tolerated very little dissent, we may well wonder whether it was the result of a flash of insight, or of conscious reliance upon a wider European tradition. (My guess is that Poe's idea of "mathematical reasoning" was derived in part from Pascal's *L'esprit de géométrie,* his "taste" from *L'esprit de finesse.* This is a scholarly question that cannot be investigated here.)

A clue to the connection between Poe's historical and metaphysical insight, on the one hand, and the mode of his literary imagination, on the other, may be found in Paul Valéry's essay, "The Position of Baudelaire," where he says:

> . . . *the basis of Poe's thoughts is associated with a certain personal metaphysical system. But this system, if it directs and dominates and suggests the* [literary] *theories . . .* by no means penetrates them [*roman mine*].[5]

His metaphysics was not available to him as experience; it did not *penetrate* his imagination. It we will consider together the "harsh mathematical reasoning of the schools" and the theory of the corruption of taste, we shall get a further clue to the Christian philosophical tradition in which Poe consciously or intuitively found himself. Taste is the discipline of feeling according to the laws of the natural order, a discipline of submission to a permanent limitation of man; this discipline has been abrogated by the "mathematical reasoning" whose purpose is the control of nature. Here we have the Cartesian split—taste, feeling, respect for the depth of nature, resolved into a subjectivism which denies the sensible world; for nature has become geometrical, at a high level of abstraction, in which "clear and distinct ideas" only are workable. The sensibility is frustrated, since it is denied its perpetual refreshment in nature: the operative abstraction replaces the rich perspectives of the concrete object. Reason is thus detached from feeling, and likewise from the moral sense, the third and executive member of the psychological triad, moving through the will. Feeling in this scheme being isolated or—as Mr. Scott Buchanan might put it—"occulted," it is strictly speaking without content, and man has lost his access to material forms. We get the hypertrophy of the intellect and the hypertrophy of the will. When neither intellect nor will is bound to the human scale, their projection becomes god-like, and man becomes an angel, in M. Maritain's sense of the term:

Cartesian dualism breaks man up into two complete substances, joined to one another none knows how: on the one hand, the body which is only geometrical extension; on the other, the soul which is only thought—an angel inhabiting a machine and directing it by means of the pineal gland.

. . . for human intellection is living and fresh only when it is centered upon the vigilance of sense perception. The natural roots of our knowledge being cut, a general drying up in philosophy and culture resulted, a drought for which romantic tears were later to provide only an insufficient remedy. . . . Affectivity will have its revenge.[6]

One cannot fail to see here a resemblance, *up to a point,* between the insights of Poe and of Maritain; but at that point appears the profound difference between a catastrophic acceptance and a poised estimation, of the Cartesian dualism. *The Colloquy of Monos and Una* is in the end a romantic tear, and in Poe's tales of perverted nature "affectivity" takes its terrible revenge.

We may discern the precise point at which Poe betrays his surrender to what I shall call the angelic fallacy: it is the point at which his conception of the "poetic intellect" becomes contradictory and obscure. This intellect speaks to us, he says, "by analogy," in "proof tones to the imagination alone." The trap is the adverb *alone,* which contradicts the idea of analogy. He may have meant analogy to the natural world, the higher truths emerging, as they do in Dante, from a rational structure of natural analogy; but he could not have meant all this. And I suppose nobody else in the nineteenth century understood analogy as a mode of knowledge. If the poetic intellect speaks "by analogy" it addresses more than the "imagination alone"; it engages also reason and cognition; for if it alone is addressed there is perhaps a minimum of analogy; if the imagination can work alone, it does so in direct intuition. And in fact in none of the essays and reviews does Poe even consider the idea of analogy. Its single mysterious appearance, in anything like its full historical sense, is in *The Colloquy of Monos and Una.* (It reappears in *Eureka,* where it means simple exemplification or parallelism.) In the "Poetic Principle," the poetic intellect moves independently, with only "incidental" connections with Pure Intellect and the Moral Sense; it is thus committed exclusively to Taste raised to an autonomous faculty. "Imagination is, possibly in man," says Poe in a footnote to his famous review of Halleck and Drake, "a lesser degree of the creative power of God." This is not far from the "esemplastic power" of the Primary Imagination, a Teutonic angel inhabiting a Cartesian machine named Samuel Taylor Coleridge.

Poe's exaltation of the imagination in its Cartesian vacuum foreshadows a critical dilemma of which we have been acutely aware in our own time. His extravagant claims for poetry do not in any particular exceed, except perhaps in their "period" rhetoric, the claims made by two later generations of English critics represented by Arnold and Richards. "Religion," said Arnold, "is morality touched with emotion." But religion, he said elsewhere, has attached itself to the "fact," by which he meant science; so religion has failed us. Therefore "the future of poetry is immense" because it is its own fact; that is to say, poetry is on its own, whatever its own may be—perhaps its own emotion, which now "touches" poetry instead of religion. Therefore poetry will save us, although it has no connection with the Cartesian machine running outside my window, or inside my vascular system. (Mr. Richards' early views I have discussed on several occasions over many years; I am a little embarrassed to find myself adverting to them again.) In Richards' writings, particularly in a small volume entitled *Science and Poetry* (1926), he tells us that the pseudo-statements of poetry—poetry on its own—cannot stand against the "certified scientific statement" about the facts which for Arnold had already failed both religion and poetry. Nevertheless poetry will save us because it "orders our minds"—but with what? For Mr. Richards, twenty-five years ago, the Cartesian machine was doing business as usual. Poetry would have to save us by ordering our minds with something that was not true.

Poe's flash of unsustained insight, in *The Colloquy of Monos and Una,* has, I submit, a greater dignity, a deeper philosophical perspective, and a tougher intellectual fibre, than the academic exercises of either Arnold or Mr. Richards. (I still reserve the right to admire both of these men.) Poe is not so isolated as they, in a provincialism of *time.* He still has access, however roundabout, to the great framework of the Aristotelian psychology to which the literature of Europe had been committed for more than two thousand years: this was, and still is for modern critics, an empirical fact that must be confronted if we are to approach literature with anything better than callow systems of psychological analysis, invented overnight, that put the imaginative work of the past at a distance seriously greater than that of time.

Poe with perfect tact puts his finger upon the particular function, feeling, that has been blighted by the abstraction of the pure intellect into a transcendental order of its own. He will let neither pure intellect nor the pure moral will (both having been purified of "nature") dominate poetry; he sees that poetry must be centered in the disciplined sense-perception which he inadequately calls taste; and he thus quite rightly opposes the "heresy of the didactic" and the "mathematical reasoning of the schools." He opposes both, but he gives in to the latter. Poe's idolatry of reason, ranging from the cryptogram and the detective story to the panlogism of *Eureka,* is too notorious to need pointing out. The autonomy of the will is in part the theme of the greater stories; and the autonomy of poetry, rising contradictorily and mysteriously from the ruin of its source in feeling, reflects "a lesser degree of the creative power of God." It is the creative power of the Word, man's *spoken* word, an extravagant and slippery pun on the Logos.

I now come to the third dialogue, *The Power of Words,* published in 1845, a fable in which the angelic imagination[7] is pushed beyond the limits of the angelic intelligence to the point at which man considers the possibility of creative power through verbal magic. The angels in this dialogue not only know essence directly; they also have the power of physical creation by means of *words.* We may ask here why, if Poe's insight was as profound as I think it was, he succumbed to a force of disintegration that he understood? An answer to this question is difficult. Insights of the critical intelligence, however impressive, will not always correct, they may never wholly rise above, the subtle and elusive implications of the common language to which the writer is born. As Dante well understood, this is the primary fact of his culture that he has got to reckon with. The culture of the imaginative writer is, first of all, the elementary use of language that he must hear and learn in childhood, and, in the end, not much more than a conscious manipulation of what he had received from life before the age of seven. Poe understood the spiritual disunity that had resulted from the rise of the demi-religion of scientism, but by merely opposing its excesses with equally excessive claims for the "poetic intellect," he subtly perpetuated the disunity from another direction. He set up, if we may be allowed the figure, a parallelogram of forces colliding by chance from unpredicted directions, not proceeding from a central unity. Although he was capable of envisaging the unified action of the mind through the three faculties, his own mind acted upon its materials now as intellect, now as feeling, now as will; never as all three together. Had he not been bred in a society committed to the rationalism of Descartes and Locke by that eminent angel of the rationalistic Enlightenment, Thomas

Jefferson? [8] Such commitments probably lie so deep in one's sensibility that mere intellectual conviction, Poe's "unaided reason," can scarcely reach them. Perhaps this discrepancy of belief and feeling exists in all ages, and creates the inner conflicts from which poetry comes. If this points to something in the nature of the literary imagination, we are bound to say that it will always lie a little beyond our understanding.

By the time Poe came to write his fable of the power of words, the angels of omnipotent reason could claim a victory. The scene is again the after-life; the characters two angels who meet in interstellar space after the destruction of the earth—a disaster assumed in all three of the dialogues and in *Eureka,* and a possible eventuality in most of Poe's tales. (One scarcely needs to be reminded of the collapse of the world of Roderick Usher.) The probable meaning of this omnivorous symbol I shall try to glance at presently. The climax of the angels' talk will reveal the long way that Poe had come from the philosophic insight of 1841 to the full angelic vision of 1845:

Oinos—*But why, Agathos, do you weep—and why, Oh why do your wings droop as we hover over this fair star— which is the greenest and yet most terrible of all we have encountered in our flight. Its brilliant flowers look like a fairy dream—but its fierce volcanoes like the passions of a turbulent heart.*

Agathos—*They* are—*they* are! *This wild star it is now three centuries since, with clasped hands, and with streaming eyes, at the feet of my beloved—I spoke it—with a few passionate sentences—into birth. Its brilliant flowers* are *the dearest of all unfulfilled dreams, and its raging volcanoes* are *the passions of the most turbulent and unhallowed of hearts.*

How had Agathos created this beautiful but unhallowed object? By the "physical power of words," he tells Oinos. Madame Maritain is the only critic I have read who has had the perception to take seriously this dialogue; her comment is of great interest:

Eh bien, ce texte se réfère-t-il vraiment à une conception magique de la poésie et de la parole? Je ne crois pas. Nous avons affaire ici, comme dans Eureka, *à une philosophie et une cosmologie panthéistiques, où tout mouvement et toute action participent à l'efficicacité d'une action divine.*

[*Does the text then really refer to a magical conception of poetry and of the word? I do not think so. We have to do here, as in* Eureka, *with a pantheistic philosophy and cosmology, where every movement and every action participates in the efficiency of a divine action.*]

There can be no doubt about Poe's pantheism here and in *Eureka,* but in both works we cannot fail to detect special variations in the direction of deism. Madame Maritain quotes Léon Bloy on the eternal consequences of every action of divine grace for the human spirit, an ancient Christian doctrine connected with the belief in the Community of Saints, for which Pascal invented the great natural analogy:

The slightest movement affects the whole of nature; a stone cast into the sea changes the whole face of it. So, in the realm of Grace, the smallest act affects the whole by its results. Therefore everything has its importance.

In every action we must consider, besides the act itself, our present, past, and future conditions, and others whom it touches, and must see the connections of it all. And so we shall keep ourselves well in check.[9]

It almost seems as if Poe had just read this passage and had gone at once to his desk to begin *The Power of Words;* as if he had deliberately ignored the moral responsibility, the *check* upon human power, enjoined in the last sentence, and had concentrated upon Pascal's physical analogy for divine grace: "The slightest *movement* affects the whole of nature." One more step, and the "slightest movement," a spoken *word,* will act creatively. A failure of moral responsibility towards the universe would not necessarily issue in an act of physical creation; nor would action undertaken in the state of sanctifying grace produce stars that are both beautiful and hallowed, unless, of course, the *word* is a "magic recipe," incantatory magic, which I believe we undoubtedly get in *The Power of Words.* This is not the same presumption as our own timid, superstitious reverence for an order of poetic language which creates its own reality, but rather a grandiose angelic presumption on the part of man. As usual, Poe is at least partly aware of what he is doing; for Agathos explains:

This power of retrogradation [Pascal's "the smallest action affecting the whole by its results"] in its absolute fulness and perfection—this faculty of referring all *epochs, all effects to all causes—is of course the prerogative of the Deity alone—but in every variety of degree, short of absolute perfection, is the power itself exercised by the whole host of the Angelic intelligences.*

This "power," of course, is not at this stage magical; it represents angelic knowledge rather than power. But when Agathos created his green star he was not yet an angel; he was still man, but man with the creative power, just short of divine perfection, of the angelic intelligences. Wasn't his power on earth actually greater than that of the angels of Christian theology? For they are not primary creators; they are the powerful but uncreative executives of the divine will. Agathos' doctrine transcends the ideal of mere angelic knowledge: it is superangelism. Man is not only an angel, he is God in his aspect of creativity. I remark almost with regret, mingled with uneasiness, that Poe proves my argument, perhaps too well. (When criticism thinks that it has proved anything, it has become angelic itself.) But this is not all: Oinos tells Agathos that he "remembers many successful experiments in what some philosophers were weak enough to denominate animalculae." And Agathos bows to the mathematicians: "Now the mathematicians . . . saw that the results of any given impulse were absolutely endless . . . these men saw, at the same time, that this species of analysis itself had within itself a capacity for indefinite progress. . . ." Mathematicians were about to achieve the omniscience of the Son, and biologists the creative power of the Father.

Are we to conclude that in these fantasies Poe "appears to yield himself completely to the idea of the moment"? I believe that Mr. Eliot's observation is inaccurate. Poe is quite capable of faking his science, and of appearing to take seriously his own wildest inventions; but the invention is the creaking vehicle of something deeper. What he really takes seriously, and what he yields to in the end, is not an *idea* of the moment. He is progressively mastered by one great idea, deeper than any level of conscious belief and developing to the end of his life at an ever increasing rate, until at last he is engulfed by it. It is his own descent into the maelstrom.

He arrives at it, or reaches the bottom of it, in *Eureka*, which he wrote in 1848, the year before his death. I shall not go so far as to connect, symbolically or prophetically, his death and the vision of the pit at the end of *Eureka*. We may only observe that the complete vision, of which the early works represent an approximation, immediately precedes his death. The proposition of which *Eureka* is to provide the "proof," he states at the beginning:

In the original unity of the first thing lies the secondary cause of all things, with the germ of their inevitable annihilation.

This "nothingness" is a dialectical conversion, not of one symbol into its opposite by analogy, as we see it in Dante, or even in Donne, but of an abstraction into its antithesis. Thesis: the omniscient intellect of man (of Poe as man) achieves a more than angelic knowledge in comprehending the structure and purpose of the created universe. Antithesis: the final purpose of the created universe is the extinction in its own unity of the omniscient intellect of man. There is no Hegelian synthesis. After the original act of divine creation, God withdraws into his deistic aloofness, leaving the separate and local acts of creation to man. This is the sphere of secondary creations which man as angelic delegate of God is empowered to perform. Thus, says Poe at the end of *Eureka,* not only is every man his own God, every man *is* God: every man the non-spatial center into which the universe, by a reverse motion of the atoms, will contract, as into its annihilation. God destroys himself in the eventual recovery of his unity. Unity equals zero. If Poe must at last "yield himself unto Death utterly," there is a lurid sublimity in the spectacle of his taking God along with him into a grave which is not smaller than the universe.

The material universe is in a state of radical disequilibrium, every atom striving to disengage itself from material forms and to return to the original center; but this is not a center in space. It is the Pascalian center which is the everywhere and nowhere, occupied by nothing. Since matter is merely the dialectical movement of attraction and repulsion, it will have ceased to exist when it rejoins the everywhere and nowhere. Space being emptied of matter, there is not even space, for space is that which is occupied by something. We are beyond the topless and bottomless abyss of Pascal.

The image of the abyss is in all of Poe's serious writings: the mirror in "William Wilson"; burial alive; the "tarn" into which the House of Usher plunges; the great white figure towards which Pym is being borne by a current of the sea; the pit over which the pendulum swings; the dead body containing the living soul of M. Valdemar; being walled up alive; the vertigo of the maelstrom.

Poe's most useful biographer, Professor Quinn, exhibits testimonials from modern physicists to bolster up with scientific authority a work in which he probably has little confidence. Let us assume, what may well be false, that *Eureka* from the scientific point of view of any age is nonsense. That would not make *Eureka* nonsense. "The glory of man," says Valéry in his essay on *Eureka,* "and something more than his glory, is to waste his powers on the void. . . . Thus it would seem that the history of thought can be summarized in these words: *It is absurd by what it seeks; great by what it finds.*" What did Poe's "absurd" essay in eschatology inadvertently find, if indeed it found anything but nothing? Valéry again (and again the French instruct us in Poe) points, in another context, to the central meaning of *Eureka,* without perhaps quite knowing that he has done so (for Paul Valéry was himself an archangel); he says: "As soon as we leave the bounds of the moment, as soon as we attempt to enlarge and extend our presence outside of itself, our forces are exhausted in our liberty." Is this always and under all conditions necessarily true? I think not; but it was particularly true of Poe.

It was true of him because in *Eureka* he circumvented the natural world and tried to put himself not in the presence of

God, but in the seat of God. *The exhaustion of force as a consequence of his intellectual liberation from the sensible world*—that is my reading of Valéry as a gloss upon the angelism of Poe. The intellectual force is exhausted because in the end it has no real object. The human intellect cannot reach God as essence; only God as analogy. Analogy to what? Plainly analogy to the natural world; for there is nothing in the intellect that has not previously reached it through the senses. Had Dante arrived at the vision of God by way of sense? We must answer yes, because Dante's Triune Circle is light, which the finite intelligence can see only in what has already been seen by means of it. But Poe's center is that place—to use Dante's great figure— "where the sun is silent." Since he refuses to see nature, he is doomed to see nothing. He has overleaped and cheated the condition of man. The reach of our imaginative enlargement is perhaps no longer than the ladder of analogy, at the top of which we may see all, if we still wish to *see* anything, that we have brought up with us from the bottom, where lies the sensible world. If we take nothing with us to the top but our emptied, angelic intellects, we shall see nothing when we get there. Poe as God sits silent in darkness. Here the movement of tragedy is reversed: there is no action. Man as angel becomes a demon who cannot initiate the first motion of love, and we can feel only compassion with his suffering, for it is potentially ours.

I have not supposed it necessary to describe in detail the structure of *Eureka,* or to call attention to its great passages of expository prose, which seem to me unsurpassed in their kind in the nineteenth century. I have not discussed Poe from what is commonly known as the literary point of view. I have tried to expound one idea, the angelism of the intellect, as one aspect of one writer. I do not hesitate in conclusion to commit Poe's heresy of the didactic, and to point a moral. We shall be so exhausted in our liberty that we shall have to take our final rest, not in the cool of the evening, but in the dark, if any one of our modes decides to set up in business for itself.

OUR COUSIN, MR. POE

When I was about fourteen there were in our house, along
with the novels of John Esten Cooke, E. P. Roe, and
Augusta Evans, three small volumes of Edgar Allan Poe.
That, by my reckoning, was a long time ago. Even then the
books were old and worn, whether from use (I suppose not)
or from neglect, it did not occur to me to enquire. I
remember, or imagine I remember the binding, which was
blue, and the size, which was small, and the paper, which
was yellow and very thin. One volume contained the Poems,
prefaced by Lowell's famous "biography." In this volume I
am sure, for I read it more than the others, was the well-
known, desperate, and asymmetrical photograph, which I
gazed at by the hour and which I hoped that I should some
day resemble. Another volume contained most, or at least the
most famous of the Tales: "Ligeia," which I liked best (I
learned in due time that Poe had, too); "Morella" and
"William Wilson," which I now like best; and "The Fall of
the House of Usher," which was a little spoiled for me even
at fourteen by the interjection of the "Mad Tryst of Sir
Launcelot Canning." Perhaps it was in this volume that I
admired "Marginalia," the first "criticism" I remember reading;
but I did not discern either the bogus erudition or the sense
of high literature which Poe was the first American to distinguish from entertainment and self-improvement through
books; the merits as well as the defects went over my head.
"Marginalia" could not at any rate have been in the third
volume, which was given to a single long work: *Eureka—
A Prose Poem.* This astrophilosophical discourse, which the
late Paul Valéry took more seriously than any English or
American critic ever did, fell in with my readings in popular astronomical books. In the back yard I arranged in a
straight line peas, cherries, and oranges, in the proportionate

sizes and distances of the sun and planets, and some hundreds of feet away (an inch perhaps to a thousand light-years) an old volley ball of my elder brothers' to represent Alpha Lyrae.

Later, on another occasion, I expect to examine *Eureka* at length, as I read it now, not as I read it at fourteen; yet before I leave it I must mention two other circumstances of my boyhood reading and the feeling that accompanied it. It lives for me as no later experience of ideas lives, because it was the first I had. The "proposition" that Poe undertook to demonstrate has come back to me at intervals in the past thirty-six years with such unpredictable force that now I face it with mingled resignation and dismay. I can write it without looking it up:

In the original unity of the first thing lies the secondary cause of all things, with the germ of their inevitable annihilation.

This is not the place to try to say what Poe meant by it. I could not, at fourteen, have guessed what it meant even after I had read the book; yet it is a fact of my boyhood (which I cannot suppose unique) that this grandiose formula for cosmic cataclysm became a part of my consciousness through no effort of my own, but seemed to come to me like a dream, and came back later, like a nursery rhyme, or a tag from a popular song, unbidden.

The other circumstance I am surer of because it was a visible fact, a signature in faded brown ink on the fly-leaf of *Eureka*: it told me years later that the three volumes had been printed earlier than 1870, the year the man who had owned them died. He was my great-grandfather. My mother had said, often enough, or on some occasion that fixed it in memory, that her grandfather had "known Mr. Poe." (She was of the era when all eminent men, living or recently dead, were "Mr.") I knew as a boy that my great-grandfather had been a "poet," and in 1930 I found some of his poems, which I forbear to discuss. He had for a while been editor of the *Alexandria Gazette* at about the time of Mr. Poe's death. Both were "Virginians," though Virginians of somewhat different schools and points of view. I can see my great-grandfather in Poe's description of a preacher who called upon him in the summer of 1848: "He stood smiling and bowing at the madman Poe."

I have brought together these scattered memories of my first reading of a serious writer because in discussing any writer, or in coming to terms with him, we must avoid the trap of mere abstract evaluation, and try to reproduce the actual conditions of our relation to him. It would be difficult for me to take Poe up, "study" him, and proceed to a critical judgment. One may give these affairs the look of method, and thus deceive almost everybody but oneself. In reading Poe we are not brought up against a large, articulate scheme of experience, such as we see adumbrated in Hawthorne or Melville, which we may partly sever from personal association, both in the writer and in ourselves. Poe surrounds us with Eliot's "wilderness of mirrors," in which we see a subliminal self endlessly repeated or, turning, a new posture of the same figure. It is not too harsh, I think, to say that it is stupid to suppose that, by "evaluating" this forlorn demon in the glass, we dispose of him. For Americans, perhaps for most modern men, he is with us like a dejected cousin: we may "place" him but we may not exclude him from our board. This is the recognition of a relationship, almost of the blood, which we must in honor acknowledge: what destroyed him is potentially destructive of us. Not only this; we must acknowledge another obligation, if, like most men of my generation, we were brought up in houses where the works of Poe took their easy place on the shelf with the family Shakespeare and the early novels of Ellen Glasgow. This is the obligation of loyalty to one's experience: he was in our lives and we cannot pretend that he was not. Not even Poe's great power in Europe is quite so indicative of his peculiar "place" as his unquestioned, if unexamined, acceptance among ordinary gentle people whose literary culture was not highly developed. The horrors of Poe created not a tremor in the bosoms of young ladies or a moment's anxiety in the eyes of vigilant mothers. I suppose the gentlemen of the South did not read him much after his time; in his time, they could scarcely have got the full sweep and depth of the horror. Nothing that Mr. Poe wrote, it was said soon after his death, could bring a blush to the cheek of the purest maiden.

But I doubt that maidens read very far in the Tales. If they had, they would have found nothing to disconcert the image that Miss Susan Ingram recorded from a visit of Poe to her family a few weeks before his death:

Although I was only a slip of a girl and he what seemed to me then quite an old man, and a great literary one at that, we got on together beautifully. He was one of the most courteous gentlemen I have ever seen, and that gave great charm to his manner. None of his pictures that I have ever seen look like the picture of Poe that I keep in my memory . . . there was something in his face that is in none of them. Perhaps it was in the eyes.

If he was a madman he was also a gentleman. Whether or not we accept Mr. Krutch's theory,[1] we know, as this sensible young lady knew, that she was quite safe with him. A gentleman? Well, his manners were exemplary (when he was not drinking) and, to the casual eye at any rate, his exalted idealization of Woman (even of some very foolish women) was only a little more humorless, because more intense, than the standard cult of Female Purity in the Old South.

What Mr. Poe on his own had done with the cult it was not possible then to know. A gentleman and a Southerner, he was not quite, perhaps, a Southern gentleman. The lofty intellect of Ligeia, of Madeline, of Berenice, or of Eleanora, had little utility in the social and economic structure of Virginia, which had to be perpetuated through the issue of the female body, while the intellect, which was public and political, remained under the supervision of the gentlemen. Although Morella had a child (Poe's only heroine, I believe, to be so compromised), she was scarcely better equipped than Virginia Clemm herself to sustain more than the immaculate half of the vocation of the Southern lady. "But the fires," writes Morella's narrator-husband, "were not of Eros." And we know, at the end of the story, that the daughter is no real daughter but, as Morella's empty "tomb" reveals, Morella herself come back as a vampire to wreak upon her "lover" the vengeance due him. Why is it due him? Because, quite plainly, the lover lacked, as he always lacked with his other heroines, the "fires of Eros." The soul of Morella's husband "burns with fires it had never before known . . . and bitter and tormenting to my spirit was the gradual conviction that I could in no manner define their unusual meaning, or regulate their vague intensity." Perhaps in the soul of John Randolph alone of Virginia gentlemen strange fires burned. The fires that were not of Eros were generally for the land and oratory, and the two fires were predictably regulated.

Poe's strange fire is his leading visual symbol, but there is not space in an essay to list all its appearances. You will see it in the eye of the Raven; in "an eye large, liquid, and luminous beyond comparison," of Roderick Usher; in the burning eye of the old man in "The Tell-Tale Heart"; in "Those eyes! those large, those shining, those divine orbs," of the Lady Ligeia. Poe's heroes and heroines are always burning with a hard, gem-like flame—a bodyless exaltation of spirit that Poe himself seems to have carried into the drawing-room, where its limited visibility was sufficient guarantee of gentlemanly behavior. But privately, and thus, for him, publicly, in his stories, he could not "regulate its vague intensity."

I cannot go into this mystery here as fully as I should like; yet I may, I think, ask a question: Why did not Poe use explicitly the universal legend of the vampire? Perhaps some instinct for aesthetic distance made him recoil from it; perhaps the literal, businesslike way the vampire went about making its living revolted the "ideality" of Poe. At any rate, D. H. Lawrence was no doubt right in describing as vampires his women characters; the men, soon to join them as "undead," have, by some defect of the moral will, made them so.

The mysterious exaltation of spirit which is invariably the unique distinction of his heroes and heroines is not quite, as I have represented it, bodyless. *It inhabits a human body but that body is dead. The spirits prey upon one* another with destructive fire which is at once pure of lust and infernal. All Poe's characters represent one degree or another in a movement towards an archetypal condition: the survival of the soul in a dead body; but only in "The Facts in the Case of Monsieur Valdemar" is the obsessive subject explicit.

In none of the nineteenth-century comment on "The Fall of the House of Usher" that I have read, and in none of our own period, is there a feeling of shock, or even of surprise, that Roderick Usher is in love with his sister: the relation not being physical, it is "pure." R. H. Stoddard, the least sympathetic of the serious early biographers, disliked Poe's morbidity, but admitted his purity. The American case against Poe, until the First World War, rested upon his moral indifference, or his limited moral range. The range is limited, but there is no indifference; there is rather a compulsive, even a profound, interest in a moral problem of universal concern. His contemporaries could see in the love stories neither the incestuous theme nor what it meant, because it was not represented literally. The theme and its meaning as I see them are unmistakable: the symbolic compulsion that drives through, and beyond, physical incest moves towards the extinction of the beloved's will in complete possession, not of her body, but of her being; there is the reciprocal force, returning upon the lover, of self-destruction. Lawrence shrewdly perceived the significance of Poe's obsession with incestuous love. Two persons of the least dissimilarity offer the least physical resistance to mutual participation in the *fire* of a common being. Poe's most casual reader perceives that his lovers never do anything but contemplate each other, or pore upon the rigmarole of preposterously erudite, ancient books, most of which never existed. They are living in each other's insides, in the hollows of which burns the fire of will and intellect.

The fire is a double symbol; it lights and it burns. It is overtly the "light" of reason, but as action it becomes the consuming fire of the abstract intellect, without moral significance, which invades the being of the beloved. It is the fire that, having illuminated, next destroys. Lawrence is again right in singling out for the burden of his insight the epigraph to "Ligeia," which Poe had quoted from Glanvill: "Man does not yield himself to the angels, nor unto death utterly, save through the weakness of his own feeble will." Why do these women of monstrous will and intellect turn into vampires? Because, according to Lawrence, the lovers have not subdued them through the body to the biological level, at which sanity alone is possible, and they retaliate by devouring their men. This view is perhaps only partly right. I suspect that the destruction works both ways, that the typical situation in Poe is more complex than Lawrence's version of it.

If we glance at "The Fall of the House of Usher" we shall be struck by a singular feature of the catastrophe. Bear in mind that Roderick and Madeline are brother and sister, and that the standard hyperaesthesia of the Poe hero acquires in Roderick a sharper reality than in any of the others, except perhaps William Wilson. His naked sensitivity to sound and light is not "regulated" to the forms of the human situation; it is a mechanism operating apart from the moral consciousness. We have here something like a capacity for mere sensation, as distinguished from sensibility, which in Usher is atrophied. In terms of the small distinction that I am offering here, sensibility keeps us in the world; sensation locks us into the self, feeding upon the disintegration of its objects and absorbing them into the void of the ego. The lover, circumventing the body into the secret being of the beloved, tries to convert the spiritual object into an object of sensation: the intellect which knows and the will which possesses are unnaturally turned upon that center of the beloved which should remain inviolate.

As the story of Usher opens, the Lady Madeline is suffering from a strange illness. She dies. Her brother has, of course, possessed her inner being, and killed her; or thinks he has, or at any rate wishes to think that she is dead. This is all a little vague: perhaps he has deliberately entombed her alive, so that she will die by suffocation—a symbolic action for extinction of being. Why has he committed this monstrous crime? Sister though she is, she is nevertheless not entirely identical with him: she has her own otherness, of however slight degree, resisting his hypertrophied will. He puts her alive, though "cataleptic," into the "tomb." (Poe never uses graves, only tombs, except in "Premature Burial." His corpses, being half dead, are thus only half buried; they rise and walk again.) After some days Madeline breaks out of the tomb and confronts her brother in her bloody cerements. This is the way Poe presents the scene:

". . . *Is she not hurrying to upbraid me for my haste? Have I not heard her footsteps on the stair? Do I not distinguish the heavy and horrible beating of her heart? Madman!"—here he sprang furiously to his feet, and shrieked out his syllables, as if in his effort he were giving up his soul—*"Madman! I tell you that she now stands without the door!"

As if in the superhuman energy of his utterance there had been found the potency of a spell, the huge antique panels to which the speaker pointed threw slowly back, upon the instant, their ponderous and ebony jaws. It was the work of the rushing gust—but then without those doors there did stand the lofty and enshrouded figure of the Lady Madeline of Usher. There was blood upon her white robes, and the evidence of some bitter struggle upon every portion of her emaciated frame. For a moment she remained trembling to and fro upon the threshold—then, with a low moaning cry, fell heavily inward upon the person of her brother, and in her violent and now final death-agonies, bore him to the floor a corpse, and a victim to the terrors he had anticipated.

Madeline, back from the tomb, neither dead nor alive, is in the middle state of the unquiet spirit of the vampire, whose heart-beats are "heavy and horrible." There is no evidence that Poe knew any anthropology; yet in some legends of vampirism the undead has a sluggish pulse, or none at all. In falling prone upon her brother she takes the position of the vampire suffocating its victim in a sexual embrace. By these observations I do not suggest that Poe was conscious of what he was doing; had he been, he might have done it even worse. I am not saying, in other words, that Poe is offering us, in the Lady Madeline, a vampire according to Bram Stoker's specifications. An imagination of any power at all will often project its deepest assumptions about life in symbols that duplicate, without the artist's knowledge, certain meanings, the origins of which are sometimes as old as the race. If a writer ambiguously exalts the "spirit" over the "body," and the spirit must live wholly upon another spirit, some version of the vampire legend is likely to issue as the symbolic situation.

Although the action is reported by a narrator, the fictional point of view is that of Usher: it is all seen through his eyes. But has Madeline herself not also been moving towards the cataclysmic end in the enveloping action outside the frame of the story? Has not her *will to know* done its reciprocal work upon the inner being of her brother? Their very birth had violated their unity of being. They must achieve spiritual identity in mutual destruction. The physical symbolism of the fissured house, of the miasmic air, and of the special order of nature surrounding the House of Usher and conforming to the laws of the spirits inhabiting it—all this supports the central dramatic situation, which moves towards spiritual unity through disintegration.

In the original unity of the first thing lies the secondary cause of all things, with the germ of their inevitable annihilation.

Repeated here, in the context of the recurrent subject of the Tales, the thesis of *Eureka* has a sufficient meaning and acquires something of the dignity that Valéry attributed to it. Professor Quinn adduces quotations from mathematical physicists to prove that Poe, in *Eureka,* was a prophet of science. It is a subject on which I am not entitled to an opinion. But even if Professor Quinn is right, the claim is irrelevant, and is only another version of the attempt today to make religion and the arts respectable by showing that they are semi-scientific. Another sort of conjecture seems to me more profitable: that in the history of the moral imagination in the nineteenth century Poe occupies a special place. No other writer in England or the United States, or so far as I know, in France, went so far as Poe in his vision of dehumanized man.

His characters are, in the words of William Wilson's

double, "dead to the world"; they are machines of sensation and will, with correspondences, in the physical universe, to particles and energy. Poe's engrossing obsession in *Eureka* with the cosmic destiny of man issued in a quasi-cosmology, a more suitable extension of his vision than any mythology, homemade or traditional, could have offered him. The great mythologies are populous worlds, but a cosmology need have nobody in it. In Poe's, the hyperaesthetic egoist has put all men into his void: he is alone in the world, and thus dead to it. If we place Poe against the complete Christian imagination of Dante, whom he resembles in his insistence upon a cosmic extension of the moral predicament, the limits of his range are apparent, and the extent of his insight within those limits. The quality of Poe's imagination can be located, as I see it, in only two places in Dante's entire scheme of the after-life: Cantos XIII and XXXII of the *Inferno*. In Canto XIII, the Harpies feed upon the living trees enclosing the shades of suicides—those "violent against themselves," who will not resume their bodies at the Resurrection, for "man may not have what he takes from himself." In XXXII, we are in Caïna, the ninth circle, where traitors to their kin lie half buried in ice, up to the public shadow—"where the doleful shades were . . . sounding with their teeth like storks." Unmotivated treachery, for the mere intent of injury, and self-violence are Poe's obsessive subjects. He has neither Purgatory nor Heaven, and only two stations in Hell.

Let us turn briefly to the question of Poe's style. He has several styles, and it is not possible to damn them all at once. The critical style, which I shall not be able to examine here, is on occasion the best; he is a lucid and dispassionate expositor, he is capable of clear and rigorous logic (even from mistaken premises, as in "The Rationale of Verse"), when he is not warped by envy or the desire to flatter. He is most judicial with his peers, least with his inferiors, whom he either overestimates or wipes out. As for the fictional style, it, too, varies; it is perhaps at its sustained best, in point of sobriety and restraint, in the tales of deduction. Exceptions to this observation are "Descent into the Maelström," "The Narrative of Arthur Gordon Pym," and perhaps one or two others in a genre which stems from the eighteenth-century "voyage." These fictions demanded a Defoe-like verisimilitude which was apparently beyond his reach when he dealt with his obsessive theme. Again I must make an exception: "William Wilson," one of the serious stories (by serious, I mean an ample treatment of the obsession), is perspicuous in diction and on the whole credible in realistic detail. I quote a paragraph:

The extensive enclosure was irregular in form, having many capacious recesses. Of these, three or four of the largest constituted the play-ground. It was level, and covered with a hard fine gravel. I well remember it had no trees, nor benches, nor anything similar within it. Of course it was in the rear of the house. In front lay a small parterre, planted with box and other shrubs, but through this sacred division we passed only upon rare occasions indeed—such as a first advent to school or a final departure hence, or perhaps, when a parent or a friend having called upon us, we joyfully took our way home for the Christmas or midsummer holidays.

It is scarcely great prose, but it has an eighteenth-century directness, and even elegance, of which Poe was seldom capable in his stories. I surmise that the playground at Dr. Bransby's school at Stoke-Newington, where, as a child, he was enrolled for five years, recalled one of the few periods of his life which he could detach from the disasters of manhood and face with equanimity. Now a part of the description of the Lady Ligeia:

. . . I examined the contour of the lofty and pale forehead—it was faultless—how cold indeed that word when applied to a majesty so divine!—the skin rivalling the purest ivory, the commanding extent and repose, the gentle prominence of the regions above the temples; and the raven-black, the glossy, the luxuriant, the naturally curling tresses, setting forth the full force of the Homeric epithet, "hyacinthine." I looked at the delicate outline of the nose. . . .

But I refrain. It is easy enough to agree with Aldous Huxley and Yvor Winters, and dismiss this sort of ungrammatical rubbish as too vulgar, or even too idiotic, to reward the time it takes to point it out. But if Poe is worth understanding at all (I assume that he is), we might begin by asking why the writer of the lucid if not very distinguished passage from "William Wilson" repeatedly fell into the bathos of "Ligeia." I confess that Poe's serious style at its typical worst makes the reading of more than one story at a sitting an almost insuperable task. The Gothic glooms, the Venetian interiors, the ancient winecellars (from which nobody ever enjoys a vintage but always drinks "deep")—all this, done up in a glutinous prose, so fatigues one's attention that with the best will in the world one gives up, unless one gets a clue to the power underlying the flummery.

I have tried in the course of these remarks to point in the direction in which the clue, as I see it, is to be found. I do not see it in the influence of the Gothic novel. This was no doubt there; but no man is going to use so much neo-Gothic, over and over again, unless he means business with it; I think that Poe meant business. If the Gothic influence had not been to hand, he would have invented it, or something equally "unreal," to serve his purpose. His purpose in laying on the thick décor was to simulate sensation. Poe's sensibility, for reasons that I cannot surmise here, was almost completely impoverished. He could feel little but the pressure of his predicament, and his perceptual powers remained undeveloped. Very rarely he gives us a real perception because he is not interested in anything that is alive. Everything in Poe is dead: the houses, the rooms, the furniture, to say nothing of nature and of human beings. He is like a child—all appetite without sensibility; but to be in manhood all appetite, all will, without sensibility, is to be a monster: to feed spiritually upon men without sharing with them a real world is spiritual vampirism. The description of Ligeia's head is that of a dead woman's.

Does it explain anything to say that this is necrophilism? I think not. Poe's prose style, as well as certain qualities of his verse,[2] expresses the kind of "reality" to which he had access: I believe I have indicated that it is a reality sufficiently terrible. In spite of an early classical education and a Christian upbringing, he wrote as if the experience of these traditions had been lost: he was well ahead of his time. He could not relate his special reality to a wider context of insights—a discipline that might have disciplined his prose. From the literary point of view he combined the primitive and the decadent: primitive, because he had neither history nor the historical sense; decadent, because he was the conscious artist of an intensity which lacked moral perspective.

But writers tend to be what they are; I know of no way to make one kind into another. It may have been a condition of Poe's genius that his ignorance should have been what it was. If we read him as formal critics we shall be ready to see that it was another condition of his genius that he should never produce a poem or a story without blemishes, or a critical essay that, despite its acuteness in detail, does not evince provincialism of judgment and lack of knowledge. We must bear in mind Mr. Eliot's remark that Poe must be viewed as a whole. Even the fiction and the literary journalism that seem without value add to his massive impact upon the reader.

What that impact is today upon other readers I cannot pretend to know. It has been my limited task to set forth here a little of what one reader finds in him, and to acknowledge in his works the presence of an incentive (again, for one man) to self-knowledge. I do not hesitate to say that, had Poe not written *Eureka,* I should have been able, a man of this age, myself to formulate a proposition of "inevitable annihilation." I can only invite others to a similar confession. Back of the preceding remarks lies an ambitious assumption, about the period in which we live, which I shall not make explicit. It is enough to say that, if the trappings of Poe's nightmare strike us as tawdry, we had better look to our own. That particular vision in its purity (Poe was very pure) is perhaps not capable of anything better than Mr. Poe's ludicrous décor. Nor have persons eating one another up and calling it spiritual love often achieved a distinguished style either in doing it or in writing about it. It was not Ugolino, it was Dante who wrote about Ugolino with more knowledge than Ugolino had. Mr. Poe tells us in one of his simple poems that from boyhood he had "a demon in my view." Nobody then—my great-grand-father, my mother, three generations—believed him. It is time we did. I confess that his voice is so near that I recoil a little, lest he, Montressor, lead me into the cellar, address me as Fortunato, and wall me up alive. I should join his melancholy troupe of the undead, whose voices are surely as low and harsh as the grating teeth of storks. He is so close to me that I am sometimes tempted to enter the mists of pre-American genealogy to find out whether he may not actually be my cousin.

1949

THE HOVERING FLY

*A Causerie on the Imagination and the
Actual World*

Of the three great novels of Dostoevsky, *The Idiot* has
perhaps the simplest structure. In the center of the action
there are only three characters. The development of the plot
is almost exclusively "scenic" or dramatic; that is to say, a
succession of scenes with episodic climaxes leads, with more
than Dostoevsky's usual certainty of control, to the catastrophe at the end. There is very little summary or commentary by the author; here and there a brief lapse of time
is explained, or there is a "constatation," a pause in the action
in which the author assumes the omniscient view and reminds us of the position and plight of the other characters,
who are complicating the problem of the hero. I emphasize
here the prevailing scenic method because at the catastrophe
the resolution of the dramatic forces is not a statement about
life, or even about the life that we have seen in this novel:
the resolution is managed by means of that most difficult
of all feats, a narrow scene brought close up, in which the
"meaning" of the action is conveyed in a dramatic visualization so immediate and intense that it creates its own symbolism. And it is the particular symbolism of the fly in the
final scene of *The Idiot* which has provided the spring-board,
or let us say the catapult, that will send us off into the unknown regions of "actuality," into which we have received
orders to advance.[1]

What is *The Idiot* about? In what I have said so far I
have purposely evaded any description of the novel; I have
not tried to distinguish the experience which it offers, a kind
of experience that might start a wholly different train of
speculation upon actuality from that which will be our spe-
146

cial concern in these notes. But now, before we get into the
last scene, where the three main characters find themselves in
a dark room, alone for the first time, we must drop them,
and go a long way round and perhaps lose our way on a
road that has no signs at the forks to tell us which turn to
take.

II

When we say poetry *and* something else—poetry and science, poetry and morality, or even poetry and mathematics—it
makes little difference in dialectical difficulty what the coor-
dinate field may be: all problems are equally hard and in the
end they are much the same. The problem that I shall skirt
around in these notes is a very old one, going back to the first
records of critical self-consciousness. Aristotle was aware of it
when he said that poetry is more philosophical than history.
Although the same quagmire awaits us from whatever direction we come upon it, the direction itself and the way we tum-
ble into the mud remain very important. Perhaps the crucial
value of the critical activity—given the value of the directing
mind, a factor that "systematic" criticism cannot find—will be
set up or cast down by the kind of tact that we can muster for
the "approach," a word that holds out to us a clue.

Armies used to besiege towns by "regular approaches"; or
they took them by direct assault; or they maneuvered the enemy out of position, perhaps into ambuscade. These strategies
are used today, for in war as in criticism the new is usually
merely a new name for something very old. When Caesar laid
waste the country, he was using a grand tactics that we have
recently given a new name: infiltration, or the tactics of getting effectively into the enemy's rear. When you have total war
must you also have total criticism? In our time critics are supposed to know everything, and we get criticism on all fronts.
Does this not outmode the direct assault? When there are so
many "problems" (a term equally critical and military) you
have got to do a little here and a little there, and you may not
be of the command that enters the suburbs of Berlin.

At any rate, the world outside poetry, which continues to disregard the extent that it is also *in* poetry, resists and eludes our best understanding. When and why did it begin to behave in this way? When we had the Truce of God for three days a week, we attacked, with a great deal of military rhetoric and pageantry, the enemy, on the fourth day, and the attack was a frontal assault; both sides knew the rules. But we do not know them. And in the critical manual of war there has been nothing comparable to the rules since Arnold's doctrine of the "criticism of life" could still engage the non- or anti-poetic forces of the world head on.

But suppose there isn't an enemy? Suppose the war figure is misleading? Henry James (one of the great critics) wrote to Stevenson in 1891 that "No theory is kind to us that cheats us of seeing." What did he mean? In this instance he meant Stevenson's refusal to visualize his scene. "It struck me," says James, "that you either didn't feel— through some accident—your responsibility on this article quite enough; or, on some theory of your own, had declined it." We know that Stevenson did have a theory that made him generalize his scenes.

It is not necessary to find out here what Stevenson missed, or what, missing that, he did actually succeed in seeing. Every imaginative writer has a theory, whether he recognize it or not; it may operate for him at some dynamic level where it can liberate all that writer's power; but in so far as it participates in the exclusive nature of theory, it must entail upon some phase of his work very great risks, even perils. "Thus Hardy," says William Empson, "is fond of showing us an unusually stupid person subjected to very unusually bad luck, and then a moral is drawn, not merely by inference but by solemn assertion, that we are all in the same boat as this person whose story is striking precisely because it is unusual." The "solemn assertion" in Hardy and in many other writers, critics no less than novelists and poets, must always either limit or somehow illegitimately extend what the writer has actually seen.

What I want to end these beginning remarks with is an observation that has been too little acknowledged. The art of criticism must inevitably partake of the arts on which it lives, and in a very special and niggling way. I refer to the "approach," the direction of attack, the strategy; and in terms of the strategy of this occasion, I mean the "point of view," as Percy Lubbock understands that phrase when he tells us that very nearly the whole art of fiction is in it. From what position shall the critic, who is convinced that the total view is no view at all, the critic not being God, and convinced too that even if (which is impossible) he sees everything, he has got to see it from somewhere, like the painter Philippoteaux who placed himself under a tree in his picture of the Battle of Gettysburg to warn you that what you see is only what he sees, under that tree: under what tree, then, or from what hill, or under what log or leaf, shall the critic take his stand, which may be less than an heroic stand, to report what he sees, infers, or merely guesses? Merely to ask this question is enough to indicate something of the post which I am trying to find and hold. You may locate it far to the sinister side of the line which divides the arts and the sciences. Even if this spectator succeeds in holding his ground, you may be sure that he will not be able to give you a scientific report.

III

Suppose we take two terms and relate them. The two terms for this occasion are, first, Poetry, and, second, the Actual World. Do we mean then by the actual world a world distinguished from one which is less actual or not actual at all? I suppose we mean both things; else we should say: Poetry and the World. We might again alter the phrase and get: Poetry and Actuality, which by omitting the world would give us a clue to its bearing in the preceding phrase; that is, world might then mean region, realm, field of observation, or experience. So I take it that the bearing of the phrase "actual world" is towards something outside us, something objective, whose actuality is somehow an empirical one which tends to look after its own affairs without consulting us, and even at times resisting whatever it is in us which we like to call by names like subjective, private, human as opposed to non-human, although even the human and the subjective lie ready for objective scrutiny if we change our vantage-point and let them stand opposite us rather than let them oppose a third thing, a world, beyond them. It is, in fact, no mere quibble of idealism if we decide to call this subjective field not only the world but the actual world, taking our stand on the assumption that it sufficiently reflects or gathers in or contains all that we can ever know of any other world or worlds that appear to lie beyond it.

Are we prepared to take this stand? Perhaps we are if we are philosophers of a certain logical stubbornness; but as poets our zeal for subjectivism might seem to be good only at times, at certain places and moments. And are we, here in this kind of enquiry, either philosophers or poets? To ask that question is to diminish or perhaps to reduce to zero any degree of confidence that we may have enjoyed in trying to sort out, however provisionally, some of the bearings of our phrase "actual world." When we are sorting them out are we outside them, or inside, or partly inside and partly outside?

If we go back for another glimpse of a suggestion that I merely threw down at the outset of this discussion, we shall drop to a degree somewhere below zero in our confidence of certainty in this enquiry. From what position is the critic looking at the object of his enquiry? That was our suggestion, but we have now identified the critic's object as the actual world, whatever that is, as that world is related to poetry, whatever that is.

If I seem to be making this matter obscure, let me plead my ignorance, and if you will, add your own ignorance to my plea; or if you like it better, add your skepticism to mine; and we shall examine together our riddle, so far as we can, as if nobody had seen it before: which, I take it, is the *action* of skepticism as distinguished from the mere feeling of the skeptic.

I suppose the easiest and, for all I know, the best way to establish our post of observation to look at the actual world, under our given condition, is to look at it through poetry. But here again we encounter difficulties as harassing as those we almost had to give up when we plumped ourselves down into the actual world. Even if we knew what poetry is, we should have to find it in particular poetic works: you see in that abstract phrase—"particular poetic works"—how difficult it is to face the paralyzing simplicity of our problem at this stage. We should have to find poetry in poems. Does not that make it look easier? It does, until we remember that even the man who may have read five thousand poems, an anthologist, for example, could lay claim to real mastery of not more than a few hundred.

What, then, is poetry? The innocence of the question ought to excuse it. Were we German idealists of the past century, or their disciples of today, we might easily begin "poetry" with a capital P, and putting initial capitals before "actual" and "world," start Poetry and the Actual World off on their historic merry-go-round; or perhaps Poetry could pursue the Actual World as the Lord, in the Gullah sermon, chased Adam and Eve "round and round dat Gyarden, round and round"; or again there are the standard clowns in the bestiary of the animated cartoon that chase each other's tail until at last all that is left on the screen is a whirling vortex. Any of these similes will do that testify to our helplessness before the fenced-in apriorism of the merely philosophical approach: its conclusions are impressive and are usually stated at length, but I have never seen one of them that increased my understanding of the XXVIIIth Canto of the *Paradiso,* or even of "Locksley Hall."

But if we cannot say philosophically what poetry is, or even how it functions, how shall we know from any point of view what post of observation we are taking when we decide to look at the actual world through poetry? From now on this is what I shall be trying to get at. We shall certainly not be looking on as a spectator who has no stake in the scene; and yet to say that, as a man who has written verse, I have a special tact which will lead me to the right hill and turn my eyes in the right direction smacks a little of our national reliance upon expert testimony. For even if a poet, some other poet, seems in his verse to have given us flashes of what we may provisionally call actuality, he is not, as he talks about poetry, inside his verse, but outside it; and his report is as much under the obligation to make good as yours.

IV

I am sorry to introduce another complication before we go further. I must introduce a broader term, and the broader term usually lifts the spirits for a brief span, until somebody reminds us that it may be an evasion of the harder distinctions enjoined by the narrower term. The broader term is Imagination. If we say that we are trying to discover the relation between the Imagination and the Actual World, we find ready to run to our aid a host of comforting saws that could easily turn this vacillating discourse into an oration— and may actually do so before we are done. The Imagination is superior to Reality. Imagination is the rudder, Fancy the sails. Imagination is the esemplastic power. There are others as good, perhaps even better; and I do not deny the probability that before I am through I shall have spoken in substance one of these doctrines.

Yet I have brought in the Imagination for a more empirical reason. The great prose dramatists and novelists are makers and thus poets, and they give us something that is coherent and moving about human life which partakes of actuality but which is not actuality as it is reported to me by my senses as I look about me at a given moment. How does their report differ from mine? How does it differ from the report of the poet who writes, either lyrically or dramatically, in verse? Perhaps we had better take the risk and decide that the two reports seem to differ, verse being the occasion of the difference but not its explanation; and yet, bearing in mind a few of the examples and comparisons which I shall produce or refer to in a few minutes, I make a large reservation about a categorical difference between the imagination in prose and the imagination in verse: Whether verse be expressive or formal in its function, it nevertheless becomes a sort of medium through which the poet may convey a deeper and wider heterogeneity of material than the prose vehicle will ordinarily carry. My reservation about this difference simply acknowledges the probability that it may be only a difference of degree, of intensity, of scope, with respect to the material, or, if it is a real distinction, it cannot be said to hold all the time, but only as a rule. I admire, for example, the late Robert Bridges' poetry, but I see in it a failure or, if you will, a refusal to go all the way for as much of the richness of image as his magnificent control of verse-technique would have justified. On the other hand, if you will recall the cutting up of the whale in *Moby Dick* you will see at once the long reach of a prose style that is probably richer and more fluent than any verse style of its century, and far more dynamic than the style of *Dawn in Britain,* which perhaps alone in nineteenth-century poetry equals *Moby Dick* in rhetorical ambition. Bridges and Melville, then, might be seen as the exceptions in their respective mediums; and yet, in order to see them that way, we should have to establish a middle point at which the prose imagination and the verse imagination pass each other on the way to their proper extremes; and no such point exists except in books on the differential calculus.

But if we look at this matter empirically, not claiming too much for any differences or for our more confident distinctions, we may succeed in taking up an attitude towards a very real problem; for I take it that nobody denies the value of what seems to go on in sound works of the imagination. In what respects does this value belong to an actual world? In that spirit, we may phrase the question more narrowly, even finically, and ask it in terms of motion or process, or as Mr. Kenneth Burke would have it, of drama. In what ways, then, does an actual world *get into* the imagination?

Thus I turn to another line of speculation, with an observation that ought to arrest some of the vacillation of my opening trial flights, and at the same time fix our point of view. If we think of the actual world as either a dead lump or a whirling wind somewhere outside us, against which we bump our heads or which whirls us around, we shall never be able to discover it: we have got to try to find it in terms of one of our chief interests. Let us call that interest the imagination.

v

There is now raging in one of our best journals a controversy about a human crisis which the editors of that journal call "The Failure of Nerve." [2] The full implications of the controversy are irrelevant to the end of my discussion; yet there is one issue, perhaps the central issue, of that controversy which may instruct us, or at any rate prepare us for what follows. Professors Dewey, Hook, and Nagel are anxious and at moments even a little angry about the disorderly rebirth of certain beliefs about man that tend to reject scientific positivism and the reliance upon what they, in their tradition of thought, are pleased to call reason. The answers to these challenging blasts are scarcely developed; the editors of *Partisan Review* have so far relegated them to their correspondence columns; and I do not know whether or not there will be more considered replies. As an old anti-positivist, I cannot do less than to point out a standard objection to the positivist program, reminding its adherents that our supposed "failure of nerve" might actually turn out to be the positivists' failure to allow for all that our nerve-ends are capable of taking in.

The positivist program for the complete government of man may perhaps be a form of what Scott Buchanan has called "occultation," a term that I should apply to positivism somewhat as follows: Positivism offers us a single field of discourse which may be briefly labeled as physicalism; and it pretends that this is the sole field of discourse, all the others being illusion, priestcraft, superstition, or even Nazism. Now as this single field of discourse is directed towards works of the imagination it carries with it a certain test of validity, which is usually the semantical test; and I hold that when this test becomes the pragmatic test and usurps the business of other tests, from other fields of discourse, pretending to be the sole test, it is performing an act of occultation upon these tests—a hiding away, an ascription of dark motives, even an imputation of black art.

Is there failure of nerve in a recognition of the failure of positivism even at its subtlest level to deliver all the goods? Are men the victims of a failure of nerve if, standing on a precipice from which there is no retreat, they prepare to make the best jump possible, and refuse to mumble to themselves that their fall will only exemplify the laws of gravity? There is no doubt that the fall will offer this confirmation of positivism; for positivism is a highly efficient technique of our physical necessities; it is the creation of the practical reason which organizes our physical economy, without which we cannot live. But under the rule of a positivism which has become a group of self-sufficient sciences, the organization has grown exclusive. What is it that is excluded? What is *occulted?*

There are two answers to this question which are two ways of giving the same answer. But before I try to give this single-double answer I ought to say that my purpose here is not to berate the sciences but only the positivist religion of scientists. I am even more concerned with what it leaves out, or at least to "point" towards that omitted thing, as one nods in the direction of a good landscape which one might have missed, driving by it at seventy miles an hour.

What is excluded, what is occulted? First, the actual world; second, Dostoevsky's hovering fly; I shall be saying presently that in terms of the dramatic imagination the world and the fly are the same thing. Our skepticism—and as I say it I have my own doubt—our doubt of this identification proceeds from what we ordinarily call our common sense, a good thing to have, but not good enough if it is all we have. Let me put the matter somewhat differently. We may *look* at the hovering fly; we can to a degree *know* the actual world. But we shall not know the actual world by looking at it; we know it by looking at the hovering fly.

I am sorry that this sounds a little gnomic; and it is time to remember James' remark again: No theory is kind to us that cheats us of seeing. But it is also time to amend James:

No theory is kind to us that cheats us of seeing what path we ought to be on. What is our path? When we do not know, we may get a vision, and then hope that all visions appear on the road to Damascus. Before we may build our hope so high we had better confront Pascal: "We run carelessly to the precipice, after we have put something before us to prevent us seeing it."

VI

The fly appears out of nowhere in the last scene in *The Idiot:* out of nowhere, but only if we limit our apperception of place to the scale of the human will. There are, as I have said, three persons in the scene, but one of them is dead, and her place is taken by the hovering fly. Nastasya Filippovna has appeared less directly in the action than other women characters of the story; but she is the heroine; for it is she who creates for the hero his insoluble problem. She is a beautiful and gifted orphan of good family who has been seduced by her guardian, a libertine of high political and social connections at the court. There is Rogozhin, who, as the story opens, has just inherited a fortune; he is in love with Nastasya and he offers her the worldly solution of money and marriage, a solution that she will not accept; and it is he, of course, who murders her at the end, since in no other way may he possess her. From the beginning Prince Myshkin, our hero, has been in his special way in love with Nastasya. He is the "idiot," the man whom epilepsy has removed from the world of action. I am not prepared to add to our critical knowledge of Myshkin. He has a marvelous detachment and receptivity, and a profundity of insight into human motives which I believe nobody but Dostoevsky has ever succeeded so perfectly in rendering dramatically. (It is always easy for the novelist to *say* that a character is profound; it is quite another matter to dramatize the profundity, to make it *act*.) Nastasya's agony of guilt, the conviction of sin, mirrors an almost Christ-like perception of the same potentialities on the part of Myshkin; and it is Nastasya who creates Myshkin's problem. Nastasya is tortured by those oscillating extremes, personal degradation and nobility of motive; and Myshkin alone in his world knows that she is not a "bad woman." But she will not marry Myshkin either. Marriage to Myshkin would be the symbolic signal that the pressure of her conflict had abated, and that Myshkin's problem had found solution in Nastasya's solution of her own. She cannot marry Rogozhin because she is too noble; she cannot marry Myshkin because she is too degraded. Thus we get in Rogozhin's murder of Nastasya the deeply immoral implications of Rogozhin's character, and the dramatically just irony of the good in her being destroyed by the lover who was indifferent to it. When the murder is done, Myshkin feels no resentment: he can accept that too. The lovers stand over the dead body of the murdered girl:

[Myshkin's] eyes were by now accustomed to the darkness, so that he could make out the whole bed. Someone lay asleep on it, in a perfectly motionless sleep; not the faintest stir, not the faintest breath could be heard. The sleeper was covered over from head to foot with a white sheet and the limbs were vaguely defined; all that could be seen was that a human figure lay there, stretched at full length. All around in disorder at the foot of the bed, on chairs beside it, and even on the floor, clothes had been flung; a rich white silk dress, flowers, and ribbons. On a little table at the head of the bed there was the glitter of diamonds that had been taken off and thrown down. At the end of the bed there was a crumpled heap of lace and on the white lace the toes of a bare foot peeped out from under the sheet; it seemed as though it had been carved out of marble and it was horribly still. Myshkin looked and felt that as he looked, the room became more and more still and death-like. Suddenly there was the buzz of a fly which flew over the bed and settled on the pillow.

I assume that the minimum of exposition is necessary; it is one of the great and famous scenes of modern literature; and I hope that seeing it again you recalled the immense drama preceding it and informing it and stretching the tensions which are here let down, eased, and resolved for us. I am not sure that the power of the scene would be diminished by the absence of the fly; but at any rate it is there; and its buzz rises like a hurricane in that silent room, until, for me, the room is filled with audible silence. The fly comes to stand in its sinister and abundant life for the privation of life, the body of the young woman on the bed. Here we have one of those conversions of image of which only great literary talent is capable: life stands for death, but it is a wholly different order of life, and one that impinges upon the human order only in its capacity of scavenger, a necessity of its biological situation which in itself must be seen as neutral or even innocent. Any sinister significance that the fly may create for us is entirely due to its crossing our own path: by means of the fly the human order is compromised. But it is also extended, until through a series of similar conversions and correspondences of image the buzz of the fly distends, both visually and metaphorically, the body of the girl into the world. Her degradation and nobility are in that image. Shall we call it the actual world?

Or is there another adjective that we could apply to this world? There doubtless is; but I cannot, for my purpose, find it short of an adjectival essay, which this essay largely is, of another sort. With some propriety we might call it *an* actual world, which resembles other worlds equally actual, like Dante's or some of Shakespeare's, in its own final completeness, its coherence, depth, perspective. Yet I suspect that this side of the very great men we seldom get magnitude with actuality. We get magnitude in Thackeray and actuality in James; but not both in either. We get both in Tolstoy; but I take it that we accept his magnitude because it is actual, not because it is large. Thackeray's hurly-burly over the Battle of Waterloo is pleasant, empty, and immemorable; Prince André lying wounded under the infinite sky is all the world so lying; and we suspect that Tolstoy's magnitude is only a vast accumulation of little actualities—young Rostov on his horse at the bridgehead, the "little uncle" serving tea to the young people, Natasha weeping over Anatol in her room.

Whither do these casual allusions take us? They might take us far, on some other occasion, at a time when we had the heart for the consideration of actual worlds. But now we are in an occult world, from which actualities, which in their nature are quiet and permanent, are hard to find. As we face the morning's world we see nothing, unless we have the peculiar though intermittent talent for it, so actual as Dostoevsky's fly or Prince André's empty heavens. For if the drift of this essay have anything of truth in it, then our daily suffering, our best will towards the world in which we with difficulty breathe today, and our secret anxieties, however painful these experiences may be, must have something of the occult, something of the private, even something of the willful and obtuse, unless by a miracle of gift or character, and perhaps of history also, we command the imaginative power of the relation of things.

VII

It is a gift that comes and goes; its story is so long that neither time nor understanding has permitted me to tell it here. Yet I think that the risk, the extreme risk that I have so far faced, of some general commitments concerning the function of the imagination as a black art will be worth taking, if only to challenge a fierce denial. It ought to be plain to us, who share a common experience of two conflicts in a single war and who continue to wonder at the ingenious failure of our time, that although human powers are by no means depleted, something has gone wrong with their direction. No man but acknowledges this commonplace; yet how shall we imbed it, ground it, in some conceivable knowledge of the actuality of a world?

It must be plain also that the very instruments of our daily economy have more and more dictated our ends, or at best have suggested to an obscure power within us how we shall conduct our lives. The possibilities latent in our situation must make us falter. The obscure power within us we have made into an occult power; we are no longer conscious of its limits, its function, its purposes. Is that not the meaning of an occult power? One that we sway under but cannot know?

Here again I come up against formidable hazards, and I feel as if I had gone round the flank only to lose direction and to be cut off; but these perils will be plain enough although I shall not describe them. This occult power that seems to overwhelm us must, in times past, have enjoyed the fullness of light; but even underground it will not be gainsaid. If it does not have the privilege of its rational place in the order of human experience, it will take irrational toll of that order. Human violence is an historical constant; yet how shall we come to terms with a violence that is rationally implemented, an efficient, a total violence? It seems to me that the answer of our time to this problem is at present the historical answer of the dead-end, of the stalemate, of the facile optimism of decay. In a time like ours you may be sure of this: that men will be easy and hopeful, and will try a little of the medicine of the bridge-expert along with the elixirs of the innumerable Gerald Heards. Why? Because, although historically man may be a social being before he is a religious being, he is, after he achieves society, primarily religious, and remains incurably so. If he is told that mere "operational techniques" will see him through, whether these are put to work in society, or in the laboratory, or in industry, or in the arts, he may believe it for a while, and try to realize it; but, like a child after the game is over and the fingers are uncrossed, he will return to the real world, unprepared and soon to be overwhelmed by it because he has been told that the real world does not exist.

Or perhaps you would prefer to call it merely another world, after the analogy of *an* actual world; not *the* other world and *the* actual world. For there must be a great many of these worlds, all actual, all to be participated in, all participating in us; yet I prefer the frank Platonism of *the* actual world, as Socrates himself preferred it when he told Ion that "poetry is one." And the impulse to reality which drives us through the engrossing image to the rational knowledge of our experience which, without that image, is mere process, must also be one. Once more the professed skeptic of thirty minutes ago reaches an immoderate deduction beyond any preparation that he has been able to ground it in.

For I should be chagrined could I feel that I have carried you, as well as myself, beyond known depths: are we not committed to the affirmation that actuality and poetry are respectively and even reciprocally one? If we are so committed, we must not affirm otherwise of humanity, which has been one from the beginning. And we cannot allow any novelty to our attempted insights.

Are we not saying something very old when we assert that we may know an actual world in the act of seeing the hovering fly? We are saying that our minds move through three necessities which, when in proper harmony and relation, achieve a dynamic and precarious unity of experience. Now that our oration is over I may say quite plainly that the three necessities—necessities at any rate for Western man— are the three liberal arts. And any one of them practiced to the exclusion of the others retires a portion of our experience into the shadows of the occult, the contingent, the uncontrolled. The grammarians of the modern world have allowed their specialization, the operational technique, to drive the two other arts to cover, whence they break forth in their own furies, the one the fury of irresponsible abstraction, the other the fury of irresponsible rhetoric. The philosopher serves the operational technique, whether in the laboratory or on the battlefield. The poet—and the poet is the rhetorician, the specialist in symbol—serves the operational technique because, being the simplest mind of his trinity, his instinct is to follow and to be near his fellow men.

In a last glance at the last scene of *The Idiot* let us imagine that Myshkin and Rogozhin do not appear. The body of Nastasya Filippovna lies indefinitely upon the narrow bed, the white toe exposed, the fly intermittently rising and falling over the corpse. The dead woman and the fly are a *locus* of the process of decomposition. But, of course, we cannot imagine it, unless like a modern positivist we can imagine ourselves out of our humanity; for to imagine the scene is to be there, and to be there, before the sheeted bed, is to have our own interests powerfully affected. The fiction that we are neither here nor there, but are only spectators who, by becoming, ourselves, objects of grammatical analysis, can arrive at some other actuality than that of process, is the great modern heresy: we can never be mere spectators, or if we can for a little time we shall probably, a few of us only, remain, until there is one man left, like a solitary carp in a pond, who has devoured all the others.

1943

IS LITERARY CRITICISM POSSIBLE?

The questions that I propose to discuss in this essay will fall
into two main divisions. I shall undertake to discuss, first, the
teaching of literary criticism in the university. Since I am not
able to *define* literary criticism I shall be chiefly concerned
with the idea of a formal relation; that is to say, supposing
we knew what criticism is, what relation would it have to the
humanities, of which it seems to be a constituent part? In
the second division I shall try to push the discussion a little
further, towards a question that has been acute in our time:
Is literary criticism possible at all? The answer to this question
ought logically to precede the discussion of a formal relation,
for we ought to know what it is that we are trying to relate
to something else. But we shall never know this; we shall
only find that in teaching criticism we do not know what we
are teaching, even though criticism daily talks about a vast
material that we are in the habit of calling the humanities.
The mere fact of this witnesses our sense of a formal relation
that ought to exist between two things of the nature of
which we are ignorant.

I

Literary criticism as a member of the humanities I take to
be a problem of academic statesmanship inviting what we
hopefully call "solutions" of both the theoretical and the
practical sort. Is literary criticism properly a branch of humanistic study? That is the theoretical question, to which I shall
avoid the responsibility of giving the answer. Without this
answer, we cannot hope to understand the practical question:
What is the place of criticism in the humanities program; on
what grounds should it be there (if it should be there at all),

162

given the kind of education that the present teachers of the humanities bring to their work?

The two questions, the theoretical and the practical, together constitute the formal question; that is to say, whatever criticism and the humanities may be, we should have to discuss their relation in some such terms as I am suggesting. But before we follow this clue we must address ourselves more candidly to the fact of our almost total ignorance.

The three grand divisions of higher education in the United States are, I believe, the Natural Sciences, the Social Sciences, and the Humanities. Of the first, I am entirely too ignorant to speak. Of the social sciences I know little, and I am not entitled to suspect that they do not really exist; I believe this in the long run because I want to believe it, the actuality of a science of human societies being repellent to me, apart from its dubious scientific credentials. Of the humanities, the division with which as poet and critic I am presumably most concerned, one must speak with melancholy as well as in ignorance. For into the humanistic bag we throw everything that cannot qualify as a science, natural or social. This discrete mixture of hot and cold, moist and dry, creates in the bag a vortex, which emits a powerful wind of ineffectual heroics, somewhat as follows: We humanists bring within the scope of the humanities all the great records— sometimes we call them the remains: poetry, drama, pre-scientific history (Herodotus, Joinville, Bede)—of the experience of man *as* man; we are not concerned with him as vertebrate, biped, mathematician, or priest. Precisely, reply the social scientists; that is just what is wrong with you; you don't see that man is not man, that he is merely a *function;* and your records (or remains) are so full of error that we are glad to relegate them to professors of English, poets, and other dilettanti, those "former people" who live in the Past. The Past, which we can neither smell, see, taste, nor touch, was well labeled by our apostle, Mr. Carl Sandburg, as a bucket of ashes . . . No first-rate scientific mind is guilty of his vulgarity. Yet as academic statesmen, the humanists must also be practical politicians who know that they cannot stay in office unless they have an invigorating awareness of the power, and of the superior foot-work, of the third-rate mind.

As for literary criticism, we here encounter a stench and murk not unlike that of a battlefield three days after the fighting is over and the armies have departed. Yet in this war nobody has suggested that criticism is one of the social sciences, except a few Marxists, who tried fifteen years ago to make it a branch of sociology. History not long ago became a social science, and saved its life by losing it; and there is no reason why sociology "oriented" toward literature should not be likewise promoted, to the relief of everybody concerned. And whatever criticism may be, we should perhaps do well to keep it with the humanities, where it can profit by the sad example of Hilaire Belloc's Jim, who failed "To keep ahold of Nurse/For fear of getting something worse."

It may not be necessary to know what criticism is; it may be quite enough to see that it is now being written, that a great deal of it was written in the past, that it is concerned with one of the chief objects of humanistic study: literature. And we therefore study it either as an "area" in itself—that is, we offer courses in its history; or as a human interest in some past age—that is, we use criticism as one way of understanding the age of Johnson or the high Renaissance. Guided by the happy theory of spontaneous understanding resulting from the collision of pure intelligence with its object—a theory injected into American education by Charles W. Eliot —we expose the student mind to "areas" of humanistic material, in the confident belief that if it is exposed to enough "areas" it will learn something. If we expose it to enough "areas" in all three grand divisions, the spontaneous intelligence will automatically become educated without thought.

The natural sciences have a high-powered rationale of their daily conquests of nature. The social sciences have a slippery analogical [1] metaphor to sustain their self-confidence. The humanities modestly offer the vision of the historical lump. This lump is tossed at the student mind, which is conceived as the miraculous combination of the *tabula rasa* and innate powers of understanding. In short, the humanities have no rationale. We suppose that it is sufficient to show that a given work—a poem, a play, a critical "document"—came before or after some other poem, play, or critical "document," or was written when something else was happening, like Alexander's invasion of India or the defeat of the Armada. When these and other correlations are perceived, the result is understanding. But the result of correlation is merely the possibility of further correlation. Our modest capacity for true understanding is frustrated. For the true rationale of humanistic study is now what it has always been, even though now it is not only in decay, but dead. I allude to the arts of rhetoric.

By rhetoric I mean the study and the use of the figurative language of experience as the discipline by means of which men govern their relations with one another in the light of truth. Rhetoric presupposes the study of two prior disciplines, grammar and logic, neither of which is much pursued today, except by specialists.

These disciplines are no longer prerequisite even to the study of philosophy. An Eastern university offers a grandiose course in Greek philosophical ideas to sophomores who will never know a syllogism from a handsaw. A graduate student who, I was told, was very brilliant in nuclear physics, decided that he wanted to take a course in *The Divine Comedy*. (Why he wanted to study Dante I do not know, but his humility was impressive.) I was assured by the academic grapevine that he understood difficult mathematical formulae, but one day in class he revealed the fact that he could neither define nor recognize a past participle. At the end of the term he confessed that nobody had ever told him that the strategies of language, or the arts of rhetoric, could be as important and exacting a discipline as the theory of equations. He had thought courses in English a little sissified; he had not been told that it might be possible, after severe application, to learn how to read. He had learned to talk without effort in infancy, in a decadent democracy, and no doubt supposed that grammar came of conditioning, and that he would get it free.

Back of this homely exemplum stands a formidable specter whose name is Cultural Decay—at a time when men are more conscious of cultures than ever before, and stock their universities and museums with lumps of cultures, like inert geological specimens in a glass case. I am far from believing that a revival of the trivium, or the three primary liberal arts, would bring the dead bodies to life: revivals have a fatal incapacity to revive anything. But unless we can create and develop a hierarchy of studies that can lead not merely to further studies but to truth, one may doubt that the accelerating decline of modern culture will be checked.

Without quite knowing what literary criticism is, let us assume again that we are teaching it within the humanities division, usually in the English Department, either because it ought to be there or because nobody else wants it. For convenience we may think of the common relations between the work of the imagination and the teaching activity under four heads, which I shall put in the form of rhetorical questions:

(1) Can a given work, say *Clarissa Harlowe* or *Kublai Khan,* be "taught," in such a way as to make it understood, without criticism?

(2) Can the work be taught first, and the criticism then applied as a mode of understanding?

(3) Can the criticism be presented first and held in readiness for the act of understanding which could thus be simultaneous with the act of reading the novel or the poem?

(4) Is the purpose of teaching imaginative works to provide materials upon which the critical faculty may exercise itself in its drive toward the making of critical systems, which then perpetuate themselves without much reference to literature?

These four versions of the relation by no means exhaust its possible variations. The slippery ambiguity of the word criticism itself ought by now to be plain. But for the purposes of this localized discussion, which I am limiting for the moment to the question of how to teach, we may think of criticism as three familiar kinds of discourse about works of literature. (We must bear in mind not only our failure to know what criticism is, but another, more difficult failure resulting from it: the failure to know what literature is.) The three kinds of critical discourse are as follows: (1) acts of evaluation of literature (whatever these may be); (2) the communication of insights; and (3) the rhetorical study of the language of the imaginative work.

I am not assuming, I am merely pretending that any one of the three activities is to be found in its purity. To the extent that they may be separated, we must conclude that the two first, acts of evaluation and the communication of insights, cannot be taught, and that the third, rhetorical analysis, has not been taught effectively in this country since the rise of the historical method in literary studies.

When I first taught a college class, about eighteen years ago, I thought that anything was possible; but with every year since it has seemed a little more absurd to try to teach students to "evaluate" works of literature, and perhaps not less absurd to try to evaluate them oneself. The assumption that we are capable of just evaluation (a word that seems to have got into criticism by way of Adam Smith) is one of the subtler, if crude, abuses of democratic doctrine, as follows: all men ought to exercise independent judgment, and all men being equal, all are equally capable of it, even in literature and the arts. I have observed that when my own opinions seem most original and independent they turn out to be almost wholly conventional. An absolutely independent judgment (if such a thing were possible) would be an absolutely ignorant judgment.

Shall the instructor, then, set before the class his own "evaluations"? He will do so at the risk of disseminating a hierarchy that he may not have intended to create, and thus may be aborted, or at least stultified, the student's own reading. It is inevitable that the instructor shall say to the class that one poem is "better" than another. The student, in the degree of his intelligence, will form clear preferences or rejections that will do little harm if he understands what they are. But the teaching of literature through the assertion of preference will end up either as mere impressionism, or as the more sinister variety of impressionism that Irving Babbitt detected in the absorption of the literary work into its historical setting.

As to the communication of "insights," it would perhaps be an inquiry without benefit to anybody to ask how this elusive maid-of-all-work got into modern criticism. She is here, and perhaps we ought to be grateful, because she is obviously willing to do all the work. Insight could mean two things, separately or taken together: the perception of meanings ordinarily or hitherto undetected, and/or the synthetic awareness that brings to the text similar or contrasting qualities from other works. These awarenesses are the critical or receiving end of the Longinian "flash" proceeding from varying degrees of information and knowledge, unpredictable and largely unviable. They are doubtless a good thing for a teacher to have, but they cannot be taught to others; they can be only exhibited. If insight is like faith, a gift by the grace of God, there is no use in teaching at all—if insight-teaching is our only way of going about it. But if it is partly a gift and partly the result of labor (as Longinus thought), perhaps the teacher could find a discipline of language to expound to the class, with the hope that a latent gift of insight may be liberated.

Rhetoric is an unpopular word today, and it deserves to be, if we understand it as the "pragmatic dimension" of discourse as this has been defined by Charles W. Morris, and other semanticists and positivists. In this view rhetoric is semantically irresponsible; its use is to move people to action which is at best morally neutral; or if it is good action, this result was no necessary part of the rhetorician's purpose. The doctrine is not new; it is only a pleasantly complex and double-talking revival of Greek sophistry. But if we think of rhetoric in another tradition, that of Aristotle and of later, Christian rhetoricians, we shall be able to see it as the study of the full language of experience, not the specialized languages of method.[2] Through this full language of experience Dante and Shakespeare could arrive at truth.

This responsible use implies the previous study of the two lower, but not inferior, disciplines that I have already mentioned. One of these was once quaintly known as "grammar," the art that seems to be best learned at the elementary stage in a paradigmatic language like Latin. I think of a homely exemplum that will illustrate one of the things that have happened since the decay of grammar. I had a student at the University of Chicago who wrote a paper on T. S. Eliot's religious symbolism, in which he failed to observe that certain sequences of words in "Ash Wednesday" are without verbs: he had no understanding of the relation of the particulars to the universals in Eliot's diction. The symbols floated, in this student's mind, in a void of abstraction; the language of the poem was beyond his reach. Is the domination of historical scholarship responsible for the decline of the grammatical arts? I think that it may be; but it would not follow from its rejection that these arts or their equivalent would rise again. (One must always be prepared for the rise of nothing.) My Chicago student was laudably trying to read the text of the poem; he had nothing but a good mind and good intentions to read it with. What he had done, of course, was to abstract Eliot's symbols out of their full rhetorical context, so that they had become neither Eliot's nor anybody else's symbols. They were thus either critically useless, or potentially useful in a *pragmatic dimension* of discourse where ideas may be *power:* as the fullback is said to "bull" through the opposing line. The rhetorical disciplines, which alone seem to yield something like the full import of the work of imagination, are by-passed; and we by-pass these fundamentals of understanding no less when we read our own language. All reading is translation, even in the native tongue; for translation may be described as the act of mediation between universals and particulars in the complex of metaphor. As qualified translators we are inevitably rhetoricians. One scarcely sees how the student (like the Chicago student, who is also the Minnesota, the Harvard, and the Cornell student) can be expected to begin the study of rhetoric at the top, particularly if below it there is no bottom. If he begins at the top, as a "critic," he may become the victim of "insights" and "evaluations" that he has not earned, or he may parrot critical systems that his instructors have expounded or perhaps merely alluded to, in class. In any case, man being by nature, or by the nature of his language, a rhetorician, the student becomes a bad rhetorician. It is futile to expect him to be a critic when he has not yet learned how to read.

How can rhetoric, or the arts of language, be taught today? We are not likely to begin teaching something in which we do not believe: we do not believe in the uses of rhetoric because we do not believe that the full language of the human situation can be the vehicle of truth. We are not facing the problem when we circumvent it by asking the student to study the special languages of "criticism," in which we should like to believe. Can we believe in the language of humane truth without believing in the possibility of a higher unity of truth, which we must posit as *there,* even if it must remain beyond our powers of understanding? Without such a belief are we not committed to the assumption that literature has nothing to do with truth, that it is only illusion, froth on the historical current, the Platonic *gignomenon?* We languish, then, in the pragmatic vortex where ideas are disembodied into power; but power for what it is not necessary here to try to say. I turn now to literary criticism as it seems to be in itself, apart from any question of teaching it.

II

We have reached the stage of activity in individual criticism at which we begin to ask whether what we severally do has, or ought to have, a common end. What has a common end may be better reached, or at any rate more efficiently pursued, if the long ways to it are by-passed for the short ways—if happily we can agree on a common methodology, or at worst a few cooperating methodologies. The image that this enticing delusion brings to mind is that of the cheerful, patient bulldozer leveling off an uncharted landscape. The treeless plain thus made could be used as a desert—by those who can use deserts—or as an airfield from which to fly somewhere else.

The notes that follow I have put in the form of propositions, or theses, which either I or some imaginable person might be presumed to uphold at the present time. Some will be found to contradict others; but this is to be expected when we try to distinguish the aims and habits of literary critics over a period so long as a quarter of a century. The ten theses will affirm, deny, or question a belief or a practice.

I. Literary criticism is in at least one respect (perhaps more than one) like a mule: it cannot reproduce itself, though, like a mule, it is capable of trying. Its end is outside itself. If the great formal works of literature are not wholly autonomous, criticism, however theoretical it may become, is necessarily even less so. It cannot in the long run be practiced apart from what it confronts, that gives rise to it. It has no formal substance: it is always *about* something else. If it tries to be about itself, and sets up on its own, it initiates the infinite series: one criticism within another leading to another criticism progressively more formal-looking and abstract; or it is progressively more irrelevant to its external end as it attends to the periphery, the historical buzz in the ear of literature.

II. The more systematic and methodical, the "purer," criticism becomes, the less one is able to feel in it the presence of its immediate occasion. It tends more and more to *sound* like philosophical discourse. There are countless degrees, variations, and overlappings of method, but everyone knows that there are three typical directions that method may take: (1) Aesthetics, which aims at the ordering of criticism within a large synthesis of either experimental psychology or ontology; from the point of view of which it is difficult to say anything about literature that is not merely pretentious. For example: Goethe's Concrete Universal, Coleridge's Esemplastic Power, Croce's Expression. (2) Analysis of literary language, or "stylistics" (commonly supposed to be the orbit of the New Criticism). Without the correction of a total rhetoric, this *techné* must find its limit, if it is not at length to become only a habit, in the extreme "purity" of nominalism ("positivism") or of metaphysics. (3) Historical scholarship, the "purest" because the most methodical criticism of all, offers the historical reconstruction as the general possibility of literature, without accounting for the unique, miraculous superiority of *The Tempest* or of *Paradise Lost*.

III. When we find criticism appealing to phrases like "frame of reference," "intellectual discipline," or even "philosophical basis," it is not improper to suspect that the critic is asking us to accept his "criticism" on the authority of something in which he does not believe. The two first phrases contain perhaps hidden analogies to mathematics; the third, a metaphor of underpinning. This is nothing against them; all language is necessarily figurative. But used as I have indicated, the phrases have no ontological, or substantive, meaning. The critic is only avoiding the simple word truth, and begging the question. Suppose we acknowledge that the critic, as he begs this question, gives us at the same moment a new and just insight into a scene in *The Idiot* or *King Lear*. Yet the philosophical language in which he visibly expounds the insight may seem to reflect an authority that he has not visibly earned. The language of criticism had better not, then, try to be univocal. It is neither fish nor fowl, yet both, with that unpleasant taste that we get from fishing ducks.

IV. Literary criticism may become prescriptive and dogmatic when the critic achieves a coherence in the logical and rhetorical orders which exceeds the coherence of the imaginative work itself in those orders. We substitute with the critic a dialectical order for the elusive, and perhaps quite different, order of the imagination. We fall into the trap of the logicalization of parts discretely attended. This sleight of hand imposed upon the reader's good faith invites him to share the critic's own intellectual pride. Dazzled by the refractions of the critic's spectrum, the reader accepts as his own the critic's dubious superiority to the work as a whole. He is only attending serially to the separated parts in which he worships his own image. This is critical idolatry; the idols of its three great sects are the techniques of purity described in Thesis II.

V. If criticism undertakes the responsibility and the privilege of a strict theory of knowledge, the critic will need all the humility that human nature is capable of, almost the self-abnegation of the saint. Is the critic willing to test his epistemology against a selfless reading of *The Rape of the Lock, War and Peace,* or a lyric by Thomas Nashe? Or is his criticism merely the report of a quarrel between the imagined life of the work and his own "philosophy"? Has possession of the critic by a severe theory of knowledge interfered with the primary office of criticism? What is the primary office of criticism? Is it to expound and to elucidate, with as little distortion as possible, the knowledge of life contained by the novel or the poem or the play? What critic has ever done this?

VI. A work of the imagination differs from a work of the logical intellect in some radical sense that seems to lie beyond our comprehension. But this much may be said: the imaginative work admits of neither progressive correction nor substitution or rearrangement of parts; it is never obsolete, it is always up-to-date. Dryden does not "improve" Shakespeare; Shakespeare does not replace Dante, in the way that Einstein's physics seems to have "corrected" Newton's. There is no competition among poems. A good poem suggests the possibility of other poems equally good. But criticism is perpetually obsolescent and replaceable.

VII. The very terms of elucidation—the present ones, like any others—carry with them, concealed, an implicated judgment. The critic's rhetoric, laid out in his particular grammar, is the critic's mind. This enables him to see much that is there, a little that is there, nothing that is there, or something that is not there; but none of these with perfect consistency. We may ask again: to what extent is the critic obligated to dredge the bottom of his mind and to exhibit to an incredulous eye his own skeleton? We might answer the question rhetorically by saying: We are constantly trying to smoke out the critic's "position." This is criticism of criticism. Should we succeed in this game to our perfect satisfaction, we must be on guard lest our assent to or dissent from a critic's "position" mislead us into supposing that his gift of elucidation is correspondingly impressive or no good. If absolutely just elucidation were possible, it would also be philosophically sound, even though the critic might elsewhere announce his adherence to a philosophy that we should want to question.

VIII. If the implicated judgment is made overt, is there not in it an invitation to the reader to dismiss or to accept the work before he has read it? Even though he "read" the work first? (Part of this question is dealt with in Thesis V.) Is *a priori* judgment in the long run inevitable? What unformulated assumption lurks, as in the thicket, back of T. S. Eliot's unfavorable comparison of "Ripeness is all" with *"E la sua voluntade è nostra pace"*? Is Shakespeare's summation of life naturalistic, pagan, and immature? J. V. Cunningham has shown that "Ripeness is all" is a statement within the natural law, quite as Christian as Dante's statement within the divine law. The beacon of conceptual thought as end rather than means in criticism is a standing menace to critical order because it is inevitable, human nature being what it is. One thing that human nature is, is "fallen."

IX. In certain past ages there was no distinct activity of the mind conscious of itself as literary criticism; for example, the age of Sophocles and the age of Dante. In the age of Dante the schoolmen held that poetry differed from scriptural revelation in its *historia,* or fable, at which, in poetry, the literal event could be part or even all fiction. But the other, higher meanings of poetry might well be true, in spite of the fictional plot, if the poet had the gift of anagogical, or spiritual, insight. Who was capable of knowing when the poet had achieved this insight? Is literary criticism possible without a criterion of absolute truth? Would a criterion of absolute truth make literary criticism as we know it unnecessary? Can it have a relevant criterion of truth without acknowledging an emergent order of truth in its great subject matter, literature itself?

X. Literary criticism, like the Kingdom of God on earth, is perpetually necessary and, in the very nature of its middle position between imagination and philosophy, perpetually impossible. Like a man, literary criticism is nothing in itself; criticism, like man, embraces pure experience or exalts pure rationality at the price of abdication from its dual nature. It is of the nature of man and of criticism to occupy the intolerable position. Like man's, the intolerable position of criticism has its own glory. It is the only position that it is ever likely to have.

1950–1951

LONGINUS AND THE "NEW CRITICISM"

To begin an essay with a silent apology to the subject is commendable, but one should not expect the reader to be interested in it. I allude to the ignorance in which I had underestimated Longinus, before I reread him after twenty years, because I am convinced that it is typical. Who reads Longinus? I do not mean to say literally that he is not read. There is an excellent recent study by Mr. Elder Olson; there are the fine books by Mr. T. R. Henn and Mr. Samuel H. Monk, [1] which persons of the critical interest should know something about and doubtless do. Until these books appeared, there had been no serious consideration of Longinus since Saintsbury's *A History of Criticism* (1900). In some twenty-five years of looking at criticism in the United States and England, I have not seen, with the exceptions already noticed, a reference to the περὶ ὕψους which is of more than historical interest. One might, with misplaced antiquarian zeal, find the name, if not much more, of Aristotle in the pages of a fashionable journal like *Horizon;* one would have to go to the learned journals, which few critics see, to find even the name of Longinus. Until Mr. Henn and Mr. Monk reminded us of him, he had been dropped out of active criticism since the end of the eighteenth century. I should like to believe that these excellent scholars have brought about a Longinian revival. Mr. Herbert Read informs me that Coleridge in *Table Talk* spoke of him as "no very profound critic." It must seem to us today that Coleridge buried him in that remark. I am not confident that I shall succeed where Mr. Monk and Mr. Henn failed (if they did fail), that what I am about to say will exhume Longinus.

I

This is not the occasion to establish a correct English title for περὶ ὕψους. (In the New Testament ὕψος means not the physical heavens [οὐρανός] but something like "on high.") To my mind, the idea of height or elevation contained in the title, *Of the Height of Eloquence,* which was given to the work by the first English translator, John Hall, in 1652, is more exact than *On the Sublime,* which carries with it the accretions of Boileau and the English eighteenth century, and the different meanings contributed later by Burke and Kant, which are far removed from anything that I have been able to find in this third- (or is it first-?) century treatise. So far from Kant's is Longinus' conception of "sublimity" that one pauses at the marvelous semantic history of the word. In Chapter IX Longinus quotes a passage from the *Iliad,* Book XX, about the war of the gods, and comments: "Yet these things terrible as they are, if they are not taken as an allegory are altogether blasphemous and destructive of what is seemly." To allegorize infinite magnitude, quantity beyond the range of the eye, is to reduce it to the scale of what Kant called the Beautiful as distinguished from the Sublime. The "sublimity" of the passage, in the Kantian sense, Longinus could not accept. These shifts of meaning are beyond the scope of my interest and my competence. Three other brief and confusing parallels will fix in our minds the difficulties of Longinus' title. His insight, perhaps unique in antiquity, which is contained in the distinction between the "persuasion" of oratory and the "transport" of what, for want of a better phrase, one may call the literary effect, reappears in this century as neo-Symbolism and Surrealism. Some twenty years ago the Abbé Bremond decided that "transport" meant religious mysticism, and wrote a book called *La Poésie pure.* In England, about thirty years ago, Arthur Machen, of whom few people of the generations younger than mine have heard, the author of *The Hill of Dreams* and other novels after Huysmans, wrote a small critical book called *Hieroglyphics.* Machen proposed to discern the real thing in literature with a test that he called "ecstasy," but what made Machen ecstatic left many persons cold. At any rate, the Greek word in Longinus that we translate as "transport" is ἔκστασις. Had Boileau not stuffed Longinus with neoclassical "authority," would he have been discovered by the French and English romantics, to whom he could have spoken from another if equally wrong direction? This topic may be dropped with the observation that literary history is no more orderly than any other history.

I shall, then, in the following remarks, think of the two key terms in Longinus, ὕψος and ἔκστασις, as respectively Elevation of Language and Transport; but I cannot expect to disentangle them from each other. They contain, in their interrelations, a version of a persistent ambiguity of critical reference which appeared with Aristotle, had vigorous life up to Coleridge (with whom it comes back disguised), and now eggs on an edifying controversy of the contemporary English and American critics: Ransom, Cleanth Brooks, Read, Leavis, Richards, Blackmur, and Winters. Is Elevation an objective quality of the literary work? Is Transport its subjective reference denoting the emotions of the reader— or the "hearer," as Longinus calls him—as he receives the impact of Elevation? Does either word, Elevation or Transport, point to anything sufficiently objective to be isolated for critical discussion?

This is not the moment to answer that question, if I were competent to answer it. Our first duty is to find out how Longinus asks it. After defining Elevation tautologically, in Chapter I, as "a kind of supreme excellence of discourse" (ἐξοχή τις λόγων ἐστὶ τὰ ὕψη), he describes its effect:

For what is out of the common *affects the hearer not to persuade but to entrance* (οὐ γὰρ εἰς πειθὼ τοὺς ἀκροωμένους ἀλλ᾽ εἰς ἔκστασιν ἄγει τὰ ὑπερφυᾶ). *It moves to wonder and surprise, and always wins against what is merely delightful or persuasive. It is not enough in one or two passages of a work to exhibit invention schooled by experience, nor again the fine order and distribution of its parts, nor even these qualities displayed throughout. Rather, I suggest, does the sublime, fitly expressed, pierce everything like a flash of lightning. . . .*[2]

Not to persuade, but to entrance, like a flash of lightning. In these words Longinus breaks with the rhetoricians who had dominated ancient criticism since Aristotle, four to six hundred years before him, and who continued to dominate it until the seventeenth century. Neither Longinus nor Dante, in *De Vulgari Eloquentia,* had any influence on critical theory after them, until the time of Boileau, when Longinus was used to justify rules that he had never made. Dante's criticism has languished in the department of biography; at best, in the history of criticism, as a document of the time.

II

Chapter II opens with the question: "We must first discuss whether there is an art of the sublime." In the Greek, the phrase is ὕψους τις ἢ βάθους τέχνη—"an art of height or of depth"; but the word we should attend is τέχνη, "art," which the Greeks used for any teachable skill, from metal-working to music and medicine. They applied the term to all the skills of making for which an objective rationale could be devised. Longinus explains the views of Caecilius, the opponent of uncertain identity whom the περὶ ὕψους was written to refute, who believed that elevation of language came through nature alone, that the great writer, born great, needs nothing but his birth. In this controversy of lively acrimony with a man who may have been dead three hundred years (such was the leisure of antiquity), Longinus at the beginning of his essay opposes, in opposing Caecilius, both the Platonic and the Aristotelian doctrines, and holds that style is a compound of natural talent and conscious method. He thus parts with Plato's "divine madness" in the *Ion,* and implicitly claims for Thought and Diction, two of the nonstructural elements in Aristotle's analysis of tragedy, a degree of objectivity that Aristotle's rhetorical view of poetic language could not include.

If literary method cannot alone produce a style, the judgment of which, says Longinus, "is the last fruit of long experience," it can "help us to speak at the right length and to the occasion." How much interpretation of a casual observation such as this, which is only common sense, the modern scholiast is entitled to develop, I do not know. Although Longinus may have in mind merely the orator and the *public* occasion, may we just see him reaching out for a criterion of objectivity for any sort of literary composition? The "right length" is the adaptation of form to subject; and is not the "occasion" the relation between the poet and the person to whom the poem is addressed? We have, foreshadowed here, I think, a principle of dramatic propriety, a sense of the "point of view" in composition, the prime literary strategy which can never be made prescriptive, but which exhibits its necessity equally in its operation and in its lapse. Later, discussing meter, Longinus tells us that Elevation cannot be achieved in the trochaic, or tripping, meter, and we may dismiss the remark as the perennial fallacy which identifies certain fixed effects with certain meters. But if we can imagine "Lycidas" written in trochees and "The Raven" in iambuses, we might suppose the one would be worse, the other considerably better. And if we look at "length" and "occasion" in somewhat different terms, we shall find ourselves again in the thick of one of our own controversies. Does not the occasion force upon the poet the objective and communicable features of his work? Are they not Mr. Winters' theory of the relation of "feeling" to "rational content" and Mr. Ransom's theory of a "texture" within a "structure"?

In exceeding the literal text of Longinus in this matter, I hope that I have not also stretched two living critics into an agreement which they have scarcely acknowledged; nor should I ask them to asknowledge Longinus as their forerunner. I suggest that Longinus' question, "Is there an art of Elevation?" is the question we are asking today, somewhat as follows: Can there be a criticism of convincing objectivity which approaches the literary work through the analysis of style and which arrives at its larger aspects through that aperture?

That is the question of our time. In asking it, are we not following Longinus rather than Aristotle? Aristotle began with the conspicuous "larger aspects" of a mature literary genre, Greek tragedy, and got around to the problems of poetic language only at the end, and as a rhetorician (except for one curious remark about metaphor) who offers us shrewd but merely schematic advice about the use of figures.

III

If there is an art of Elevation, if there is possible a coherent criticism of literature through its language, it follows that we must examine good and bad writers together, in order to arrive, not at rules, but at that "judgment of style which is the fruit of long experience"; to arrive at that sense of the length and the occasion which will permit us, as poets, to imitate not Homer's style but its excellence, in our own language. It is here that intensive literary criticism and literary tradition work together; it is here that we arrive at the idea of a literary tradition which does not enjoin the slavery of repetition, but the emulation which comes of insight. We shall have of course to deal as best we can with the ambiguity of Longinus' word $\tau\acute{\epsilon}\chi\nu\eta$. By the "art of height or of depth" does he mean criticism? Or does he mean the "art" of the poet? He means, I take it, both; and it is proper that he should. For our sense of the achievement of the past may issue in a critical acquisition of knowledge which is not to be put away in the attic when the creative moment comes. At this point one may profitably notice two characteristic defects, defects of its quality, that proud and self-sufficient writers fall into in attempting the elevated style. "Frigidity," says Longinus, is the over-elaboration of the academic writer, a violation of length due to aiming at "the curious and the artificial." The "feeling" (or the detail) is unreal in the sense that it is on a scale smaller than its intelligible form. Likewise, the opposite fault—and in describing it Longinus has written as good criticism as any I know—of Thomas Wolfe and the contemporary lyrical novel; he says:

Theodorus calls it the mock-inspired. It is emotion out of place and empty where there is no need of it, or lack of proportion where proportion is needed. Some writers fall into a maudlin

*mood and digress from their subject into their own tedious
emotion. Thus they show bad form and leave their audience
unimpressed: necessarily, for they are in a state of rapture,
and the audience is not.*

If this is the performance of the writer great by nature and
beyond "art," Henry James gives us his dreary portrait: "The
writer who cultivates his instinct rather than his awareness
sits by finally in a stale and shrinking puddle." His awareness of what? I should say of the "occasion" and the "length,"
the sense of limiting structure and of what, within that limit,
is to be objectively communicated and made known. This
sense becomes operative through "art," $\tau \acute{\epsilon} \chi \nu \eta$, technique, the
controlled awareness *through* language of what can be made
actual *in* language, resulting in a just, if unpredictable, proportion between what Longinus calls the "emotion" and the
"subject." Doubtless, any experienced reader of literature can
point to the failures of great writers in the two extremes of
disproportion corresponding to two forms of pride that prevent the complete discovery of the subject: the pride of intellect and the pride of feeling, the pride of will and the
pride of instinct. (Perhaps the history of the imagination is
the pendulum between these extremes.) Mr. Blackmur has
shown us in the past few years how the thesis in Dostoevsky
distorts or even wrecks the theme, the imaginative actuality
in which the form ought to have been discovered under pressure of its internal necessity. In a more recent writer, D. H.
Lawrence, we get both extremes of pride: the attack on the
intellect on behalf of instinct, instinct itself hardening into a
core of abstraction which operates as intellectual pride, as
thesis; not as realized form.

The instances of "disproportion" could be multiplied, but
I pause to remark my own digression, and to ask, as the
eighteenth-century critics seem not to have done, whether
there is not already, in what I have said, a certain excess of
gloss, commentary cut loose from the text commented upon,
a self-indulgence which seems to attribute to Longinus a
comprehension which one is covertly claiming for oneself?
Criticism should no doubt observe the same proprieties of

occasion and length that we require of the imagination; but
it has seldom done so, and I think with good reason. If criticism is only secondary to literature, it is thus the dependent
partner, and for the hazards that it must face in every generation it must constantly worry the past for support, and make
too much of what it revives, or perhaps even make it into
something different. Perhaps I have got out of the περὶ ὕψους
at this stage of the discussion only a general insight available,
if not always used, as common property since Coleridge. Yet
we should remember that Longinus alone seems to have
achieved it in the ancient world.

I have been trying to see the outlines, before I move on
to some of the particular judgments in the περὶ ὕψους, of a
possible framework into which to put Longinus' profound
but topical dialectic. In the same chapter (II) in which the
proportions of length and occasion are held to be established
through "art" or method, he writes this crucial passage:

*Demosthenes says somewhere that in ordinary life luck is the
greatest good, and that it cannot exist without another which
is not inferior to it, namely prudent conduct. Following him,
we might say, in the case of style, that nature takes the place
of good luck; and art, of prudent conduct.* Most important of
all, we must learn from art the fact that some elements of
style depend upon nature alone.

At this point four pages of the manuscript disappear, a loss
of the first importance to critical theory. If the amateur
Hellenist reads from classical criticism a passage in which
the word "nature" occurs, he is likely to read it with Boileau
or the English eighteenth century, and get entangled in the
thickets of "nature," which they opposed to "art," when they
were not effecting a compromise by making art nature to
advantage dressed; and so on. It seems to me that we ought
to support the passage just quoted with a full sense of the
special kind of judgment that Longinus brings to bear upon
the actual texture of Greek literature; he produces many examples which cannot be cited here. We could then just see
in it the first declaration of independence from the practical,
forensic eloquence of the rhetoricians.

"Most important of all, we must learn from art the fact that some elements of style depend upon nature alone." In trying to understand this nice oxymoron, I shall take risks which are perhaps not greater than those taken by most commentators on the *Poetics*. Most important of all, I make Longinus say, we learn from the development of technique that stylistic autonomy is a delusion, because style comes into existence only as it discovers the subject; and conversely the subject exists only after it is formed by the style. No literary work is perfect, no subject perfectly formed. Style reveals that which is not style in the process of forming it. Style does not create the subject, it discovers it. The fusion of art and nature, of technique and subject, can never exceed the approximate; the margin of imperfection, of the unformed, is always there—nature intractable to art, art unequal to nature. The converse of Longinus' aphorism will further elucidate it: we must learn from nature that some elements of subject matter, in a literary work, "depend" upon art alone. There is a reciprocal relation, not an identity—not, certainly, the identity of form and content—a dynamic, shifting relation between technique and subject; and they reveal each other. This is my sense of Longinus' primary insight. It is an insight of considerable subtlety that has a special claim to the attention of our generation.

IV

I suppose we should agree that by and large the critical method of the *Poetics* is inductive. Aristotle's generalizations proceed from a scrutiny of one kind of literature, drama, chiefly from one kind of drama, tragedy, and from one kind of tragedy, Greek. Longinus repeats Aristotle's animadversions on "character," which Aristotle seems to think need not be much developed if the "plot" is good. We must constantly remind ourselves of the narrow range of literature at the command of the two great critics of antiquity; they lacked the novel, for one thing, and Aristotle evidently did not consider the works of his great predecessor and teacher worthy of the name of "poetry." The larger conception of *literature* does not appear in the *Poetics*. Although Longinus, trained as he must have been in the rhetorical schools, did not see clearly whither he was heading, it is just the awareness of *literature at large* which raises his theory of the relation of language and subject to a higher degree of useful generality than any literary theory before him had reached. He is the first, though necessarily incomplete, literary critic. His question, put again, in its wider implications, is: what distinguishes literature from practical oratory, from history? A quality, he says in effect, beyond an immediate purpose. His discussion of imagination is what we should expect: it is the classical rhetorician's view of the image as a "mental picture," which he, along with his age, seems to believe must be laid on the work discreetly from the top. Yet the distinction between two widely different purposes in the controlled use of language puts his doctrine on a high yet accessible level of empirical generalization, and makes it possible for him to look beyond specific conventions to estimate the value of a literature offering a great variety of forms and structures.

It has been supposed by many critics that Longinus is not interested in structure, that his doctrine of "transport" and the "lightning flash" anticipates the romantic *frisson,* or that Pope did it justice when he called in Longinus to help him "snatch a grace beyond the reach of art." I think I have shown that Longinus would reject that art which is beyond its own reach. And what, in fact, I now wish to show is that Longinus is quite prepared to put his finger directly upon the problem of structure, and by implication to tell us that structure is not in the formal "type" or genre, a viable body of special conventions, such as the lyric, the ode, or the epic provides, but exists in the language of the poem.

After discussing, in Chapters VIII and IX, the five sources of Elevation in language (to which I shall return), he analyzes the effect, from the point of view of structure, of Sappho's Ode to Anactoria, beginning: φαίνεταί μοι κῆνος ἴσος θεοῖσιν . The analysis is brief (everything in Longinus is brief but the lacunae in the text), yet it is probably the first example in criticism of structural analysis of a lyric poem. (I ought for my purpose here to know more than I do, which is virtually nothing, about the ancient theory of the Passions.) I quote the entire passage:

Let us now go on to see whether we have anything further by means of which we can raise our words to the sublime. Since, then, in the substance of everything, we find certain elements which naturally belong to it, we should of course find one cause of the sublime by always choosing the most relevant circumstances and by compounding them (ἐπισυνθέσει) to make, so to speak, one body (ἕν τι σῶμα ποιεῖν). For the audience is attracted, first by our choice of topics (ὁ μὲν γὰρ τῇ ἐκλογῇ . . . τῶν λημμάτων), and second, by the conciseness of our exposition. For example, Sappho takes from their actual setting the feelings that accompany the frenzy of love. Where then does she display her skill? In the tact with which she chooses and binds together supreme and intense feelings.

*Peer of Gods he seemeth to me, the blissful
Man who sits and gazes at thee before him,
Close beside thee sits, and in silence hears thee
   Silverly speaking,*

*Laughing love's low laughter. Oh this, this only
Stirs the troubled heart in my breast to tremble!
For should I but see thee a little moment,
   Straight is my voice hushed;*

*Yea, my tongue is broken, and through and through me
'Neath the flesh impalpable fire runs tingling;
Nothing see mine eyes, and a noise of roaring
   Waves in my ear sounds;*

*Sweat runs down in rivers, a tremor seizes
All my limbs, and paler than grass in autumn,
Caught by pains of menacing death, I falter,
   Lost in the love trance. . . .*

Do you not wonder how she gives chase at once to soul and body, to words and tongue, to sight and color, all as if scattered abroad, how uniting contradictions,[3] she is frozen and

*burns, she raves and is wise? For either she is panic-stricken
or at point of death; she is haunted not by a single emotion
but their* whole company.[4]

Towards the end of the περὶ ὕψους there is some scattered commentary on the rhetorical figures; but in the criticism of
Sappho the language is not that of the tropes and figures. In
so far as it concerns emotion, it is "psychological," if not very
exact, even in the terms of the classical psychology of the
passions; yet perhaps it is not too much to claim for
Longinus' perception of opposites in this poem, of the positive compulsion given tension by its negative, that it goes
deeper and is more attentive to what the poem says than
anything that Arnold has to say about Keats' or Milton's
poetry. *He is trying to see what is happening in the poem.*
If he is hampered by his affective terms, so was Mr. T. S.
Eliot when, in an early essay, he was getting at a similar play
of opposites (what Mr. Cleanth Brooks has since called
"paradox") by proposing his theory of the "positive" and the
"negative" emotion, and more especially the theory of the
central "emotion" gathering up and controlling a variety of
contingent "feelings." Mr. Eliot's early theory I should call
advanced romantic criticism: it was struggling through the
subjective effect towards the objective structure of the work.
Longinus' criticism of Sappho is advanced romantic criticism, as advanced as Mr. Eliot's.

One hesitates to present to Longinus a theory which I
hope is not implicit in his phrase ἕν τι σῶμα ποιεῖν, "to make
into one body"; it looks like an organic theory of poetry, but
if we suppose that he is merely using the phrase analogically,
and means by it no more than he means a moment later,
when he says that the poem is a result of choosing and binding together intense feelings, we shall have to acknowledge
the presence of a quite modern piece of criticism. At the
least, he is telling us that in this poem contradictions are
united, bound together, not that Sappho was expressing herself. We are a long step on the way to that critical moment
when the affective vocabulary goes over into linguistic analysis, when, instead of what the poem "feels like," we try to

decide what it says. That Longinus was farther along this road than we may at a glance suspect, there is evidence in the remarkable sentence that he plumps down before us without explanation: ". . . the sublime is often found where there is no emotion." There will be something to say about this when we come to the discussion of "harmony," or composition.

V

The promise at the beginning of the treatise to produce the elements of an Art of Elevation leads to a good deal of miscellaneous specification, under five heads, for its achievement; but the dialectical links among the categories are not distinct. If we think of Longinus as Pascal's man of *finesse*, man of insights, and of Aristotle as a man of *géométrie*, man of deduction, we shall have to look twice at Mr. Olson's observation that, "Unlike Edmund Burke, who finds the sources of sublimity in qualities of the subject matter of art, Longinus finds them in the faculties of the author." This is partly true; but it is misleading, if we are led to suppose that Longinus tried but failed to erect a systematic philosophy of art, comparable to Burke's *A Philosophical Enquiry into the Origins of Our Ideas of the Sublime and Beautiful,* but placing the origin of the ideas in the author. He is ambiguous at this point, but I have shown, I hope, that his considerable originality consists in shifting the center of critical interest, without rejecting it as an "interest," from the genetic and moral judgment to the aesthetic, from the subject matter and the psychology of the author to the language of the work. When he describes the first of his five sources of Elevation as the "impulse towards what is great in thought," he speaks perhaps as a casual Platonist, but primarily as a rhetorician in the great tradition reaching from Aristotle to Cicero.

In distinguishing a critical insight from the intellectual discipline from which, to an extent, it may be a departure, we tend to assume that the insight has replaced the discipline; whereas it may merely alter it. It is not certain that

we need a philosophical aesthetics in order to produce a
work of art; at the Renaissance, I need hardly to observe, an
education in rhetoric and oratory produced poets. Sidney is
not too apologetic for "straying from Poetrie to Oratorie";
for, he says, "both have such an affinity in this wordish
consideration. . . ." It was the point of view of his age. Dis-
ciplining that point of view was the art of rhetoric, one
member of a tripartite whole completed by ethics and politics; rhetoric was the ethics of the public man in its appropriate discipline, the art of the enthymeme, or rhetorical
syllogism.

The second of Longinus' categories, "strong and inspired
emotion," proceeds from the first, or from a common source;
it also is "due to nature." Here we come upon a curious and,
as usual, undeveloped observation. Strong and inspired emotion is one source of, but it is not the same as, style. Pity,
grief, and fear, he says, are "humble [$\tau\alpha\pi\epsilon\iota\nu\acute{\alpha}$: lowly, mean]
and without the note of the Sublime"—as if in "pity" and
"fear" he had a critical eye to Aristotle, whose doctrine of
katharsis was practical and even "sociological." The curious
observation honors the critic who puts "awareness" above system, for it enters an exception to the rule: "The masters of
panegyric," Longinus says, "are seldom given to emotion."
What, then, are they given to? An English instance will be
helpful. The epigraph to "Lycidas" tells us that "The Author
bewails a Learned Friend"—but the author does nothing of
the sort; [5] the strong feeling is directed at the clergy, and
even it is sufficiently assimilated into the rich pastoral texture.

I pass over sources two and three, the "framing of rhetorical figures" and "nobility of expression," with the remark
that Longinus is prudential, like a good teacher, and on these
topics not more rewarding than the rhetoricians, Demetrius
and Dionysius. But number five, "Composition and distribution of words and phrases into a dignified and exalted unit,"
heads up the entire argument. "It is a unity of composition,"
he says, "attained through language." If it is so attained, it is
not attained, though it may originate, in the inaccessible
nobility of the author's mind. Observe again the superiority

of Longinus' insight, with the specific work in mind, to his critical apparatus, which tends to the moralistic and academic. We may see composition here as *ordonnance,* "the best words in the best order." It is more than that. Composition is the total work, not the super-addition of method. Its effect is not to persuade but to entrance; it is "out of the common," not uncommon words, but words used uncommonly well. It is clear that Longinus, by and large, is not recommending the "grand style"; his translators have probably done him a disservice in rendering his characteristic adjective μέγα as "grand"; it is, rather, great, unusual, *uncommon;* and likewise ὕψος, "height," which I understand as "excellence." ἔκστασις is our subjective acknowledgement of the presence of the uncommon, of an objective order of unpredictable distinction. He is quite explicit in this matter. By means of "an appropriate *structure,* and by this means only, as we have sufficiently shown, the best writers give the effect of stateliness and distinction which is removed from the commonplace." In illustration he quotes a line from the *Hercules Furens* of Euripides:

γέμω κακῶν δὴ κοὐκετ' ἔσθ' ὅποι τεθῇ,
I am loaded with sorrows nor can I take on more.

"The phrase is quite commonplace but it has *gained elevation* by the arrangement of the words." The fine statement that follows ought to remove any remaining misconception of the nature of "transport," if we still suppose it to be the romantic shudder; it addresses itself to the whole mind:

. . . *if a work of literature fails to disclose to the reader's intelligence an outlook beyond the range of what is said, when it dwindles under a careful and continuous inspection, it cannot be truly sublime, for it has reached the ear alone. . . . For that is truly grand* [μέγα] *of which the contemplation bears repeating.*

There must be, in short, a total quality of the work which abides its first impact; to that total quality he gives the name of composition.

It includes rhythm. Saintsbury, whose exposition of

Longinus might have revived his influence had somebody else written it, misses the originality of Longinus' treatment of this subject. Longinus' location of rhythm in the total composition, as binding and bound up with it, is perhaps the best critical insight of its kind before Coleridge. Quoting a passage from Demosthenes, he makes the experiment of adding a syllable, and observes that the "sublime phrase is loosened and undone by lengthening of the final rhythm." Likewise, if the phrase were shortened by a syllable. His principle of prose rhythm is negatively stated, but it seems to me to hold for every kind of writing. It is: prose rhythm should not have "a conspicuous movement of sound." It must seem, even if metaphysically it is not, at one with the meaning; it must not call attention to itself, unless—as in Tacitus, Gibbon, Doughty, or Sir Thomas Browne—the "conspicuous movement of sound" is a tonal vehicle that once established is not distinguishable from, but is a part of, the subject itself. But if it is a rhythm "like that of a dancer taking his step before the audience," which the audience anticipates, it distracts attention from what is being said to who is saying it. It is a disproportion in composition similar to that of the orator or the poet who "digresses from the subject into his own tedious emotions." Had Longinus been discussing the rhythm of verse, I should have been able to cite Swinburne and *The Age of Anxiety* by Mr. W. H. Auden.

VI

I have postponed consideration of the third source of Elevation to this concluding section because it pertains in part to metaphor, the *pons asinorum* of literary criticism. If on this subject Longinus is unsatisfactory, it is only a matter of degree; here everybody is unsatisfactory, even Mr. I. A. Richards, whose *Philosophy of Rhetoric* offers a good deal but promises too much. This is a field of inquiry of a difficulty equal to that of the burden of the mystery. Here again Longinus is prudential, but he no doubt gives us as good an account as any of the classical precept of nothing-too-much.

Don't use too many metaphors, unless you are overwhelmed by emotions which may make them credible. Follow Aristotle, perhaps in the *Rhetoric;* soften the metaphor up by inserting "as if" or "just as though" and making it a simile that does not assert improbable identities.

One goes through the περὶ ὕψους, and then the *Rhetoric,* half-heartedly and vainly, looking for something better than this, from the literary point of view, that Longinus might have overlooked, or for something as far-reaching as Aristotle's own Delphic pronouncement in Chapter XXII of the *Poetics,* where he says:

It is a great thing indeed to make a proper use of these poetical forms, as also of compounds and strange words. But the greatest thing by far is to be a master of metaphor. It is the one thing that cannot be learnt from others; and it is also a sign of genius, since a good metaphor implies an intuitive perception of the similarity in dissimilars.

That is very nearly the beginning and the end of our own inquiries into metaphor; but I am rash enough to question whether Aristotle, as a Greek, could know, as we have known since Shakespeare and Donne, how similar dissimilars can be made to seem, or (to take an extreme view which is not unknown today) how similar they can be made to *be.* Metaphor, says Aristotle, is the transference of names, through the permutations of genus and species, or by analogy. Metaphor by analogy takes the formula of arithmetical proportion, a quantitative and relational procedure. We are thus in the Greek Cosmos, an ordering of solid objects under a physics of motion, in which the formal object offers but a narrow margin of analogy to any other. If the ancient inquiry into the structure of metaphor was less resourceful than ours, it was not I daresay because Aristotle was less intelligent than the best modern critics. Our multiverse has increasingly, since the seventeenth century, consisted of unstable objects dissolving into energy; and there has been no limit to the extension of analogy. Criticism follows whatever it is given to follow. Are the famous lucidity and the restraint of the Greeks evidence that by nature they were more lucid and more restrained than we? I doubt it. For even the physical sight may be controlled by the religious selectivity, which fixes the height and the direction of the casement framing our inspection of the world. To introduce at the end of an essay so large and so undeveloped a conception is an impropriety of length and occasion; I offer it as historical relativism in defense of Longinus and of ourselves.

On no single kind of literature is Longinus as searching as Aristotle on tragedy. But I risk the guess that he came nearer to a comprehensive theory of literary form than any other ancient critic. If he did not quite make the leap to a complete theory of the language of imagination, we must remember that nobody in the ancient world did. He shared Aristotle's sense of the simple relation between word and thing; in a world of fixed forms, thing was unyielding; the word, like its object, retained a plastic visibility. With the Greeks the "transference" of "names" was limited to the surface designation, to the comparison of objects in the round, to sculpturesque analogy. Metaphor was a feature of discourse to be described, not a metaphysical problem to be investigated. We need not see as a critical limitation Longinus' failure to investigate a problem that for him did not exist. The permanent critics do not settle the question. They compel us to ask it again. They are the rotating chairmen of a debate only the rhetoric of which changes from time to time. Among these we may think of Longinus, if we will read him not in our age, but in his own.

1948

A READING OF KEATS

It is proper that we celebrate the hundred and fiftieth anniversary of the birth of John Keats by testing our powers of reading him. For the perpetual task of criticism, every generation or two, is to understand again the poetry of the past. Poetry which cannot survive this renewal of understanding, and live again in the critical sensibility of posterity, must contain some radical flaw of interest; it is perhaps in this sense that time is the test of poetry. This view, commonly held today, presupposes the continuity of tradition which with occasional lapses has come down to us from the Greeks; but whether the best English poets shall survive the coming age is a question bearing less upon their value for us than upon our capacity to receive it. If Keats goes unread by the next generation, whose memory will not go back to the great historical era which now seems to be closing, I cannot think that the failure will be his. He will remain one of the great English poets for a later generation to rediscover.

This sounds like the prediction of Colvin in 1917; and I see no reason to argue generally with the Victorian estimate. Perhaps of Keats alone of the English romantics does this estimate still hold, possibly because the great claims were never made for him that were made for Wordsworth and Coleridge. If definitive criticism were possible, Bridges's *A Critical Introduction to Keats* (1894, revised 1914) and A. C. Bradley's "The Letters of Keats" (*Oxford Lectures on Poetry*, 1909) might be said to realize it; and to these should be added the fine textual study, Professor Ridley's *Keats' Craftsmanship* (1933), and Professor C. D. Thorpe's *The Mind of John Keats* (1926).[1] So, apart from the three full-length biographies by Houghton, Colvin, and Miss Lowell, there are four excellent critical studies of Keats, two from the late Victorian age, two from our own: there is probably less useless writing about Keats than about the other great English romantics. The reasons for this are obvious if a little hard to state: the bulk of Keats' work is comparatively slight; at his best (the odes, "Lamia," "The Eve of St. Agnes," and parts of "Hyperion") he has a masterful simplicity of purpose and control; in these poems, with the single exception of "Hyperion," the influences are so well assimilated that only the most trivial academic mind could suppose Keats' relation to the "history of ideas" to have more than the value of a few monographs. In this I take it "he is with Shakespeare." It has been easier for the critics to get at the essentials of Keats than of Wordsworth, Coleridge, and Shelley, who conceal more traps to catch scholars.

This is not to say that Keats was, in the sense of the phrase common a few years ago, a "pure poet." He was the great poet of his age, in the fullest sense; and even Matthew Arnold almost let himself see that he was. Arnold's essay remains one of the best "estimates" of Keats in the Victorian style (which goes back to Johnson) of combined moral and critical judgment; perhaps Arnold was the last great critic to use it effectively; for since its decay in the impressionism of Pater and in the dilettantism of the "literary essay" of the nineties and early nineteen-hundreds, we have been getting a new sort of criticism which was brought in by Eliot's *The Sacred Wood* (1920).

Arnold's essay still has a certain interest in the history of Keats' reputation, yet it must concern us now as perhaps the best evidence of Arnold's almost perverse use of critical standards. More than any other poet, Keats pinned him upon the horns of his dilemma: "Natural magic" and/or "Moral interpretation." It has been said (by whom, I do not remember) that the ambiguousness of Arnold's judgment of Keats was due to his humorless sense of responsibility for the poetry of his age: Keats was the greatest "natural magician" since Shakespeare; but what poetry then *needed* was moral interpretation, and Keats had been a harmful example. This is not the place to examine Arnold's critical dialectic (that has been admirably done by Mr. Trilling); yet it is not beside the point to remark Arnold's failure to see that in Keats' "principle of beauty in all things" lay a possible way out of his dilemma. Even the *Letters* (among the great letters of the world) give a clue to its significance, to say nothing of the structure of the odes. Arnold was not interested in structure unless it was a structure of action inviting moral interpretation. He saw Keats quite simply as a "sensuous" poet.

I have belabored this question more than either Arnold or it deserves (not more than they merit) because I think it is necessary, before proceeding to Keats' poetry, to refer briefly to my own disabilities as a critic of Keats. They are not unlike Arnold's. It would be ludicrous to confess that I lack Arnold's general powers, or more particularly his capacity for awareness of what he did not like (it was this awareness that raised him above the level of the conventional Victorian moralist); but it is not beside the point to warn readers of this essay that my attitude towards Keats is reverent, yet distant without disinterestedness. Whether Keats is what we *need* I do not know; yet we neither want him nor use him. For the past fifteen years the direction of Anglo-American poetry has been rather towards Shelley than Keats, towards "Godwin-perfectibility" and social consciousness than towards a dramatic-symbolic style. I hope I shall not sound like Margaret Fuller if I say that I am not indifferent to the utmost capacity of men for social and individual perfection; I simply do not think that poetry should be limited to exhorting men to these goods. My lack of sympathy with this school nevertheless does not qualify me as a critic of Keats, in spite of my conviction (which was Arnold's unhappy conviction) that Keats was in one of the great modes of poetry. It is perhaps a mode inaccessible to us today. I shall not try, because it is too difficult, to state directly why I think this obstacle exists; my understanding of it, such as it may be, will be implied in what I am about to say of "Ode to a Nightingale," in my opinion Keats' great poem in spite of its imperfect detail, greater than "Ode to Autumn," which because of its purity of tone and style Bridges ranks first among the odes; "Ode to Autumn" is a very nearly perfect piece of style but it has little to say. Because I believe that "Ode to a Nightingale" at least tries to say everything that poetry can say I am putting it at the center of this discussion.

II

The testimony of the criticism of Keats which I have read (I cannot pause to summarize it here) is that he was a pictorial poet in the Spenserian tradition. I would add to this very general statement the observation: his progress from "Endymion" to the revised "Hyperion" is a direct line, at the end of which he achieved under Milton's influence a new kind of blank verse; but in it he could not control the heroic action. In a letter to Reynolds (September 21st, 1819), he said: "I have given up 'Hyperion'—there were too many Miltonic inversions in it . . ."; and in a letter to George Keats, written six days later: "I have but lately stood on my guard against Milton. Life to him would be death to me." I think the second of these explanations, general as it is, comes nearer to the truth: he could not write Miltonic verse without eventual frustration because he lacked a Miltonic subject; it would be "death" to him. For the framework of "Hyperion," of the more human, revised version no less than the first version, is pictorial, with declamatory summaries of action which Keats does not present. It is a succession of plastic scenes.

If this had been the only line of development from "Endymion," we should not, of course, have got the odes; and Keats would have remained a youthful experimenter of genius, considerably above Chatterton but not so impressive as Shelley. The other line runs in the order of time, from "Endymion" to the odes; but perhaps technically, as Professor Ridley has argued, the line is from the sonnets to the odes; that is to say, his experiments with the sonnet led him to modifications of the form which gave us the great stanzas of the Grecian Urn and the Nightingale. And within that narrow, lyrical, and potentially dramatic compass he had something ready to say that he could not have said in the other kinds of verse that he had tried. "The Eve of St. Agnes" is his masterpiece in the Spenserian tradition of *ut pictura, poesis,* and the originality is in the freshness of the language. Far more instructive for technical reasons (reasons which cannot be disconnected from the higher reasons) is the versification of "Lamia," based partly upon Dryden, but, as Professor Ridley shows, in no sense imitative. For example, "Lamia" has proportionately three times as many run-on lines as Dryden's "Fables" taken as a whole, thirty-three per cent being run on; there is a large number of tercets ending with alexandrines; but there are no feminine endings. The result of this adaptation of Dryden's verse is a movement of great speed and flexibility, firm yet supple; and altogether the most original contribution to narrative verse of the nineteenth century. But it should be remembered that "Lamia" is a narrative of a minor mythological incident which Keats picked up in Burton, not epic action: although Keats failed to sustain his blank verse because he could not fill it with action, he succeeded brilliantly with a new kind of verse in which the pictorial method supports the main effect, the simple action turning on a plot of recognition. For the moment we need not go into the symbolism; but it is significant that it was material which Keats found something like the perfect means to bring into form. Written in the summer of 1819 (Part I by mid-July), "Lamia" is the height of his achievement in the long poem. The important thing to remember is that Keats finished it at about the same time he abandoned "Hyperion."

I shall briefly anticipate the end that I am heading towards by setting down a few opinions which will both indicate its direction and gauge my understanding of Keats. "Lamia" is more closely related to the two great odes, the Nightingale and the Grecian Urn, than to "Hyperion," and the fact that he could successfully revise "The Eve of St. Agnes" at the time he was finishing "Lamia" is as much proof as criticism needs that it is not too far from the materials and methods of a poem which some critics would put with the other narratives, "Isabella" and the fragment "The Eve of St. Mark." Moreover, we must think of "Lamia" and "The Eve of St. Agnes" along with the great odes, as follows: "Ode to a

Nightingale," "Ode on a Grecian Urn," "Ode to Psyche," "To Autumn," and "Ode on Melancholy." This cluster of poems is the center of Keats' great work, and they all deal with the same imaginative dilemma—or, if we wish to be biographical, the same conflict in Keats' experience. (I cannot agree with Bridges that there is anything in the sonnets as good as the best Shakespeare; I am convinced that they would not have won their great reputation apart from the other work; and I shall not discuss them here.)

The imaginative dilemma of Keats is, I assume, implicit in the poems, which are at its best statement: the most that criticism ought to attempt is perhaps a kind of circulatory description of its movements, from poem to poem. Bridges' astute remark that "Keats' art is primarily objective and pictorial, and whatever other qualities it has are as it were *added on to things as perceived*," contains critical insight of the first order. I have italicized *added on to things as perceived,* and I would double the italics of the last two words; they point directly to the imaginative limit of Keats' poetry, one horn of the dilemma out of which it does not move, in which it must, if it is to exceed the *ut pictura, poesis* formula, seek some conversion of that limit.

I should thus offer (for what it is worth) the very general analysis: Keats as a pictorial poet was necessarily presenting in a given poem a series of scenes, and even in the narratives the action does not flow from inside the characters, but is governed pictorially from the outside. He is thus a painting poet and would have earned Lessing's censure. But like every great artist he knew (in his own terms, which are none of our business) that his problem was to work within his limitations, and to transcend them. He was a poet of space whose problem was to find a way of conveying what happens in time; for it is time in which dramatic conflict takes place; and it is only by conversion into dramatic actuality that the parts of the verbal painting achieve relation and significance. "The form of thought in Keats," says Mr. Kenneth Burke, "is mystical, in terms of an eternal present" —and I should add, in terms of the arrested action of painting.

III

When Keats adds to "things as perceived," what does he add? That, it seems to me, is the special problem of Keats. In the simplest language, it is the problem of adding movement to a static picture, of putting into motion the "languor which lingers in the main design" (Bridges) of even the later work.

Of the eight stanzas of "Ode to a Nightingale," six are distinctly pictorial in method; a seventh, stanza three, in which Keats expresses his complaint of common life, develops as a meditation out of the second stanza, the picture of Provence. The only stanza which does not give us or in some way pertain to a definite scene is number seven; for though the method there is pictorial, the effect is allusive: the permanence of the nightingale's song is established in a rapid series of vignettes, ending with the famous "faëry lands forlorn." It is the only stanza, as some critic has remarked, which contains a statement contradictory of our sense of common reality.

> *Thou wast not born for death, immortal Bird,*

he says to the nightingale; and we cannot agree. The assertion is out of form in an obvious sense; for the poem is an accumulation of pictorial situations; and the claim of immortality for the bird is dramatic and lyrical.

I am raising the question whether the metonymy which attributes to the literal nightingale the asserted immortality of the song is convincing enough to carry the whole imaginative insight of the poem. I think it is, given the limits of Keats' art, but I am still nagged by a difficulty that will not down. It seems to me that the ambivalence of the nightingale symbol contains almost the whole substance of the poem: the bird, as bird, shares the mortality of the world; as symbol, it purports to transcend it. And I feel that the pictorial technique has not been quite dramatic enough to give to the transcendence of the symbol life in some visibly presented experience. The far more implausible, even far-fetched, metaphor of the draughtsman's compasses, in Donne, comes out a little better because through a series of dialectical transformations, from the dying man to the Ptolemaic spheres, and then through the malleable gold to the compasses, there is a progression of connected analogies, given us step by step; and we acknowledge the identity of compasses and lovers as imaginatively possible. Keats merely *asserts:* song equals immortality; and I feel there is some disparity between the symbol and what it is expected to convey—not an inherent disparity, for such is not imaginatively conceivable; but a disparity such as we should get in the simple equation $A = B$, if we found that the assigned values of A and B were respectively 1 and 3.

This feature of Keats' art we shall find in "Ode on a Grecian Urn" but not in "Ode to Psyche." I confess that I do not know what to do about this anomalous poem, except to admire it. There appears to me to be very little genuine *sensation* in Keats (rather what Arnold and his contemporaries mistook for sensation), but there is more of it in "Ode to Psyche" than anywhere else in the great odes. Mr. T. S. Eliot puts it first among the odes, possibly because most of its detail is genuinely experienced and because it contains no developed attitude towards life. The other odes do; and it is an attitude less mature than that which Mr. Eliot finds in the *Letters.* With this part of his view of Keats one must agree. But it is a dangerous view, since it is very remotely possible that some letters from Shakespeare may turn up some day. But Mr. Eliot's preference for "Ode to Psyche" doubtless shares at bottom the common prejudice that romantic art tends not only to be pictorial but "off center" and lacking in that appearance of logical structure which we ordinarily associate with Donne and Dryden. I do not want to get into this classical-and-romantic affair, for the usual reason, and for a reason of my own, which is that it has a way of backfiring. Mr. Eliot has said that Coleridge and Wordsworth on one side are "as eighteenth century as anybody." So is Keats. The apostrophe to the nightingale, which I have been at some pains to try to understand, is quite "eighteenth century"; but it is not nearly so eighteenth century as the entire third stanza, which I shall now try to understand, assuming that what it says has a close connection with that literal part of the nightingale, the physical bird, which Keats seemed not to know what to do with (except to make it, in the last stanza, fly away). Here it is:

> *Fade far away, dissolve, and quite forget*
> *What thou among the leaves hast never known,*
> *The weariness, the fever, and the fret*
> *Here where men sit and hear each other groan;*
> *Where palsy shakes a few, sad, last gray hairs,*
> *Where youth grows pale, and spectre-thin, and dies;*
> *Where but to think is to be full of sorrow*
> *And leaden-eyed despairs,*
> *Where beauty cannot keep her lustrous eyes,*
> *Or new Love pine at them beyond tomorrow.*[2]

Looked at from any point of view, this stanza is bad; the best that one ought to say of it perhaps is that there are worse things in Shelley and Wordsworth, and in Keats himself. (Even Colvin's habitual tone of eulogy is restrained when he comes to it.[3]) It is bad in the same way as the passages in Shelley's "Adonaïs" which exhibit the troops of mourners are bad. Keats here is relapsing into weakened eighteenth-century rhetoric; Blake could have put into the personifications imaginative power, and Pope genuine feeling, or at any rate an elegance and vigor which would have carried them.

There is not space enough in an essay to go into this matter as it needs to be gone into. What I wish to indicate, for the consideration of more thorough readers, is that stanza three may be of the utmost significance in any attempt to understand the structure of Keats' poetry. It gives us a "picture" of common reality, in which the life of man is all mutability and frustration. But here if anywhere in the poem the necessity to dramatize time, or the pressure of actuality, is paramount. *Keats has no language of his own for this realm of experience.* That is the capital point. He either falls into the poetic language of the preceding age, or, if he writes spontaneously, he commits his notorious errors of taste; in either case the language is not adequate to the feeling; or, to put it "cognitively," he lacks an ordered symbolism through which he may *know* the common and the ideal reality in a single imaginative act. One would like to linger upon the possible reasons for this. I suspect that evidence from another source, which I shall point out later, will be more telling than anything, even this stanza, that we can find in the odes. The consciousness of change and decay, which can, and did in Keats, inform one of the great modes of poetry, is deeply involved with his special attitude towards sexual love. He never presents love directly and dramatically; it is in terms of Renaissance tapestry, as in "The Eve of St. Agnes," or in a fable of Italian violence, as in "Isabella"; or, most interesting of all, in terms of a little myth, Lamia the snake-woman, a symbol which permits Keats to objectify the mingled attraction and repulsion which his treatment of love requires. I sometimes think that for this reason "Lamia" is his best long poem: the symbol inherently contains the repulsive element, but keeps it at a distance, so that he does not have to face it in terms of common experience, his own, or as he was aware of it in his age. Is it saying too much to suppose that Keats' acceptance of the pictorial method is to a large extent connected with his unwillingness to deal with passion dramatically? (There is sensuous detail, but no sensation as direct experience, such as we find in Baudelaire.)

I need not labor a point which even the Victorian critics and biographers, almost without exception, remarked: Keats, both before and after his fatal illness (as other poets have been who were not ill at all), was filled with the compulsive image of the identity of death and the act of love (for example, "You must be mine to die upon the rack if I want you," he wrote to Fanny Brawne); and it is only an exaggeration of emphasis to say that death and love are interchangeable terms throughout his poetry. The "ecstasy" that the nightingale pours forth contains the Elizabethan pun on "die" with the wit omitted, and a new semi-mystical intensity of feeling added. And is it too much to say that Keats' constant tendency was to face the moment of love only in terms of an ecstasy so intense that he should not survive it? When Lamia vanishes, Lycius "dies." And this affirmation of life through death is the element that Keats "adds on to things as perceived." But life-in-death is presented pictorially, in space, as an eternal moment, not as a moment of dramatic action in time, proceeding from previous action and looking towards its consequences.

The dialectical tension underlying "Ode to a Nightingale" seems to me to be incapable of resolution, first in terms of Keats' mind as we know it from other sources, and, secondly, in terms of the pictorial technique which dominates the poetic method. This method, which seems to reflect a compulsive necessity of Keats' experience, allows him to present the thesis of his dilemma, the ideality of the nightingale symbol, but not the antithesis, the world of common experience, which is the substance of stanza three. The "resolution" is suspended in the intensity of the images setting forth the love-death identity and reaching a magnificent climax in stanza six ("Now more than ever seems it rich to die," etc.). But the climax contains a little less than the full situation; it reaches us a little too simplified, as if Keats were telling us that the best way to live is to die, or the best way to die is to live intensely so that we may die intensely. There may be concealed here one of the oldest syntheses of Christian thought, that we die only to live; but, if so, there has been a marked shrinkage in range of that conception since Donne wrote his "A Nocturnall upon S. Lucies Day."

Messrs. Brooks and Warren, in their excellent if somewhat confident analysis[4] of the Nightingale ode, argue with much conviction that the dramatic frame of the poem, the painful accession to the trance in the opening lines and the return to immediate reality ("Do I wake or sleep?") at the end, provides a sufficient form. I confess that I am not sure. I am not certain of the meaning of what happens inside the frame; but at times I am not certain that it is necessary to understand it. There is no perfection in poetry. All criticism must in the end be comparative (this does not mean critical relativity); it must constantly refer to what poetry has accomplished in order to estimate what it can accomplish, not what it ought to accomplish; we must heed Mr. Ransom's warning that perfect unity or integration in a work of art is a critical delusion. "Ode to a Nightingale" is by any standard one of the great poems of the world. Our philosophical difficulties with it are not the same as Keats' imaginative difficulties, which pertain to the order of experience and not of reason. The poem is an emblem of one limit of our experience: the impossibility of synthesizing, in the order of experience, the antinomy of the ideal and the real, and, although that antinomy strikes the human mind with a different force in different ages (Donne's dualism is not Keats'), it is sufficiently common to all men in all times to be understood.

If we glance at "Ode on a Grecian Urn," we shall see Keats trying to unify his pictorial effects by means of direct philosophical statement. "Do I wake or sleep?" at the end of the Nightingale ode asks the question: Which is reality, the symbolic nightingale or the common world? The famous Truth-Beauty synthesis at the end of the "Grecian Urn" contains the same question, but this time it is answered. As Mr. Kenneth Burke sees it, Truth is the practical scientific world and Beauty is the ideal world above change. The "frozen" figures on the urn, being both dead and alive, constitute a scene which is at once perceptible and fixed. "This transcendent scene," says Mr. Burke, "is the level at which the earthly laws of contradiction no longer prevail." [5] The one and the many, the eternal and the passing, the sculpturesque and the dramatic, become synthesized in a higher truth. Much of the little that I know about this poem I have learned from Mr. Burke and Mr. Cleanth Brooks, who have studied it more closely than any other critics; and what I am about to say will sound ungrateful. I suspect that the dialectical solution is Mr. Burke's rather than Keats', and that Mr. Brooks' "irony" and "dramatic propriety" are likewise largely his own.[6] Mr. Brooks rests his case for the Truth-Beauty paradox on an argument for its "dramatic propriety"; but this is just what I am not convinced of. I find myself agreeing with Mr. Middleton Murry (whom Mr. Brooks quotes), who admits that the statement is out of place "in the context of the poem itself." I would point to a particular feature, in the last six lines of stanza four, which I feel that neither Mr. Burke nor Mr. Brooks has taken into a certain important kind of consideration. Here Keats tells us that in the background of this world of eternal youth there is another, from which it came, and that this second world has thus been emptied and is indeed a dead world:

> *What little town by river or sea-shore*
> *Or mountain-built with peaceful citadel,*
>   *Is emptied of this folk, this pious morn?*
> *And, little town, thy streets for evermore*
> *Will silent be; and not a soul to tell*
>   *Why thou art desolate, can e'er return.*

Mr. Burke quite rightly sees in this passage the key to the symbolism of the entire poem. It is properly the "constatation" of the tensions of the imagery. What is the meaning of this perpetual youth on the urn? One of its meanings is that it is perpetually anti-youth and anti-life; it is in fact dead, and "can never return." Are we not faced again with the same paradox we had in the Nightingale ode, that the intensest life is achieved in death? Mr. Burke brings out with great skill the erotic equivalents of the life-death symbols; and for his analysis of the developing imagery throughout we owe him a great debt. Yet I feel that Mr. Burke's own dialectical skill leads him to consider the poem, when he is through with it, a philosophical discourse; but it is, if it is anything (and it is a great deal), what is ordinarily known as a work of art. Mr. Burke's elucidation of the Truth-Beauty proposition in the last stanza is the most convincing dialectically that I have seen; but Keats did not write Mr. Burke's elucidation; and I feel that the entire last stanza, except the phrase "Cold Pastoral" (which probably ought to be somewhere else in the poem) is an illicit commentary added by the poet to a "meaning" which was symbolically complete at the end of the preceding stanza, number four. Or perhaps it may be said that Keats did to some extent write Mr. Burke's elucidation; that is why I feel that the final stanza (though magnificently written) is redundant and out of form.

To the degree that I am guilty with Mr. Burke of a prepossession which may blind me to the whole value of this poem (as his seems to limit his perception of possible defects) I am not qualified to criticize it. Here, towards the end of this essay, I glance back at the confession, which I made earlier, of the distance and detachment of my warmest admiration for Keats. It is now time that I tried to state the reasons for this a little more summarily, in a brief comparison of the two fine odes that we have been considering.

Both odes are constructed pictorially in spatial blocks, for the eye to take in serially. Though to my mind this method is better suited to the subject of the Grecian Urn, which is itself a plastic object, than to the Nightingale ode, I take the latter, in spite of the blemishes of detail (only some of which we have looked at), to be the finer poem. If there is not so much in it as in the Grecian Urn for the elucidation of verbal complexity, there is nowhere the radical violation of its set limits that one finds in the last stanza of the Grecian Urn:

> *Thou shalt remain, in midst of other woes*
> *Than ours, a friend to man, to whom thou say'st,*
> *Beauty is truth, truth beauty,—that is all*
> *Ye know on earth, and all ye need to know.*

It is here that the poem gets out of form, that the break in "point of view" occurs; and if it is a return to Samuel Johnson's dislike of "Lycidas" (I don't think it is) to ask how an urn can say anything, I shall have to suffer the consequences of that view. It is Keats himself, of course, who says it; but "Keats" is here not implicit in the structure of the poem, as he is in "Ode to a Nightingale"; what he says is what the mathematicians call an extrapolation, an intrusion of matter from another field of discourse, so that, even if it be "true" philosophically, it is not a visible function of what the poem says. With the "dead" mountain citadel in mind, could we not phrase the message of the urn equally well as follows: Truth is *not* beauty, since even art itself cannot do more with death than preserve it, and the beauty frozen on the urn is also dead, since it cannot move. This "pessimism" may be found as easily in the poem as Keats' comforting paradox. So I should return to the Nightingale ode for its superior *dramatic* credibility, even though the death-life antinomy is not more satisfactorily resolved than in the Grecian Urn. The fall of the "I" of "Ode to a Nightingale" into the trance-like meditation in the first stanza and the shocked coming-to at the end *ground* the poem in imaginable action, so that the dialectics of the nightingale symbol do not press for resolution. So I confess a reserved agreement with Brooks and Warren.

The outlines of the conflicting claims of the ideal and the actual, in Keats' mind, I have touched upon; but now, with the two great odes in mind, I wish to give those hints a somewhat greater range and try, if possible, to point towards the *kind* of experience with which Keats was dealing when he came up short against the limit of his sensibility, the identity of love and death, or the compulsive image of erotic intensity realizing itself in "dying."

IV

One of Keats' annotations to Burton's *Anatomy,* in the copy given him by Brown in 1819, in the great period, is as follows:

Here is the old plague spot; the pestilence, the raw scrofula. I mean there is nothing disgraces me in my own eyes so much as being one of a race of eyes nose and mouth beings in a planet call'd the earth who all from Plato to Wesley have always mingled goatish winnyish lustful love with the abstract adoration of the deity. I don't understand Greek—is the love of God and the Love of women express'd by the same word in Greek? I hope my little mind is wrong—if not I could . . . Has Plato separated these lovers? Ha! I see how they endeavour to divide—but there appears to be a horrid relationship.[7]

Keats had just read in Burton the chapter "Love-Melancholy" in which the two Aphrodites, Urania and Pandemos,[8] appear: there is no evidence that he ever knew more about them than this quotation indicates. Professor Thorpe valiantly tries to show us that Keats must have known from his literary environment something of Plato's doctrine of love, but there

is no reason to believe that he ever felt the imaginative
shock of reading *The Symposium,* and of experiencing first-
hand an intuition of a level of experience that the Western
world, through Platonism and Christianity, had been trying
for more than two millennia to reach. He apparently never
knew that the two Aphrodites were merely the subject of
Pausanias' speech, one of the preliminaries to Socrates' great
dialectical synthesis. The curious thing about Keats' education
is that it was almost entirely literary; he had presumably read
very little philosophy and religion. He used the Greek myths,
not for the complete (if pagan) religious experience in
them, but to find a static and sculpturesque emblem of timeless experience—his own and the experience of his age;
hence the pictorial method, and hence the necessity for that
method.

In my reading of Keats I see his mind constantly reaching
towards and recoiling from the experience, greatly extended,
which is represented by the ambivalent Aphrodite. The conclusion of the sonnet "Bright Star! . . .":

> *Still, still to hear her tender-taken breath,*
> *And so live ever—or else swoon to death . . .*

is not Keats' best poetry, but it states very simply the conflict of emotion the symbolic limit of which I have tried to
see in terms of the double goddess. The immanence of the
Uranian in the Pandemic goddess was not beyond the range
of Keats' intellect, but it was at any rate, at the time of his
death, imaginatively beyond his reach. His goddess, in so far
as she is more than a decorative symbol in Keats, was all
Uranian; and to say in another way what I have already said,
his faulty taste (which is probably at its worst in one of the
lines in "Bright Star! . . .") lies in his inability to come to
terms wth her Pandemic sister. His pictorial and sculpturesque effects, which arrest time into space, tend to remove
from experience the dramatic agitation of Aphrodite Pandemos, whose favors are granted and whose woes are counted
in the actuality of time. (There is, of course, a great deal
more in Keats than this obsessive symbol through which I

see him; and there is also less of the symbol, explicitly presented, than my discussion would indicate; there are only eleven references to "Venus" in all Keats' poetry—he never calls her Aphrodite—and in no instance is very much done with her symbolically. She has only a fresh Botticellian surface; and one may observe that she is not mentioned in "Ode to Psyche.")

This "horrid relationship" between the heavenly and earthly Aphrodites had been in effect the great theme of St. Augustine, and before him of Lucretius; and it was to inform dramatically *The Divine Comedy*. It was perhaps the great achievement of the seventeenth-century English poets to have explored the relations of physical and spiritual love; of this Keats seems oblivious; yet we must admit that an awareness of the imaginative and spiritual achievements of the past would not have ensured them to him, as our own excessive awareness fails to ensure them to us. In Keats' mind there was, as I have said (why it should have had, even in so young a man, an exclusive dominance I do not know)— there was, to put it in the simplest language, a strong compulsion towards the realization of physical love, but he could not reconcile it with his idealization of the beloved. So we get what has been supposed to be a characteristically romantic attitude—that to *die* at the greatest intensity of love is to achieve that intensity without diminution. If this is the romantic attitude—and there is no reason to believe that Wordsworth's domestic pieties and evasions, or Shelley's rhetorical Godwinism and watered-down Platonism, ever achieved *as experience* a higher realization of the central human problem than Keats did—if this is romanticism, then romanticism (or romantic poetry) represents a decline in insight and in imaginative and moral power. In the interval between

> So must pure lovers soules descend
> T'affections, and to faculties,
> Which sense may reach and apprehend,
> Else a great Prince in prison lies . . .

and this:

> *But Love has pitched his mansion in*
> *The place of excrement;*
> *For nothing can be sole or whole*
> *That has not been rent . . .*

—between Donne and Yeats there was evidently a shrinkage in the range and depth of Western man's experience, as that experience was expressed in works of the imagination, and not merely in the Goethean or Wordsworthian goodwill towards comprehensiveness or the inclusion of a little of everything. Keats seems to me to have been, in England at any rate, the master of the central experience of his age. His profound honesty, his dislike of system and opinion as substitutes for what the imagination is actually abe to control, and his perfect artistic courage, will keep him not only among the masters of English poetry but among the few heroes of literature. To adapt to Keats a remark of Eliot's about Arnold, I should say that he did not know, because he lacked the maturity to know, the boredom; he knew a little of the horror; but he knew much of the glory, of human life.

1945

EMILY DICKINSON

Great poetry needs no special features of difficulty to make it mysterious. When it has them, the reputation of the poet is likely to remain uncertain. This is still true of Donne, and it is true of Emily Dickinson, whose verse appeared in an age unfavorable to the use of intelligence in poetry. Her poetry is not like any other poetry of her time; it is not like any of the innumerable kinds of verse written today. In still another respect it is far removed from us. It is a poetry of ideas, and it demands of the reader a point of view—not an opinion of the New Deal or of the League of Nations, but an ingrained philosophy that is fundamental, a settled attitude that is almost extinct in this eclectic age. Yet it is not the sort of poetry of ideas which, like Pope's, requires a point of view only. It requires also, for the deepest understanding, which must go beneath the verbal excitement of the style, a highly developed sense of the specific quality of poetry—a quality that most persons accept as the accidental feature of something else that the poet thinks he has to say. This is one reason why Miss Dickinson's poetry has not been widely read.

There is another reason, and it is a part of the problem peculiar to a poetry that comes out of fundamental ideas. We lack a tradition of criticism. There were no points of critical reference passed on to us from a preceding generation. I am not upholding here the so-called dead hand of tradition, but rather a rational insight into the meaning of the present in terms of some imaginable past implicit in our own lives: we need a body of ideas that can bear upon the course of the spirit and yet remain coherent as a rational instrument. We ignore the present, which is momently translated into the past, and derive our standards from imaginative constructions of the future. The hard contingency of fact invariably breaks these standards down, leaving us the intellectual chaos which is the sore distress of American criticism. Marxian criticism has become the latest disguise of this heresy.

Still another difficulty stands between us and Miss Dickinson. It is the failure of the scholars to feel more than biographical curiosity about her. We have scholarship, but that is no substitute for a critical tradition. Miss Dickinson's value to the research scholar, who likes historical difficulty for its own sake, is slight; she is too near to possess the remoteness of literature. Perhaps her appropriate setting would be the age of Cowley or of Donne. Yet in her own historical setting she is, nevertheless, remarkable and special.

Although the intellectual climate into which she was born, in 1830, had, as all times have, the features of a transition, the period was also a major crisis culminating in the war between the States. After that war, in New England as well as in the South, spiritual crises were definitely minor until the First World War.

Yet, a generation before the war of 1861-65, the transformation of New England had begun. When Samuel Slater in 1790 thwarted the British embargo on mill machinery by committing to memory the whole design of a cotton spinner and bringing it to Massachusetts, he planted the seed of the "Western spirit." By 1825 its growth in the East was rank enough to begin choking out the ideas and habits of living that New England along with Virginia had kept in unconscious allegiance to Europe. To the casual observer, perhaps, the New England character of 1830 was largely an eighteenth-century character. But theocracy was on the decline, and industrialism was rising—as Emerson, in an unusually lucid moment, put it, "Things are in the saddle." The energy that had built the meeting-house ran the factory.

Now the idea that moved the theocratic state is the most interesting historically of all American ideas. It was, of course, powerful in seventeenth-century England, but in America, where the long arm of Laud could not reach, it acquired an unchecked social and political influence. The important thing to remember about the puritan theocracy is that it permeated, as it could never have done in England, a whole society. It gave final, definite meaning to life, the life of pious and impious, of learned and vulgar alike. It gave—and this is its significance for Emily Dickinson, and in only slightly lesser degree for Melville and Hawthorne—it gave an heroic proportion and a tragic mode to the experience of the individual. The history of the New England theocracy, from Apostle Eliot to Cotton Mather, is rich in gigantic intellects that broke down—or so it must appear to an outsider—in a kind of moral decadence and depravity. Socially we may not like the New England idea. Yet it had an immense, incalculable value for literature: it dramatized the human soul.

But by 1850 the great fortunes had been made (in the rum, slave, and milling industries), and New England became a museum. The whatnots groaned under the load of knickknacks, the fine china dogs and cats, the pieces of Oriental jade, the chips off the leaning tower of Pisa. There were the rare books and the cosmopolitan learning. It was all equally displayed as the evidence of a superior culture. The Gilded Age had already begun. But culture, in the true sense, was disappearing. Where the old order, formidable as it was, had held all this personal experience, this eclectic excitement, in a comprehensible whole, the new order tended to flatten it out in a common experience that was not quite in common; it exalted more and more the personal and the unique in the interior sense. Where the old-fashioned puritans got together on a rigid doctrine, and could thus be individualists in manners, the nineteenth-century New Englander, lacking a genuine religious center, began to be a social conformist. The common idea of the Redemption, for example, was replaced by the conformist idea of respectability among neighbors whose spiritual disorder, not very evident at the surface, was becoming acute. A great idea was breaking up, and society was moving towards external uniformity, which is usually the measure of the spiritual sterility inside.

At this juncture Emerson came upon the scene: the Lucifer of Concord, he had better be called hereafter, for he was the light-bearer who could see nothing but light, and was fearfully blind. He looked around and saw the uniformity of life, and called it the routine of tradition, the tyranny of the theological idea. The death of Priam put an end to the hope of Troy, but it was a slight feat of arms for the doughty Pyrrhus; Priam was an old gentleman and almost dead. So was theocracy; and Emerson killed it. In this way he accelerated a tendency that he disliked. It was a great intellectual mistake. By it Emerson unwittingly became the prophet of a piratical industrialism, a consequence of his own transcendental individualism that he could not foresee. He was hoist with his own petard.

He discredited more than any other man the puritan drama of the soul. The age that followed, from 1865 on, expired in a genteel secularism, a mildly didactic order of feeling whose ornaments were Lowell, Longfellow, and Holmes. "After Emerson had done his work," says Mr. Robert Penn Warren, "any tragic possibilities in that culture were dissipated." Hawthorne alone in his time kept pure, in the primitive terms, the primitive vision; he brings the puritan tragedy to its climax. Man, measured by a great idea outside himself, is found wanting. But for Emerson man is greater than any idea and, being himself the Over-Soul, is innately perfect; there is no struggle because—I state the Emersonian doctrine, which is very slippery, in its extreme terms—because there is no possibility of error. There is no drama in human character because there is no tragic fault. It is not surprising, then, that after Emerson New England literature tastes like a sip of cambric tea. Its center of vision has disappeared. There is Hawthorne looking back, there is Emerson looking not too clearly at anything ahead: Emily Dickinson, who has in her something of both, comes in somewhere between.

With the exception of Poe there is no other American poet whose work so steadily emerges, under pressure of certain disintegrating obsessions, from the framework of moral character. There is none of whom it is truer to say that the poet *is* the poetry. Perhaps this explains the zeal of her admirers for her biography; it explains, in part at least, the gratuitous mystery that Mrs. Bianchi, a niece of the poet and her official biographer, has made of her life. The devoted controversy that Miss Josephine Pollitt and Miss Genevieve Taggard started a few years ago with their excellent books shows the extent to which the critics feel the intimate connection of her life and work. Admiration and affection are pleased to linger over the tokens of a great life; but the solution to the Dickinson enigma is peculiarly superior to fact.

The meaning of the identity—which we merely feel—of character and poetry would be exceedingly obscure, even if we could draw up a kind of Binet correlation between the two sets of "facts." Miss Dickinson was a recluse; but her poetry is rich with a profound and varied experience. Where did she get it? Now some of the biographers, nervous in the presence of this discrepancy, are eager to find her a love affair, and I think this search is due to a modern prejudice: we believe that no virgin can know enough to write poetry. We shall never learn where she got the rich quality of her mind. The moral image that we have of Miss Dickinson stands out in every poem; it is that of a dominating spinster whose very sweetness must have been formidable. Yet her poetry constantly moves within an absolute order of truths that overwhelmed her simply because to her they were unalterably fixed. It is dangerous to assume that her "life," which to the biographers means the thwarted love affair she is supposed to have had, gave to her poetry a decisive direction. It is even more dangerous to suppose that it made her a poet.

Poets are mysterious, but a poet, when all is said, is not much more mysterious than a banker. The critics remain spellbound by the technical license of her verse and by the puzzle of her personal life. Personality is a legitimate interest because it is an incurable interest, but legitimate as a personal interest only; it will never give up the key to anyone's verse. Used to that end, the interest is false. "It is apparent," writes Mr. Conrad Aiken, "that Miss Dickinson became a hermit by deliberate and conscious choice"—a sensible remark that we cannot repeat too often. If it were necessary to explain her seclusion with disappointment in love, there would remain the discrepancy between what the seclusion produced and the seclusion looked at as a cause. The effect, which is her poetry, would imply the whole complex of anterior fact, which was the social and religious structure of New England.

The problem to be kept in mind is thus the meaning of her "deliberate and conscious" decision to withdraw from life to her upstairs room. This simple fact is not very important. But that it must have been her sole way of acting out her part in the history of her culture, which made, with the variations of circumstance, a single demand upon all its representatives—this is of the greatest consequence. All pity for Miss Dickinson's "starved life" is misdirected. Her life was one of the richest and deepest ever lived on this continent.

When she went upstairs and closed the door, she mastered life by rejecting it. Others in their way had done it before; still others did it later. If we suppose—which is to suppose the improbable—that the love affair precipitated the seclusion, it was only a pretext; she would have found another. Mastery of the world by rejecting the world was the doctrine, even if it was not always the practice, of Jonathan Edwards and Cotton Mather. It is the meaning of fate in Hawthorne: his people are fated to withdraw from the world and to be destroyed. And it is one of the great themes of Henry James.

There is a moral emphasis that connects Hawthorne, James, and Miss Dickinson, and I think it is instructive. Between Hawthorne and James lies an epoch. The temptation to sin, in Hawthorne, is, in James, transformed into the temptation not to do the "decent thing." A whole world-scheme, a complete cosmic background, has shrunk to the dimensions of the individual conscience. This epoch between Hawthorne and James lies in Emerson. James found himself in the post-Emersonian world, and he could not, without violating the detachment proper to an artist, undo Emerson's work; he had that kind of intelligence which refuses to break its head against history. There was left to him only the value, the historic role, of rejection. He could merely escape from the physical presence of that world which, for convenience, we may call Emerson's world: he could only take his Americans to Europe upon the vain quest of something that they had lost at home. His characters, fleeing the wreckage of the puritan culture, preserved only their honor. Honor became a sort of forlorn hope struggling against the forces of "pure fact" that had got loose in the middle of the century. Honor alone is a poor weapon against nature, being too personal, finical, and proud, and James achieved a victory by refusing to engage the whole force of the enemy.

In Emily Dickinson the conflict takes place on a vaster field. The enemy to all those New Englanders was Nature, and Miss Dickinson saw into the character of this enemy more deeply than any of the others. The general symbol of Nature, for her, is Death, and her weapon against Death is the entire powerful dumb-show of the puritan theology led by Redemption and Immortality. Morally speaking, the problem for James and Miss Dickinson is similar. But her advantages were greater than his. The advantages lay in the availability to her of the puritan ideas on the theological plane.

These ideas, in her poetry, are momently assailed by the disintegrating force of Nature (appearing as Death) which, while constantly breaking them down, constantly redefines and strengthens them. The values are purified by the triumphant withdrawal from Nature, by their power to recover from Nature. The poet attains to a mastery over experience by facing its utmost implications. There is the clash of powerful opposites, and in all great poetry—for Emily Dickinson is a great poet—it issues in a tension between abstraction and sensation in which the two elements may be, of course, distinguished logically, but not really. We are shown our roots in Nature by examining our differences with Nature; we are renewed by Nature without being delivered into her hands. When it is possible for a poet to do this for us with the greatest imaginative comprehension, a possibility that the poet cannot himself create, we have the perfect literary situation. Only a few times in the history of English poetry has this situation come about: notably, the period between about 1580 and the Restoration. There was a similar age in New England from which emerged two talents of the first order—Hawthorne and Emily Dickinson.

There is an epoch between James and Miss Dickinson. But between her and Hawthorne there exists a difference of intellectual quality. She lacks almost radically the power to seize upon and understand abstractions for their own sake; she does not separate them from the sensuous illuminations that she is so marvelously adept at; like Donne, she *perceives abstraction* and *thinks sensation*. But Hawthorne was a master of ideas, within a limited range; this narrowness confined him to his own kind of life, his own society, and out of it grew his typical forms of experience, his steady, almost obsessed vision of man; it explains his depth and intensity. Yet he is always conscious of the abstract, doctrinal aspect of his mind, and when his vision of action and emotion is weak, his work becomes didactic. Now Miss Dickinson's poetry often runs into quasi-homiletic forms, but it is never didactic. Her very ignorance, her lack of formal intellectual training, preserved her from the risk that imperiled Hawthorne. She cannot reason at all. She can only *see*. It is impossible to imagine what she might have done with drama or fiction; for, not approaching the puritan temper and through it the puritan myth, through human action, she is able to grasp the terms of the myth directly and by a feat that amounts almost to anthropomorphism, to give them a luminous tension, a kind of drama, among themselves.

One of the perfect poems in English is "The Chariot," and it illustrates better than anything else she wrote the special quality of her mind. I think it will illuminate the tendency of this discussion:

> *Because I could not stop for death,*
> *He kindly stopped for me;*
> *The carriage held but just ourselves*
> *And immortality.*

We slowly drove, he knew no haste,
And I had put away
My labor, and my leisure too,
For his civility.

We passed the school where children played,
Their lessons scarcely done;
We passed the fields of gazing grain,
We passed the setting sun.

We paused before a house that seemed
A swelling of the ground;
The roof was scarcely visible,
The cornice but a mound.

Since then 'tis centuries; but each
Feels shorter than the day
I first surmised the horses' heads
Were toward eternity.

If the word "great" means anything in poetry, this poem is one of the greatest in the English language. The rhythm charges with movement the pattern of suspended action back of the poem. Every image is precise and, moreover, not merely beautiful, but fused with the central idea. Every image extends and intensifies every other. The third stanza especially shows Miss Dickinson's power to fuse, into a single order of perception, a heterogeneous series: the children, the grain, and the setting sun (time) have the same degree of credibility; the first subtly preparing for the last. The sharp *gazing* before *grain* instills into nature a cold vitality of which the qualitative richness has infinite depth. The content of death in the poem eludes explicit definition. He is a gentleman taking a lady out for a drive. But note the restraint that keeps the poet from carrying this so far that it becomes ludicrous and incredible; and note the subtly interfused erotic motive, which the idea of death has presented to most romantic poets, love being a symbol interchangeable with death. The terror of death is objectified through this figure of the genteel driver, who is made ironically to serve the end of Immortality. This is the heart of the poem: she has presented a typical Christian theme in its final irresolution, without making any final statements about it. There is no solution to the problem; there can be only a presentation of it in the full context of intellect and feeling. A construction of the human will, elaborated with all the abstracting powers of the mind, is put to the concrete test of experience: the idea of immortality is confronted with the fact of physical disintegration. We are not told what to think; we are told to look at the situation.

The framework of the poem is, in fact, the two abstractions, mortality and eternity, which are made to associate in equality with the images: she sees the ideas, and thinks the perceptions. She did, of course, nothing of the sort; but we must use the logical distinctions, even to the extent of paradox, if we are to form any notion of this rare quality of mind. She could not in the proper sense think at all, and unless we prefer the feeble poetry of moral ideas that flourished in New England in the eighties, we must conclude that her intellectual deficiency contributed at least negatively to her great distinction. Miss Dickinson is probably the only Anglo-American poet of her century whose work exhibits the perfect literary situation—in which is possible the fusion of sensibility and thought. Unlike her contemporaries, she never succumbed to her ideas, to easy solutions, to her private desires.

Philosophers must deal with ideas, but the trouble with most nineteenth-century poets is too much philosophy; they are nearer to being philosophers than poets, without being in the true sense either. Tennyson is a good example of this; so is Arnold in his weak moments. There have been poets like Milton and Donne, who were not spoiled for their true business by leaning on a rational system of ideas, who understood the poetic use of ideas. Tennyson tried to mix a little Huxley and a little Broad Church, without understanding either Broad Church or Huxley; the result was fatal, and what is worse, it was shallow. Miss Dickinson's ideas were deeply imbedded in her character, not taken from the latest tract. A conscious cultivation of ideas in poetry is always dangerous, and even Milton escaped ruin only by having an instinct for what in the deepest sense he understood. Even at that there is a remote quality in Milton's approach to his material, in his treatment of it; in the nineteenth century, in an imperfect literary situation where literature was confused with documentation, he might have been a pseudo-philosopher-poet. It is difficult to conceive Emily Dickinson and John Donne succumbing to rumination about "problems"; they would not have written at all.

Neither the feeling nor the style of Miss Dickinson belongs to the seventeenth century; yet between her and Donne there are remarkable ties. Their religious ideas, their abstractions, are momently toppling from the rational plane to the level of perception. The ideas, in fact, are no longer the impersonal religious symbols created anew in the heat of emotion, that we find in poets like Herbert and Vaughan. They have become, for Donne, the terms of personality; they are mingled with the miscellany of sensation. In Miss Dickinson, as in Donne, we may detect a singularly morbid concern, not for religious truth, but for personal revelation. The modern word is self-exploitation. It is egoism grown irresponsible in religion and decadent in morals. In religion it is blasphemy; in society it means usually that culture is not self-contained and sufficient, that the spiritual community is breaking up. This is, along with some other features that do not concern us here, the perfect literary situation.

II

Personal revelation of the kind that Donne and Miss Dickinson strove for, in the effort to understand their relation to the world, is a feature of all great poetry; it is probably the hidden motive for writing. It is the effort of the individual to live apart from a cultural tradition that no longer sustains him. But this culture, which I now wish to discuss a little, is indispensable: there is a great deal of shallow nonsense in modern criticism which holds that poetry—and this is a half-truth that is worse than false—is essentially revolutionary. It is only indirectly revolutionary: the intellectual and religious background of an age no longer contains the whole spirit, and the poet proceeds to examine that background in terms of immediate experience. But the background is necessary; otherwise all the arts (not only poetry) would have to rise in a vacuum. Poetry does not dispense with tradition; it probes the deficiencies of a tradition. But it must have a tradition to probe. It is too bad that Arnold did not explain his doctrine, that poetry is a criticism of life, from the viewpoint of its background: we should have been spared an era of academic misconception, in which criticism of life meant a diluted pragmatism, the criterion of which was respectability. The poet in the true sense "criticizes" his tradition, either as such, or indirectly by comparing it with something that is about to replace it; he does what the root-meaning of the verb implies—he *discerns* its real elements and thus establishes its value, by putting it to the test of experience.

What is the nature of a poet's culture? Or, to put the question properly, what is the meaning of culture for poetry? All the great poets become the material of what we popularly call culture; we study them to acquire it. It is clear that Addison was more cultivated than Shakespeare; nevertheless Shakespeare is a finer source of culture than Addison. What is the meaning of this? Plainly it is that learning has never had anything to do with culture except instrumentally: the poet must be exactly literate enough to write down fully and precisely what he has to say, but no more. The source of a poet's true culture lies back of the paraphernalia of culture, and not all the historical activity of an enlightened age can create it.

A culture cannot be consciously created. It is an available source of ideas that are imbedded in a complete and homogeneous society. The poet finds himself balanced upon the moment when such a world is about to fall, when it threatens to run out into looser and less self-sufficient impulses. This world order is assimilated, in Miss Dickinson, as medievalism was in Shakespeare, to the poetic vision; it is brought down from abstraction to personal sensibility.

In this connection it may be said that the prior conditions for great poetry, given a great talent, may be reduced to two: the thoroughness of the poet's discipline in an objective system of truth, and his lack of consciousness of such a discipline. For this discipline is a number of fundamental ideas the origin of which the poet does not know; they give form and stability to his fresh perceptions of the world; and he cannot shake them off. This is his culture, and, like Tennyson's God, it is nearer than hands and feet. With reasonable certainty we unearth the elements of Shakespeare's culture, and yet it is equally certain—so innocent was he of his own resources—that he would not know what our discussion is about. He appeared at the collapse of the medieval system as a rigid pattern of life, but that pattern remained in Shakespeare what Shelley called a "fixed point of reference" for his sensibility. Miss Dickinson, as we have seen, was born into the equilibrium of an old and a new order. Puritanism could not be to her what it had been to the generation of Cotton Mather—a body of absolute truths; it was an unconscious discipline timed to the pulse of her life.

The perfect literary situation: it produces, because it is rare, a special and perhaps the most distinguished kind of poet. I am not trying to invent a new critical category. Such poets are never very much alike on the surface; they show us all the varieties of poetic feeling; and, like other poets, they resist all classification but that of temporary convenience. But, I believe, Miss Dickinson and John Donne would have this in common: their sense of the natural world is not blunted by a too-rigid system of ideas; yet the ideas, the abstractions, their education or their intellectual heritage, are not so weak as to let their immersion in nature, or their purely personal quality, get out of control. The two poles of the mind are not separately visible; we infer them from the lucid tension that may be most readily illustrated by polar activity. There is no thought as such at all; nor is there feeling; there is that unique focus of experience which is at once neither and both.

Like Miss Dickinson, Shakespeare is without opinions; his peculiar merit is also deeply involved in his failure to think about anything; his meaning is not in the content of his expression; it is in the tension of the dramatic relations of his characters. This kind of poetry is at the opposite of intellectualism. (Miss Dickinson is obscure and difficult, but that is not intellectualism.) To T. W. Higginson, the editor of *The Atlantic Monthly,* who tried to advise her, she wrote that she had no education. In any sense that Higginson could understand, it was quite true. His kind of education was the conscious cultivation of abstractions. She did not reason about the world she saw; she merely saw it. The "ideas" implicit in the world within her rose up, concentrated in her immediate perception.

That kind of world at present has for us something of the fascination of a buried city. There is none like it. When such worlds exist, when such cultures flourish, they support not only the poet but all members of society. For, from these, the poet differs only in his gift for exhibiting the structure, the internal lineaments, of his culture by threatening to tear them apart: a process that concentrates the symbolic emotions of society while it seems to attack them. The poet may hate his age; he may be an outcast like Villon; but this world is always there as the background to what he has to say. It is the lens through which he brings nature to focus and control—the clarifying medium that concentrates his personal feeling. It is ready-made; he cannot make it; with it, his poetry has a spontaneity and a certainty of direction that, without it, it would lack. No poet could have invented the ideas of "The Chariot"; only a great poet could have found their imaginative equivalents. Miss Dickinson was a deep mind writing from a deep culture, and when she came to poetry, she came infallibly.

Infallibly, at her best; for no poet has ever been perfect, nor is Emily Dickinson. Her precision of statement is due to the directness with which the abstract framework of her thought acts upon its unorganized material. The two elements of her style, considered as point of view, are immortality, or the idea of permanence, and the physical process of death or decay. Her diction has two corresponding features: words of Latin or Greek origin and, sharply opposed to these, the concrete Saxon element. It is this verbal conflict that gives her verse its high tension; it is not a device deliberately seized upon, but a feeling for language that senses out the two fundamental components of English and their metaphysical relation: the Latin for ideas and the Saxon for perceptions—the peculiar virtue of English as a poetic language.

Like most poets Miss Dickinson often writes out of habit; the style that emerged from some deep exploration of an idea is carried on as verbal habit when she has nothing to say. She indulges herself:

> *There's something quieter than sleep*
> *Within this inner room!*
> *It wears a sprig upon its breast,*
> *And will not tell its name.*
>
> *Some touch it and some kiss it,*
> *Some chafe its idle hand;*
> *It has a simple gravity*
> *I do not understand!*
>
> *While simple hearted neighbors*
> *Chat of the "early dead,"*
> *We, prone to periphrasis,*
> *Remark that birds have fled!*

It is only a pert remark; at best a superior kind of punning —one of the worst specimens of her occasional interest in herself. But she never had the slightest interest in the public. Were four poems or five published in her lifetime? She never felt the temptation to round off a poem for public exhibition. Higginson's kindly offer to make her verse "correct" was an invitation to throw her work into the public ring—the ring of Lowell and Longfellow. He could not see that he was tampering with one of the rarest literary integrities of all time. Here was a poet who had no use for the supports of authorship—flattery and fame; she never needed money.

She had all the elements of a culture that has broken up, a culture that on the religious side takes its place in the museum of spiritual antiquities. Puritanism, as a unified version of the world, is dead; only a remnant of it in trade may be said to survive. In the history of puritanism she comes between Hawthorne and Emerson. She has Hawthorne's matter, which a too irresponsible personality tends to dilute into a form like Emerson's; she is often betrayed by words. But she is not the poet of personal sentiment; she has more to say than she can put down in any one poem. Like Hardy and Whitman, she must be read entire; like Shakespeare, she never gives up her meaning in a single line.

She is therefore a perfect subject for the kind of criticism which is chiefly concerned with general ideas. She exhibits one of the permanent relations between personality and objective truth, and she deserves the special attention of our time, which lacks that kind of truth.

She has Hawthorne's intellectual toughness, a hard, definite sense of the physical world. The highest flights to God, the most extravagant metaphors of the strange and the remote, come back to a point of casuistry, to a moral dilemma of the experienced world. There is, in spite of the homiletic vein of utterance, no abstract speculation, nor is there a message to society; she speaks wholly to the individual experience. She offers to the unimaginative no riot of vicarious sensation; she has no useful maxims for men of action. Up to this point her resemblance to Emerson is slight: poetry is a sufficient form of utterance, and her devotion to it is pure. But in Emily Dickinson the puritan world is no longer self-contained; it is no longer complete; her sensibility exceeds its dimensions. She has trimmed down its supernatural proportions; it has become a morality; instead of the tragedy of the spirit there is a commentary upon it. Her poetry is a magnificent personal confession, blasphemous and, in its self-revelation, its honesty, almost obscene. It comes out of an intellectual life towards which it feels no moral responsibility. Cotton Mather would have burnt her for a witch.

1932

YEATS' ROMANTICISM

Notes and Suggestions

The profundity of Yeats' vision of the modern world and the width of its perspective have kept me until this occasion[1] from writing anything about the poetry of our time which I most admire. The responsibility enjoins the final effort of understanding—an effort that even now I have not been able to make. The lesser poets invite the pride of the critic to its own affirmation; the greater poets—and Yeats is among them—ask us to understand not only their minds but our own; they ask us in fact to have minds of a related caliber to theirs. And criticism must necessarily remain in the presence of the great poets a business for the anthill: the smaller minds pooling their efforts. For the power of a Yeats will be given to the study of other poets only incidentally, for shock and technique and for the test of its own reach: this kind of power has its own task to perform.

Ours is the smaller task. The magnitude of Yeats is already visible in the failure of the partial, though frequently valuable, insights that the critics have given us in the past twenty years. There is enough in Yeats for countless studies from many points of view, yet I suspect that we shall languish far this side of the complete version of Yeats until we cease to look into him for qualities that neither Yeats nor any other poet can give us; until we cease to censure him for possessing "attitudes" and "beliefs" which we do not share. Mr. Edmund Wilson's essay on Yeats in the influential study of Symbolism *Axel's Castle* asks the poet for a political and economic philosophy; or, if this is unfair to Mr. Wilson, perhaps it could be fairly said that Mr. Wilson, when he was writing the essay, was looking for a political and economic philosophy, and inevitably saw in Yeats and the other heirs of Symbolism an evasion of the reality that he, Mr. Wilson, was looking for. (If you are looking for pins you do not want needles, though both will prick you.) Mr. Louis MacNeice's book-length study of Yeats says shrewd things about the poetry, but on the whole we get the impression that Yeats had bad luck in not belonging to the younger group of English poets, who had a monopoly on "reality." (The word is Mr. MacNeice's.) Those were the days when not to be a communist was to be fascist, which is what Mr. MacNeice makes Yeats out to be. (Yeats liked the ancient "nobility," of which for Mr. MacNeice, Wall Street and the City offer examples.)

I cite these two writers on Yeats because in them we get summed up the case for Yeats' Romanticism, the view that he was an escapist retiring from problems, forces, and theories "relevant" to the modern world. While it is true that Yeats, like every poet in English since the end of the eighteenth century, began with a Romantic use of language in the early poems, he ended up very differently, and he is no more to be fixed as a Romantic than Shakespeare as a Senecan because he wrote passages of Senecan rhetoric. If one of the historic marks of Romanticism is the division between sensibility and intellect, Yeats' career may be seen as un-Romantic (I do not know the opposite term) because he closed the gap. His critics would then be the Romantics. I do not think that these squabbles are profitable. It is still true that Yeats had a more inclusive mind than any of his critics has had.

II

Two years before Yeats died he wrote to Dorothy Wellesley: "At this moment all the specialists are about to run together in our new Alexandria, thought is about to be unified as its own free act, and the shadow in Germany and elsewhere is an attempted unity by force. In my life I have never felt so acutely the presence of a spiritual virtue and that is accompanied by intensified desire."

Scattered throughout Yeats' prose there are similar passages, but this one is only from a letter, and it lacks the imaginative reach and synthesis of the great passages towards the end of *A Vision,* where I recall particularly the fine paragraph on early Byzantium and Section III of "Dove or Swan" in which Yeats describes the annunciation to Leda which brought in the classical civilization, as the annunciation to the Virgin brought in the Christian. Of Byzantium he says:

"I think that in early Byzantium, maybe never before or since in recorded history, religious, aesthetic, and practical life were one, that architect and artificers—though not, it may be, poets, for language had been the instrument of controversy and must have gone abstract—spoke to the multitude and the few alike. The painter, the mosaic worker, the worker in gold and silver, the illuminator of sacred books, were almost impersonal, almost perhaps without the consciousness of individual design, absorbed in their subject-matter and that the vision of a whole people."

Mr. Cleanth Brooks has shown that the great sonnet "Leda" is no pretty picture out of mythology, that it gets its power from the powerful forces of the imagination behind it. Section III of "Dove or Swan" begins:

"I imagine the annunciation which founded Greece as made to Leda, remembering that they showed in a Spartan temple, strung up to the roof as a holy relic, an unhatched egg of hers; and that from one of her eggs came Love and from the other War. But all things are from antithesis, and when in my ignorance I try to imagine what older civilization that annunciation rejected I can but see bird and woman blotting out some corner of the Babylonian mathematical starlight."

In these three passages I believe that we get the main threads of Yeats' thought expressed in language which refers to the famous "system" but which is nevertheless sufficiently clear to persons who have not mastered the system or who even know nothing of it. Study of the Great Wheel with its gyres and cones might give us extensive references for certain ideas in the passage from the letter. We should learn that we are now in the twenty-third phase of our historical cycle, in which thought is abstract and unity of life must be imposed by force, and that culture is Alexandrian. The picture of a perfect culture that he gives us in Byzantium (which in the poem of that name becomes something more than mere historical insight), where men enjoy full unity of being, has too many features in common with familiar Western ideas to be seen as an eccentric piece of utopianism. Byzantium is a new pastoral symbol and will be taken as that by anybody who sees more in the pastoral tradition than ideal shepherds and abstract sheep. The annunciation to Leda offers historical and philosophical difficulties; yet in spite of Yeats' frequently expressed belief that he had found a new historical vision, the conception is not historical in any sense that we understand today. It is a symbol established in analogical terms; that is, our literal grasp of it depends upon prior knowledge of the Annunciation to the Virgin. The "Babylonian mathematical starlight" is self-evidently clear without Yeats' scattered glosses on it: it is darkness and abstraction, quantitative relations without imagination; and I doubt that Yeats' definitions make it much clearer than that. If Leda rejected it, we only learn from Yeats' "system" that the coming of Christ brought it back in; for an entire cultural cycle can be predominantly antithetical or predominantly primary, at the same time that it goes through the twenty-eight phases from primary to antithetical back to primary again.

In the letter to Dorothy Wellesley occurs a sentence which sounds casual, even literally confessional; there is no harm done if we take it at that level; there is merely a loss of insight such as we get in Mr. MacNeice's *The Poetry of W. B. Yeats,* in which Yeats' myth is dismissed as "arid" and "unsound." In the midst of the "attempted unity by force," he writes: "In my own life I have never felt so acutely the presence of a spiritual virtue and that is accompanied by intensified desire." The literal student of *A Vision,* coming upon statements like this, may well wonder what has become of the determinism of the system, which, with an almost perverse ingenuity, seems to fix the individual in a system of coordinates from which he cannot escape. Mr. Cleanth Brooks believes that some measure of free will lies in Yeats' conception of the False Mask, which some unpredictable force in the individual may lead him to choose instead of the True Mask. I believe this is only part of the explanation.

Does not the true explanation lie in there being *no* explanation in terms of the system? Even if we see Yeats as he saw himself, a man of Phase 17 living in Phase 23 of our civilization, the discrepancy merely introduces a complication which the system can easily take account of. Mr. MacNeice at this point enlightens us almost in spite of himself: "Freedom for Yeats, as for Engels, was a recognition of necessity—but not of economic necessity, which he considered a vulgarism." Yes; and he would have considered psychological necessity, or any inner determinism no less than an outer, economic determinism, a vulgarism also. But in the phrase the "recognition of necessity" we get a clue to Yeats' own relation to his system and to what seems to me the right way to estimate its value. He only wanted what all men want, a world larger than himself to live in; for the modern world as he saw it was, in human terms, too small for the human spirit, though quantitatively large if looked at with the scientist. If we say, then, that he wanted a *dramatic* recognition of necessity, we shall have to look at the system not as arid or unsound or eccentric, which it well may be in itself, but through Yeats' eyes, which are the eyes of his poetry.

If we begin with the poetry we shall quickly see that there is some source of power or illumination which is also in us, waiting to be aroused; and that this is true of even the greater number of the fine poems in which the imagery appears upon later study to lean upon the eccentric system. I would say, then, that even the terms of the system, when they appear in the richer texture of the poems, share a certain large margin of significance with a wider context than they have in the system itself. May we say that Yeats' *A Vision,* however private and almost childishly eclectic it may seem, has somewhat the same relation to a central tradition as the far more rigid structure of *The Divine Comedy* has to the Christian myth? I dare say that Mr. Eliot would not chide Dante for accepting a "lower mythology." Perhaps the central tradition in Dante and Yeats lies in a force that criticism cannot specifically isolate, the force that moved both poets to the dramatic recognition of necessity; yet the visible structure of the necessity itself is perhaps not the source of that power. I do not say that Yeats is comparable in stature to Dante; only that both poets strove for a visible structure of action which is indeed necessary to what they said, but which does not explain what they said. I believe that Mr. Eliot should undertake to explain why Arnold's Higher Mythology produced poetry less interesting than Yeats' Lower Mythology, which becomes in Yeats' verse the vehicle of insights and imaginative syntheses as profound as those which Arnold talked about but never, as a poet, fully achieved. Myths differ in range and intensity, but not, I take it, as high and low; for they are in the end what poets can make of them.

If Yeats could feel in the midst of the Alexandrian rigidity and disorder the "presence of a spiritual virtue," was he denying the inclusiveness of the system; or could he have seen his senile vigor and insight in terms of the system? Possibly the latter; but it makes little difference.

III

A Vision has been described by more than one critic as a philosophy; I speak of it here as a "system"; but I doubt that it is a system of philosophy. What kind of system is it? Yeats frequently stated his own purpose, but even that is a little obscure: to put myth back into philosophy. This phrase may roughly describe the result, but it could not stand for the process; it attributes to the early philosophers a deliberation of which they would have been incapable. The language of Plotinus, whose *Enneads* Yeats read late in life, is compounded of primitive symbolism, the esoteric fragments of classical myth, and the terms of Greek technical metaphysics; but there is no calculated intention of instilling myth into philosophy.

In what sense is *A Vision* a myth? There are fragments of many myths brought in to give dramatic and sensuous body to the framework, which attains to the limit of visualization that a complex geometrical picture can provide.

A broad view of this picture, with its gyres and cones, to say nothing of the Daimons and the Principles whose relation to the Faculties defies my understanding, gleans at least two remarkable features. I merely note them:

(1) ". . . the subjective cone is called that of the *antithetical tincture* because it is achieved and defended by continual conflict with its opposite; the objective cone is called that of the *primary tincture* because whereas subjectivity—in Empedocles 'Discord' as I think—tends to separate man from man, objectivity brings us back to the mass where we began." From this simple definition—verbally simple, but very obscure—we get the first picture of the intersecting cones; and from this the whole structure is elaborated.

It is clear visually with the aid of the diagrams; but when Yeats complicates it with his Principles and Daimons, and extends the symbol of the gyres to cover historical eras, visualization breaks down. It is an extended metaphor which increasingly tends to dissolve in the particulars which it tries to bring together into unity.

When we come to the magnificent passages on history in "Dove or Swan," all the intricacies of the geometrical metaphor disappear; and the simple figure of historical cycles, which Yeats evidently supposed came out of his gyres, is sufficient to sustain his meaning. Again Yeats' "system" overlaps a body of insight common to us all.

I would suggest, then, for the study of the relation of Yeats' "system" to his vision of man, both historical and individual, this formula: As the system broadens out and merges with the traditional insights of our culture, it tends to disappear in its specific, technical aspects. What disappears is not a philosophy, but only a vast metaphorical structure. In the great elegy, "In Memory of Major Robert Gregory," we get this couplet:

> *But as the outrageous stars incline*
> *By opposition, square, and trine—*

which is the only astrological figure in the poem. Yet it must not be assumed that Yeats on this occasion turned off the system; it must be there. Why does it not overtly appear? It has been absorbed into the concrete substance of the poem; the material to be symbolized replaces the symbol, and contains its own meaning. I would select this poem out of all others of our time as the most completely expressed: it has a perfect articulation and lucidity which cannot be found in any other modern poem in English.

(2) In his early poems Yeats is concerned with the myths of ancient Ireland. We may find unreadable today a poem like "The Wanderings of Oisin" or plays like "Deirdre" or "The Land of Heart's Desire." The later poems are less dependent upon fable and fully developed mythical plots for their structures. And yet Yeats entered his later poetic phase at about the same time he began to be interested in his system, in putting myth back into philosophy. Did this mean that he was taking myth out of his poetry?

Thus the second remarkable feature of the system, as I see it, is that it is not a mythology at all, but rather an extended metaphor, as I have already pointed out, which permits him to establish relations between the tag-ends of myths eclectically gathered from all over the world. For example, there is nothing in the geometrical structure of the system which inherently provides for the annunciation to Leda; it is an arbitrary association of two fields of imagery; but once it is established, it is not hard to pass on through analogy to the Annunciation to the Virgin.

IV

Thus it is difficult for me to follow those critics who accept Yeats' various utterances that he was concerned with a certain relation of philosophy to myth. Any statement about "life" must have philosophical implications, just as any genuine philosophical statement must have, because of the nature of language, mythical implications. Yeats' doctrine of the conflict of opposites says nothing about the fundamental nature of reality; it is rather a dramatic framework through which is made visible the perpetual oscillation of man between extreme introspection and extreme loss of the self in the world of action. The intricacies of Yeats' system provide for many of the permutations of this relation; but it cannot forsee them all; and we are constantly brought back to the individual man, not as a symbolic counter, but as a personality rich and unpredictable. Yeats' preference for the nobleman, the peasant, and the craftsman does not betray, as Mr. MacNeice's somewhat provincial contention holds, the "budding fascist"; it is a "version of pastoral" which permits Yeats to see his characters acting above the ordinary dignity of men, in a concrete relation to life undiluted by calculation and abstraction. I can only repeat here that the "system" is perpetually absorbed into action. If Yeats were only an allegorist, the meaning of his poetry could be ascertained by getting hold of the right key. The poetry would serve to illustrate the "system," as the poetry of the Prophetic Books fleshes out the homemade system of Blake.

v

Mr. Eliot's view, that Yeats got off the central tradition into a "minor mythology," and Mr. Blackmur's view, that he took "magic" (as opposed to religion) as far as any poet could, seem to me to be related versions of the same fallacy. Which is: that there must be a direct and effective correlation between the previously established truth of the poet's ideas and the value of the poetry. (I am oversimplifying Blackmur's view, but not Eliot's.) In this difficulty it is always useful to ask: *Where* are the poet's ideas? Good sense in this matter ought to tell us that while the ideas doubtless exist in some form outside the poetry, as they exist for Yeats in the letters, the essays, and *A Vision,* we must nevertheless test them in the poems themselves, and not "refute" a poem in which the

gyres supply certain images by showing that gyres are amateur philosophy.

> *Turning and turning in the widening gyre*
> *The falcon cannot hear the falconer. . . .*

—the opening lines of "The Second Coming": and they
make enough sense apart from our knowledge of the system;
the gyre here can be visualized as the circling flight of the
bird constantly widening until it has lost contact with the
point, the center, to which it ought to be able to return. As
a symbol of disunity it is no more esoteric than Eliot's "Gull
against the wind," at the end of "Gerontion," which is a casual, not traditional or systematic, symbol of disunity. Both Mr.
Blackmur and Mr. Brooks—Mr. Brooks more than Mr. Blackmur—show us the systematic implications of the symbols of
the poem "Byzantium." The presence of the system at its
most formidable cannot be denied to this poem. I should like
to see, nevertheless, an analysis of it in which no special
knowledge is used; I should like to see it examined with the
ordinary critical equipment of the educated critic; I should
be surprised if the result were very different from Mr. Brooks'
reading of the poem. The symbols are "made good" in the
poem; they are drawn into a wider convention (Mr. Blackmur calls it the "heaven of man's mind") than they would
imply if taken separately.

I conclude these notes with the remark: the study of Yeats
in the coming generation is likely to overdo the scholarly
procedure, and the result will be the occultation of a poetry
which I believe is nearer the center of our main traditions of
sensibility and thought than the poetry of Eliot or of Pound.
Yeats' special qualities will instigate special studies of great
ingenuity, but the more direct and more difficult problem of
the poetry itself will probably be delayed. This is only to
say that Yeats' Romanticism will be created by his critics.

1942

A NOTE ON DONNE

Donne's modern reputation has risen so suddenly that writers born since 1900 may look back to the time when he was a name in *The Oxford Book of English Verse* at the head of seven poems, two of which we now know that he did not write. *A Garland for John Donne,*[1] the collection of essays edited by Mr. Theodore Spencer for the tercentenary of the poet's death, attempts to revalue the poetry and to inquire into the causes of its present influence. The uncertainty of these critics about Donne's place is remarkable in the case of a poet three hundred years dead. The uncertainty comes of Donne's being still alive. He "ranks" possibly a little above Marvell, but Marvell's interest for us is not nearly so great. The reasons for his influence are at once more difficult to discover and more fruitful to pursue than his rank. The essayists in this volume are united in the belief that many of Donne's problems are our own.

Johnson blamed the vices of metaphysical style upon "a voluntary deviation from nature in pursuit of something new and strange." The eighteenth century on the whole regarded Donne as a prodigy of perverse learning. Although Donne's style, the bold images and learned conceits, had a distinct effect upon Cowley and Carew, and even Richard Crashaw; although the conversational tone influenced Dryden, it has remained for our own age to relate him to the main stream of English verse. It has been our task to understand the seriousness of the impulse and the integrity, which once seemed the perversity, of style; our task to see the whole intellectual structure of the poetry, along with the rough versification, in the light of the underlying problems of the age of Donne. For the first time he is being felt as a contemporary.

The eight essays are admirably distributed over the two kinds of problem that a great poet of the past inevitably creates—the historical and the critical problem. There are five historical essays. Mr. Spencer has written, in *Donne and His Age,* a study of the intellectual climate in which Donne lived: although he suggests more problems than he can solve in so brief a space, his discussion of the revolutionary effect of the sixteenth-century "picture of the physical world" on moral ideas is a valuable contribution to Elizabethan criticism. Mr. John Sparrow's *The Date of Donne's Travels* reviews difficult and perhaps insoluble problems of the poet's biography; incidentally Mr. Sparrow throws some light on the origin of Donne's geographical allusions—whether they were bookish or drawn from observation. A *Note on Donne the Preacher,* by Mr. John Hayward, presents a side of Donne that would have only a minor historical value had he never written his verse. Mrs. Evelyn M. Simpson's analysis of the *Paradoxes and Problems* brings out the early influence of Martial, an influence that Mr. Spencer finds general in the 1590's and not peculiar to Donne; Mrs. Simpson's paper is chiefly valuable for its emphasis on his early "interest in science."

But here, just as Mr. Eliot warns us that Donne's skepticism, being mainly an uncertainty about the right terms of faith, was not like ours, Mrs. Simpson might well have distinguished between science as we know it and Donne's "interest" in the new cosmologists, Copernicus and Kepler. This was rather an anxiety about the physical limits of consciousness and the bearing of that question on the scholastic conception of body and soul, which Donne presents in the terminology of St. Thomas. Donne knew nothing of a scientific age, or of the later, open conflict between the two world-views, science and religion. Far from having a scientific attitude towards the problem of body and soul, he grapples with it, not to get any truth out of it apart from his own personality, but to use it as the dramatic framework for his individual emotion.

This is the center of Donne. Mr. Mario Praz, in *Donne's Relation to the Poetry of His Time,* says: "Donne's technique stands in the same relation to the average technique of Renaissance poetry as that of baroque to that of Renaissance painting. His sole preoccupation is with the whole effect." And involved in the whole effect is the quality of experience known to modern criticism as "emotional tone," an implicit form that is functional to the precise rendition of the individual experience. "He was," writes Mr. Praz, "like a lawyer choosing the fittest arguments for the case in hand; not a searcher after a universally valid truth": the fittest images and tropes by which to set forth, not a truth, but a complete emotion. The terms are not the terms of objective truth, to which the individual experience is trimmed down, and all the implications rejected that the terms do not contain. They are rather occasional indications of an experience that is no longer implicit in them, to be used only when they serve the purpose. The scholastic terms in "The Extasie" are quite as illustrative, and no more "philosophical," than the merely denoted violet:

> *But as all severall soules containe*
> *Mixture of things, they know not what,*
> *Love, these mixt soules, doth mixe againe,*
> *And makes both one, each this and that.*
> *A single violet transplant,*
> *The strength, the colour, and the size . . .*

Scholastic love occupies indifferent ground, with respect to truth, quite like that of the neutral conceit of the compasses in "A Valediction forbidding mourning":

> *If they be two, they are two so*
> *As stiffe twin compasses are two,*
> *Thy soule the fixt foot, makes no show*
> *To move, but doth, if the other doe.*

The conceits in both passages are "neutral" because they may be either true or false with respect to the inherent demands of the perceptions to be set forth in the poem.

This is the modernism of Donne: it is the modernism that re-establishes our own roots in the age of Donne. Mr. Praz's essay is the link between the two problems of Donne—his place in his own time and his value for us. Here Mr. T. S. Eliot, prophesying the speedy decline of Donne's new repu' tation, leaves its future ominously obscure. Mr. Eliot's belief that Donne's prose—the sermons, *Biathanatos*, the *Paradoxes and Problems*—is ready for oblivion, and quickly, is not to be questioned; the sermons have been mildly popular, among people who wish to be in the Donne fashion without taking the trouble to read the verse. But that the *Songs and Sonnets,* the *Elegies,* most of the *Satires* and the *Divine Poems,* will not continue to be read for an indefinite time is an opinion harder to maintain.

"His learning," says Mr. Eliot, "is just information suffused with emotion . . . rather a humorous shuffling of the pieces; and we are inclined to read our own more conscious awareness of the apparent unrelatedness of things into the mind of Donne."

How much longer this "unrelatedness of things" will continue to be the background of poetry; whether it is not by now an emotional convention out of which minor poetic heresies, like Imagism or the more recent Objectivism,[2] will at intervals appear; whether the local excitement of sensation will indefinitely obscure the formal qualities of the Spenserian-Miltonic kind of verse—these are questions that Mr. Spencer's memorial volume asks, but wisely does not answer. The answers, perhaps, would contain the immediate future of poetry.

II

Why we are concerned with the future of any art is a mystery that Donne and his contemporaries could not have understood. But the difference between Donne and our age is not, in this respect, a radical one, and there was a definite place in Mr. Spencer's book for an essay on the rise of the historical consciousness.

The position of Mr. George Williamson, in his excellent paper *Donne and Today,* falls into two parts that tend to undermine each other. On the one hand, he suggests abstract analogies between Donne and some living poets, which would be interesting if true, but on the other hand, his quotations from Eliot, Read, Ransom, and the late Elinor Wylie offer as little evidence of the influence of Donne, as Mr. Williamson understands it, as one might derive from Tennyson. Mrs. Ramsay, in *Donne's Relation to Philosophy,* quotes stanzas from Donne and "In Memoriam" in order to distinguish two uses of "philosophy" in verse. But the lines of Tennyson come within Mr. Williamson's formula for Donne: "One may say that Donne's emotion is commonly given 'conceptual' form, but not that he is a philosophical poet."

Mr. Eliot remarks that Donne first made it possible to *think* in English lyrical verse; but it does not follow that his thinking in verse was our kind of thought. We are actually nearer to Tennyson. What thinking there is in modern verse has the general character of historical thinking—"And all the wars have dwindled since Troy fell." Tennyson confidently culled the scraps from the tables of "culture"; but our dietetics is more self-conscious. We use the past and we think about its meaning. Our framework of idea is the cultural cycle, or the awareness of the "pastness" of the past, as in the case of Mr. Archibald MacLeish. The vulgarity of the present and the purity of the past make the framework of Mr. John Crowe Ransom's irony. Even Mr. Jeffers performs a fusion of literary psychology with a fictitious primitivism that places him in the historical consciousness. Although Mr. Ezra Pound's method is a cunning imitation of the pre-historical view that seized past and present naïvely as a whole, the *Cantos* is a monument to the historical mentality. There is none of this explicitly in Donne.

There is, so far as I know, only the slightest evidence, in seventeenth-century poetry, of a sense of historical rise-and-fall affecting the moral temper of individuals. Milton's Latin poem, *Naturam non pati senium,* argues that nature does not inwardly decay. Civilization apart from nature is not mentioned; and the poem ends with an allusion to the Christian myth: *Ingentique rogo flagrabit machina mundi.* The decay of nature was a frequent subject of controversy in the universities, and Milton must have felt its latent hostility to his own settled belief in the relation between a fixed human nature and a perfect divine order.

It is this perfect divine order that makes Milton's mythology possible. It is the threat to such an order from the
direction of the "new philosophy" which "calls all in doubt,"
the new cosmology, that compelled Donne to ignore the
popular pastoral convention of his time; nor could he rest
secure upon the more comprehensive classical or Christian
mythology. These imaginative structures (to describe them
in the lowest terms) were by habit or in essence involved
in the medieval system. Mr. Williamson remarks: "Although
mythology is banished from his verse, medieval philosophy
and Renaissance science take its place, in fact become his
mythology." The distinction between abstract ideas and mythology is extremely important in the study of Donne, and I
believe Mr. Williamson misses a capital point. Dante could
afford to be philosophical; the terms were a system that he
acknowledged as truth. But it is different with Donne; the
vocabulary is merely vocabulary, and it lacks the ultimate,
symbolic character of a myth. It is only a step from his
lawyer-like use of ingenious terms to the intricacy of personal sensation as the center of consciousness. And from this
it is but one more step, for the philosophical egoist, to the
dramatization of oneself against the background of society or
history. It is a step that Donne could not take, but doubtless would take were he alive today.

There was the mythological, pastoral school, begun by
Wyat and Surrey, and Nicholas Grimald, improved by Sidney and Spenser, and perfected by Milton at a single stroke.
There was the dramatic, introspective school which, whether
in the lyric or on the stage, centered after Chapman in the
individual sensibility. In the non-dramatic poets of this
school, of whom Donne is the great figure before Dryden, the
poet himself becomes the dramatic character: Mr. Spencer
finds an analogy between Donne and Hamlet's philosophical
egoism of inaction: the poet's ideas, now the framework of
intense excitement, are pitted against one another like characters in a play.

Therein lies the nature of the "conceit." It is an idea not
inherent in the subject, but exactly parallel to it, elaborated
beyond the usual stretch of metaphor into a supporting struc-

ture for a long passage or even an entire poem. It may be torn away from its original meaning, like the Angels in Donne's "Elegie XI," and yet remain the vehicle of "poetic truth"; that is to say, of heightened emotion in the poet's dramatization of his own personality. The conceit in itself is neither true nor false. From this practice it is but a step to Dryden and the eighteenth century, to the rise of the historical consciousness, and to ourselves. It is the peculiar fascination of Donne that he presents the problem of personal poetry in its simplest terms. There is the simple awareness, complicated at the surface by his immense intellectual resources, of frustration and bewilderment—to which, for us, is added the frustration of historical relativity. Milton stood for the historical absolute, which is the myth. And unless it will again be possible for men to give themselves up to a self-contained, objective system of truths, the principles of Donne, whether we know him or not, will continue to be our own.

1932

THE POINT OF DYING: DONNE'S "VIRTUOUS MEN"

> *As virtuous men passe mildly away*
> *And whisper to their souls, to goe,*
> *Whilst some of their sad friends do say,*
> *The breath goes now, and some say no.*
>
> *So let us melt and make no noise,*
> *No teare-floods nor sigh tempests move;*
> *'Twere prophanation of our joyes*
> *To tell the layetie our love.*

I believe that none of Donne's commentators has tried to follow up the implications of the analogy: the moment of death is like the secret communion of lovers. The first thing that we see is that lovers die *out of* something *into* something else. They die in order to live. This is the particular *virtue*, the Christian entelechy or final cause of mankind, and the actualization of what it is to be human.

The logical argument of "A Valediction: Forbidding Mourning" is a Christian commonplace. Through the higher love, lovers achieve a unity of being which physical love, the analogue of the divine, not only preserves but both intensifies and enlarges. The implicit symbol of this union is the Aristotelian circle of archetypal motion. Union is imagined first as a mathematical point where physical and spiritual union are the same; then as an expanding circle of which the point is the center. The analogy is complete when the two legs of the draftman's compasses become congruent in the lovers' embrace, so that the legs form a vertical line standing on the "same" point. Thus Donne "reduces" a Platonic abstraction to actual form by contracting the circumference, "absence," to the point, "reunion," on the human scale, of the lovers.

Logically the mathematical point precedes the circle of which it is the center; literally it also has priority, since the lover begins his journey from the point. But the poem as action, as trope, asserts the priority of the circle, for without it nothing in the poem would move: the lovers in order to be united, or reunited, have got first to be "separated," the woman at the center, the man at the enlarging circumference, even though the separation is further and larger union. The visual image of the expanding circle is the malleable gold, which by becoming materially thinner under the hammer expands indefinitely, but not into infinity; for this joint soul of the lovers is a "formulable essence" which abhors infinity. The material gold disappears as it becomes absolutely thin, and is replaced by pure, anagogical "light"—another Christian commonplace that needs no explanation. Donne fills his circle with a physical substance that can be touched and seen; but it is the particular substance which archetypally reflects the light of heaven. Yet all this light which is contained by the circle is only an expanded point; that is to say, whether we see the lovers as occupying the contracted circle in the figure of the compasses, or the expanded point of the gold, they always occupy the same "space," and are never separated. Space is here the "letter" of a non-dimensional anagoge; and likewise the circle widening towards infinity. Thus spatial essences are the analogical rhetoric of a suprarational intuition.

But "A Valediction: Forbidding Mourning" is a poem, not a philosophical discourse. And since a poem is a movement of a certain kind in which its logical definition is only a participant, we have got to try to see this poem, like any other, as an action more or less complete. For an action, even of the simplest outline, in life or in art, is not what we can say about it; it rather is what prompts us to speak. The Christian commonplaces that I have pointed out are not Donne's poem; they are, as letter and allegory, material factors that it is the business of the poet to bring to full actualization in rhetoric; and here, as always, the rhetoric, the full linguistic body of the poem which ultimately resists our analysis, is the action, the trope, the "turning" from

one thing to another: from darkness to light, from ignorance
to knowledge, from sight to insight. This tropological motion
is the final cause ($\tau o\hat{v}\ \check{\epsilon}\nu\epsilon\kappa a$) of the poem, that towards which
it moves, on account of which its logical definition, its formu-
lable essence, exists. And it is the business of criticism to examine this motion, not the formulable essence as such.

Donne's two opening stanzas announce the theme of in-
dissoluble spiritual union in an analogy to what seems at first
glance its opposite: dissolution of soul from body. First we
have dying men (not one man, not trope but allegory) who
"whisper to their souls, to goe"; then, in the second stanza,
lovers who "melt *and* [my italics] make no noise." The moment of death is a *separation* which virtuous men welcome,
and the lovers are about to *separate* in quiet joy ("no teare-
floods nor sigh-tempests move"). For the lovers too are
"virtuous"—infused with a certain power or potency to be
realized. They have no more to fear from separation from
each other than dying men from death, or separation from
life. If the lovers foresee no loss, they may expect a gain
similar to that of the dying men.

At this point we may pass to another phase of the analogy.
Here the difficult word is "melt." I cannot find in the history
of the word, even as a secondary meaning, the idea of
human separation. The meanings range from change of physical identity to feelings of tenderness. Tenderness is no
doubt felt by the lovers at parting, and by the sad friends at
the deathbed. But it is difficult to imagine these virtuous
men feeling tender towards themselves, or sorry that they
are dying. They might feel some "tenderness" for or yearn-
ing towards something beyond life, i.e., union with God, the
realization of their virtue. Here the analogy holds for both
lovers and dying men, but here also melting as tenderness
becomes very remote; and we must fall back upon change of
physical identity as the analogue to change of spiritual
identity. The figure has got to work in the first place this side
of a remote "higher" meaning, a univocal abstraction not
caught in the burning bush of rhetorical analogy. Donne is
one of the last Catholic allegorists; to him aiming high is
meaningless unless the aim is sighted from a point below.

Thus the sense in which both dying men and lovers may be said to melt is restricted to loss of physical substance, of physical identity. The verb "to goe" applies then to both lovers and dying men; both go out of the body, yet through the body, to unite with the object of love. "To goe" thus means to join, to unite with; to "melt" must be equated with "to goe"; it means going into something other than itself. Melting and going are species of dying, but the underlying universal is affirmed, implicitly, not overtly. If lovers die in this analogical sense, they lose their identity in each other, and the physical separation is the letter of the great anagoge, spiritual union. The lover dies out of himself into the beloved in order to gain spiritual union; and spiritual union having been gained, the bodies are no longer there; they are absent, separated. The lover leaves not only the body of the beloved, but his own; and the movement of action, the trope, provides for both journeys. For "mourning" is forbidden for two reasons. They must not mourn because "Donne" is going off to the continent; they must not mourn, since through the letter of sexual union they pass tropologically from body to spirit, where body is left behind for another kind of journey.

The structure of the poem, *at the level of trope,* turns on the pun *to die:* orgasmic ecstasy as the literal analogue to spiritual ecstasy; physical union as the analogue to spiritual. Between these extremes of inert analogy we find the moral, or tropological, movement of the poem, the central action—the passage in actualized experience from the lower to the higher. But without this egregious pun, the whole range of the pun, at that: its witty, anecdotal, even obscene implications: without it the poem would not move; for the pun is its mover, its propeller, its efficient cause.

A grammatical peculiarity of stanza two will offer indirect support for this argument. I refer to "and" between "melt *and* make no noise." I have, I believe, disposed of "let us be tender" as a plausible meaning of "melt." But if that were the right meaning, the conjunction should be "but," not "and." As Donne wrote the passage (we are entitled to read only what he wrote), it evidently means: Let us pass through the body, let us "die" in both senses, *and* the loss of physical self will prevent the noisy grief of "sublunary lovers" at parting and the noisy love-making of physical union. Thus if "melt" were not an extension of the pun, Donne would probably have written "but make no noise"—a prudential injunction to protect the neighbors from scandal.

Two other features of the analogy seem to me to reinforce this reading. Why are the sad friends at the deathbed incapable of detecting the exact moment of death? Affection and anxiety account for it in life. This is obviously the first and literal meaning. But here it must be considered along with the lovers' reluctance to tell their love to the "laity." For the logic of the poem contains a third Christian commonplace: death-in-life of this world, life-in-death of the next. The sad friends are a similar laity and the laity is the world, where men do not know the difference between appearance and reality, between death and life. But men at the moment of death, lovers at the moment of spiritual union (through and beyond the body), have a sacerdotal secret, access to a sacramental rite, beyond the understanding of the "laity" who have not had these ultimate experiences. The dying of the lovers into life and the dying of death into life are reciprocally analogous. Donne is not saying that death is *like* love, or that love is *like* death; there is the identity, death-love, a third something, a reality that can be found only through analogy since it has no name. This reality, whether of "dying" lovers or of "dying" men, is the ultimate experience. The reciprocal conversion of the one into the other is the moral motion of the poem, its peripety, the "action" which eventually issues in the great top-level significance that Dante understood as the anagoge. This is nothing less, as it is surely nothing more, than the entire poem, an actual linguistic object that is at once all that our discourse can make of it and nothing that at any moment of discourse we are able to make of it.

1952

A NOTE ON ELIZABETHAN SATIRE

As the Oxford anthologies come off the press, the disadvantages of dividing English poetry into exact centuries become more and more conspicuous. Sir Edmund Chambers, in his preface to *The Oxford Book of Sixteenth Century Verse*, remarks that the year 1600 "still finds a continuous flood of literature in mid-career." He points out that "Drayton and Chapman, who hopelessly overlap the dividing line, must be cut asunder." Drayton, for example, suffers for the absence of his "ballads" of Agincourt and the Virginian Voyage. Donne is wholly omitted, for reasons that we shall see. Given the limited range, which, in the poetry of Donne, Sir Edmund seems to define with excessive narrowness, he has done his work well, even brilliantly.

There is a good reason for the success of this anthology. It is the editor's superior taste, a gift that historical scholars a generation ago feared to exercise. "In the present case," writes Sir Edmund, "an attempt has been made to apply a standard of absolute poetry, rather than one of merely historical interest. . . ." It is a difficult standard to uphold, and if it cannot be said that the editor applies it infallibly, one must remember that the power to perceive the best does not always carry with it the will to reject the second rate.

A debatable assumption underlies Sir Edmund's view of the whole period, and there are some minor disproportions in the representation of the poets. The disproportion between Raleigh and Sir John Davies is enormous. Raleigh wrote less than Davies but that less is immeasurably superior; yet Davies has fifty-one pages to Raleigh's thirty-seven. Here one feels that Sir Edmund in spite of himself is beguiled by the historical interest of Davies' *Orchestra*, perhaps by the interminable facility of its versification—although

Davies at times is still as clumsy as the earlier Gascoigne or Grimald.

One mark of Davies' inferiority is the lack of tension in his style, a lack of concentrated purpose. This inferiority is at the center of the whole Spenserian school, in which, as Sir Edmund points out, "the slightness of invention is overhung with ornamental decoration, like some great composition of Paolo Veronese. . . ." This ornamental decoration of image in Spenser and Davies arose along with the historical improvement of English versification between 1557 and 1579—a springe to catch the woodcocks of the historical method. It was, actually, the resistance, in the first half of the century, of a fluid vocabulary to the poet's meaning, joined to his metrical uncertainty, that contributed to Wyat's success in "They flee from me that sometime did me seek." It is one of a half-dozen great meditative lyrics in English.

Nevertheless, Sir Edmund justly attacks, from his own point of view, one of the hoariest pedantries in English criticism: "A rather irritating kind of scholarship insists that Wyat was chiefly notable for the acclimatization of the Italian sonnet. . . . But in lyric, sung or based on the models of song, he is a master of the first order." In spite of the perhaps too generous excerpts from Davies, Daniel, and Constable, one sees everywhere the evidence of Sir Edmund's preoccupation with the quality of the verse. He has given us all of Sackville's *Induction;* sixteen poems by Fulke Greville, including the fine long piece, "Who grace for zenith had"; thirty-one pages of Sidney, who is better represented here than in any other popular collection ever made; and the ample selections from Raleigh already noticed—although a few more of his sonnets would have furthered the rising reputation of this most neglected of Elizabethan poets. Raleigh's direct, conversational ease, his intelligence and subtlety, are qualities that deserve to be better understood: it has been the custom to see in Raleigh's verse only a sort of thin lagging after Sidney. His poetry is, on the contrary, distinct, and needs separate consideration.

II

It is ungrateful to impute to Sir Edmund Chambers any trace of wrong insight into the quality of the age. The century as a whole falls into three periods—that of Skelton, lasting until the appearance of Wyat in Tottel's *Songes and Sonets* in 1557; the period of Wyat, the most considerable figure until Sidney and Spenser, whose *Shepherd's Calendar* brought in a new era in 1579. It was by then the English Renaissance full-blown. *The Shepherd's Calendar,* a dull but original exercise in theory, offered to Spenser's successors an example of new possibilities of poetic English, and set up a pastoral convention that was to reach perfection as late as 1637. In singling out the leading impulse of the Elizabethan age one is constantly guided by the genius and magnitude of Spenser. Yet it is Milton in the next age who puts the seal of perfection on the pastoral, mythological school, and who, to no little extent, permits us to rank as highly as we do merely competent poets like Davies and Constable.

Our comparatively low rating of Greville no less than of Raleigh—Saintsbury says that Greville is "sententious and difficult"—is due to the constant introspection, the difficult self-analysis, the cynical melancholy, that break through the courtly pastoral convention to a level of feeling deeper, and historically purer, than the facile despair of the Sidneian sonneteers. Doubtless both Greville and Raleigh, as minor masters, were too much impressed with the glittering style of Sidney, and, later, of Spenser, to understand that their own sensibilities deserved a more perfectly matured style. Their work has the diffuseness of divided purpose.

There has never been enough made of Elizabethan satire. While Raleigh and Fulke Greville cannot be called pure satirists, they were not comfortable in the courtly, pastoral abstractions. In this negative feature of their verse they resemble certain of the satirists, Hall, Marston, Tourneur. If we put Raleigh and Greville together against the background of the widespread influence of Martial,[1] they, too, form a background not only for the *Satires* of Donne (1593) but for much of that great poet's most characteristic later writing.

Yet Sir Edmund says: "Only for chronology, indeed, can Donne be an Elizabethan"—an opinion that obscures the still powerful strain of medieval thought at the end of the sixteenth century. By another kind of reasoning Donne cannot be a Jacobean. For we find in Donne, significantly enough, not only the influence of Martial, but a resurgence of scholasticism—a union of classical satire and medievalism. And it is significant that "Go, soul, the body's guest" was written by the same Raleigh who wrote "The Passionate Man's Pilgrimage," a poem that is, I believe, occasionally described as charming. I cannot believe that, in order to write it, Raleigh invoked a muse different from the muse of a poem that is sophisticated, consciously erudite, and subtle. "The Passionate Man's Pilgrimage" is medieval allegory furbished up with a new awareness of the sensuous world; "Go, soul, the body's guest" is satire; and the two strains are not quite the disharmony that we are accustomed to believe them.

Possibly the last use of extended medieval allegory in verse of great distinction is Sackville's *Induction*. There are the familiar personifications—Remorse, Dread, Revenge, Misery, Death. Spenser's task was to revive allegory with a new spirit alien to the medieval mind. Although Spenser's puritanism is manifest, his allegory has a voluptuous glitter that Sackville's more medieval spareness lacked; or, if you go back to Gower's treatment of the seven deadly sins, it is plain that as a medieval man he was too serious about them to dress them up.

The medieval minds left over at the end of the sixteenth century tended to see the world not in terms of a fixed moral system, but with an ingrained moral prejudice about the nature of man. I allude here to the decline of Catholic theology in England, and to the rise, conspicuously in the dramatic poets, of an unmoral and anti-doctrinal point of view. Marlowe is an example. But the moral temper of a less expansive, more melancholy age, a kind of interregnum between feudalism and Tudorism when the evil of life was expressed in ideas of all-pervasive mortality—this moral temper, having lost its theological framework, remained as an almost instinctive approach to the nature of man. And the nature of man, far from enjoying the easy conquest of evil that Spenser set forth in six books that might have been twelve, was on the whole unpleasant and depraved. This depravity is the theme of Elizabethan tragedy, I think, as early as *The Jew of Malta*. There is no need to cite Webster and Ford.

It is the prevailing attitude of the satirists and of most of those non-dramatic poets who stand apart from the Spenserian school. In such poets we find a quality that we have shortsightedly ascribed uniquely to modern verse—the analysis of emotion and an eye chiefly to the aesthetic effect. There is here the use of symbols that are too complex to retain, throughout a long work, or from one work to another, a fixed meaning. The allegorical symbol is constant and homogeneous, like the Red Cross Knight; the richer, poetic symbol, like Prospero, does not invite the oversimplification of certain of its qualities, but asks to be taken in all its manifold richness.

It is this stream of Elizabethan poetry that has never been properly evaluated. We tend to forget, in fixing the relation of the Shakespearean drama to its sources, and of its text to the texts of contemporaries, that Shakespeare stands outside the allegorical school. It is thus difficult for us to take a further step and to see that he was closely connected with a much less conspicuous type of poetry that had been only superficially affected by the Renaissance. This was the dormant medieval which, even after the new language of Wyat, survived in Sackville's *Induction*.

In a later poet like Greene the new courtly conventions are too weak to sustain his restless sensibility. Although Greene never mastered a style, his great vitality of image and rhythm is largely due to a naïvely skeptical grasp of the conventions of Sidney and Spenser. He uses them without ever quite believing them: as in the verse of Raleigh, the convention offers just enough resistance to expression to lend to the poetry tension and depth. Though Greene is imperfect, he has none of Daniel's complacently perfect dullness.

It is this resistance of the language to full expression, the strain between images and rhythm, opposites "yoked by violence together" in varying degrees of violence, that gives to English lyrical verse its true genius. It is a genius that permitted Milton to bring to the pastoral style a richness and subtlety of effect that Spenser never achieved. It is that quality of English style which is superior to age and school. It was perfectly mastered as early as Wyat:

> It was no dream; I lay broad waking:
>   But all is turned, thorough my gentleness
> Into a strange fashion of forsaking;
>   And I have leave to go of her goodness,
>   And she also to use newfangleness.
>   But since that I so kindly am served
>   I would fain know what she hath deserved.

It is in the lyrics, even in the political satires, of Dryden, but it begins to disappear in Pope, to reappear in the nineteenth century perhaps in Landor and Browning alone. It is a quality, not of system or of doctrine, but of immediate intelligence acting directly; a definite but unpremeditated limitation of moral and metaphysical idea to the problem of the work to be done. It is unmoralistic and anti-allegorical. Out of that long and neglected stream of the English tradition comes a kind of poetry that we have named in our age Symbolism—a curious misnomer borrowed from the French; for it has no elaborate symbolism at all in the Spenserian mode.

When Saintsbury thirty-five years ago issued the first edition of his *Short History of English Literature,* he announced that his chief interest throughout would be form— at that time a revolutionary point of view. But he gave to the Elizabethan satirists only a scant paragraph: they were both "coarse" and "insincere." This view will have to be changed before we shall be able to understand the early Donne—not only Donne, but a great deal of the finest work of our own time, poets like Eliot and Yeats. The satirists of the 1590's not only read Martial, they went back through Sackville to Lyndsay and Dunbar. The medieval sense of mortality, of the vanity of the world, survives in the satirists, who use it as a weapon of critical irony upon the vaunting romanticism of the Renaissance. And we, in this age, in so far as we maintain the traditions of English verse, are still criticizing the Renaissance.

III

The poetry of our own age that we find most moving and powerful, the poetry that is tough enough to reject the easy solutions of the human predicament that arise in every age, has a longer and more honorable lineage than we are accustomed to suppose. Yet Mr. Edmund Wilson, in *Axel's Castle,* would have us believe that modern Symbolism is a method, invented by the poets, of evading the problems of modern economics: our belief in the inferiority of our own age to the past is due to the palsied irresponsibility of the Ivory Tower. But this belief is the fundamental groundwork of all poetry at all times. It is the instinctive counter-attack of the intelligence against the dogma of future perfection for persons and societies. It is in this sense, perhaps, that poetry is most profoundly the criticism of life.

It must seem to readers who have preserved, in the midst of the "historical method," a vestige of the historical sense, that social and political writers wish to exempt the world of secular policy from the criticism with which the arts are constantly threatening the latest programs of social improvement. It has always been so with the proponents of "proletarian" art; it was so with Spenser. The poets are asked to oversimplify the human predicament with morality and allegory. The first great example of proletarian—that is, allegorical—poetry in English is Spenser's *Faerie Queen:* there is no real distinction possible between an art that oversimplifies our experience in favor of princes and an art that performs that callow office for the people. There has always been a small body of men—a saving remnant very different from the Victorian notion of such a minority—headed by William Shakespeare, who warn us to make haste slowly with the best-wrought schemes for the satisfaction of our desires. Let the plans be well-wrought indeed, but let the arts teach us—if we demand a moral—that the plans are not and can never be absolutes. Poetry perhaps more than any other art tests with experience the illusions that the human predicament tempts us in our weakness to believe.

1932

EZRA POUND

and as for text we have taken it
from that of Messire Laurentius
and from a codex once of the Lords Malatesta. . . .

One is not certain who Messire Laurentius was; one is not
very certain that it makes no difference. Yet one takes comfort in the vast range of Mr. Pound's obscure learning,
which no one man could be expected to know much about.
In his great work one is continually uncertain, as to space,
time, history. The codex of the Lords Malatesta is less dis-
concerting than Laurentius; for more than half of the first
thirty cantos contain long paraphrases or garbled quotations
from the correspondence, public and private, of the Renaissance Italians, chiefly Florentine and Venetian. About a
third of the lines are versified documents. Another third
are classical allusions, esoteric quotations from the ancients,
fragments of the Greek poets with bits of the Romans
thrown in; all magnificently written into Mr. Pound's own
text. The rest is contemporary—anecdotes, satirical pictures
of vulgar Americans, obscene stories, evenings in low Medi-
terranean dives, and gossip about intrigants behind the
scenes of European powers. The three kinds of material in
the *Cantos* are antiquity, the Renaissance, and the modern
world. They are combined on no principle that seems in the
least consistent to a first glance. They appear to be mixed
in an incoherent jumble, or to stand up in puzzling con-
trasts.

This is the poetry which, in early and incomplete editions,
has had more influence on us than any other of our time; it
has had an immense "underground" reputation. And de-
servedly. For even the early reader of Mr. Pound could not
fail to detect the presence of a new poetic form in the individual cantos, though the full value and intention of this

form appears for the first time in the complete work. It is
not that there is any explicit feature of the whole design
that is not contained in each canto; it is simply that Mr.
Pound must be read in bulk; it is only then that the great
variety of his style and the apparent incoherence turn into
implicit order and form. There is no other poetry like the
Cantos in English. And there is none quite so simple in form.
The form is in fact so simple that almost no one has guessed
it, and I suppose it will continue to puzzle, perhaps to en-
rage, our more academic critics for a generation to come.
But this form by virtue of its simplicity remains inviolable
to critical terms: even now it cannot be technically described.

I begin to talk like Mr. Pound, or rather in the way in
which most readers think Mr. Pound writes. The secret of
his form is this: conversation. The *Cantos* are talk, talk,
talk; not by anyone in particular to anyone else in particular; they are just rambling talk. At least each canto is a
cunningly devised imitation of a casual conversation in
which no one presses any subject very far. The length of
breath, the span of conversational energy, is the length of
a canto. The conversationalist pauses; there is just enough
unfinished business left hanging in the air to give him a new
start; so that the transitions between the cantos are natural
and easy.

Each canto has the broken flow and the somewhat elusive
climax of a good monologue: because there is no single
speaker, it is a many-voiced monologue. That is the method
of the poems—though there is another quality of the form
that I must postpone for a moment—*and that is what the
poems are about.*

There are, as I have said, three subjects of conversation—
ancient times, Renaissance Italy, and the present—but these
are not what the *Cantos* are about. They are not about Italy,
nor about Greece, nor are they about us. They are not about
anything. But they are distinguished verse. Mr. Pound himself tells us:

> *And they want to know what we talked about?* "de litteris
> et de armis, praestantibus ingeniis,

> *Both of ancient times and our own; books, arms,*
> *And men of unusual genius*
> *Both of ancient times and our own, in short the usual*
>   *subjects*
> *Of conversation between intelligent men."*

II

There is nothing in the *Cantos* more difficult than that. There is nothing inherently obscure; nothing too profound for any reader who has enough information to get to the background of the allusions in a learned conversation. But there is something that no reader, short of some years of hard textual study, will understand. This is the very heart of the *Cantos,* the secret of Mr. Pound's poetic character, which will only gradually emerge from a detailed analysis of every passage. And this is no more than our friends are constantly demanding of us; we hear them talk, and we return to hear them talk, we return to hear them again, but we never know what they talk about; we return for the mysterious quality of charm that has no rational meaning that we can define. It is only after a long time that the order, the direction, the rhythm of the talker's mind, the logic of his character as distinguished from anything logical he may say —it is a long time before this begins to take on form for us. So with Mr. Pound's *Cantos*. It is doubtless easier for us (who are trained in the more historic brands of poetry) when the poems are about God, Freedom, and Immortality, but there is no reason why poetry should not be so perplexingly simple as Mr. Pound's, and be about nothing at all.

The ostensible subjects of the *Cantos*—ancient, middle, and modern times—are only the materials round which Mr. Pound's mind plays constantly; they are the screen upon which he throws a flowing quality of poetic thought. Now in conversation the memorable quality is a sheer accident of character, and is not designed; but in the *Cantos* the effect is deliberate, and from the first canto to the thirtieth the set tone is maintained without a lapse.

It is this tone, it is this quality quite simply which is the meaning of the *Cantos,* and although, as I have said, it is simple and direct, it is just as hard to pin down, it is as hidden in its shifting details, as a running, ever-changing conversation. It cannot be taken out of the text; and yet the special way that Mr. Pound has of weaving his three materials together, of emphasizing them, of comparing and contrasting them, gives us a clue to the leading intention of the poems. I come to that quality of the form which I postponed.

The easiest interpretation of all poetry is the allegorical: there are few poems that cannot be paraphrased into a kind of symbolism, which is usually false, being by no means the chief intention of the poet. It is very probable, therefore, that I am about to falsify the true simplicity of the *Cantos* into a simplicity that is merely convenient and spurious. The reader must bear this in mind, and view the slender symbolism that I am going to read into the *Cantos* as a critical shorthand, useful perhaps, but which, when used, must be dropped.

One of the finest *Cantos* is properly the first. It describes a voyage:

> *And then went down to the ship,*
> *Set keel to breakers, forth on the godly sea, and*
> *We set up mast and sail on that swart ship,*
> *Bore sheep aboard her, and our bodies also*
> *Heavy with weeping, and winds from sternward*
> *Bore us out onward with bellying canvas,*
> *Circe's this craft, the trim-coifed goddess.*

They land, having come "to the place aforesaid by Circe"—whatever place it may be—and Tiresias appears, who says:

>   *"Odysseus*
> *Shall return through spiteful Neptune, over dark seas,*
> *Lose all companions." And then Anticlea came.*
> *Lie quiet Divus. I mean, that is, Andreas Divus,*
> *In officina Wecheli, 1538, out of Homer.*
> *And he sailed, by Sirens and thence outward and away*
> *And unto Circe.*

Mr. Pound's world is the scene of a great Odyssey, and everywhere he lands it is the shore of Circe, where men "lose all companions" and are turned into swine. It would not do at all to push this hint too far, but I will risk one further point: Mr. Pound is a typically modern, rootless, and internationalized intelligence. In the place of the traditional supernaturalism of the older and local cultures, he has a cosmopolitan curiosity that seeks out marvels, which are all equally marvelous, whether it be a Greek myth or the antics in Europe of a lady from Kansas. He has the bright, cosmopolitan *savoir faire* which refuses to be "taken in": he will not believe, being a traditionalist at bottom, that the "perverts, who have set money-lust before the pleasures of the senses," are better than swine. And ironically, being modern and a hater of modernity, he sees all history as deformed by the trim-coifed goddess.

The *Cantos* are a book of marvels—marvels that he has read about, or heard of, or seen; there are Greek myths, tales of Italian feuds, meetings with strange people, rumors of intrigues of state, memories of remarkable dead friends like T. E. Hulme, comments on philosophical problems, harangues on abuses of the age; the "usual subjects of conversation between intelligent men."

It is all fragmentary. Now nearly every canto begins with a bit of heroic antiquity, some myth, or classical quotation, or a lovely piece of lyrical description in a grand style. It invariably breaks down. It trails off into a piece of contemporary satire, or a flat narrative of the rascality of some Italian prince. This is the special quality of Mr. Pound's form, the essence of his talk, the direction of these magnificent conversations.

For not once does Mr. Pound give himself up to any single story or myth. The thin symbolism from the Circe myth is hardly more than a leading tone, an unconscious prejudice about men which he is not willing to indicate beyond the barest outline. He cannot believe in myths, much less in his own power of imagining them out to a conclusion. None of his myths is compelling enough to draw out his total intellectual resources; none goes far enough to become a belief or even a momentary fiction. They remain marvels to be looked at, but they are meaningless, the wrecks of civilization. His powerful juxtapositions of the ancient, the Renaissance, and the modern worlds reduce all three elements to an unhistorical miscellany, timeless and without origin, and no longer a force in the lives of men.

III

And that is the peculiarly modern quality of Mr. Pound. There is a certain likeness in this to another book of marvels, stories of antiquity known to us as *The Golden Ass*. The *Cantos* are a sort of *Golden Ass*. There is a likeness, but there is no parallel beyond the mere historical one: both books are the productions of worlds without convictions and given over to a hard pragmatism. Here the similarity ends. For Mr. Pound is a powerful reactionary, a faithful mind devoted to those ages when the myths were not merely pretty, but true. And there is a cloud of melancholy irony hanging over the *Cantos*. He is persuaded that the myths are only beautiful, and he drops them after a glimpse, but he is not reconciled to this aestheticism: he ironically puts the myths against the ugly specimens of modern life that have defeated them. But neither are the specimens of modernity worthy of the dignity of belief:

> She held that a sonnet was a sonnet
> And ought never to be destroyed
> And had taken a number of courses
> And continued with hope of degrees and
> Ended in a Baptist learnery
>   Somewhere near the Rio Grande.

I am not certain that Mr. Pound will agree with me that he is a traditionalist; nor am I convinced that Mr. Pound, for his part, is certain of anything but his genius for poetry. He is probably one of two or three living Americans who will be remembered as poets of the first order. Yet there is no reason to infer from that that Mr. Pound, outside his craft (or outside his written conversation) knows in the least what he is doing or saying. He is and always has been in a muddle of revolution; and for some appalling reason he identifies his crusade with liberty—liberty of speech, liberty of press, liberty of conduct—in short, liberty. I do not mean to say that either Mr. Pound or his critic knows what liberty is. Nevertheless, Mr. Pound identifies it with civilization and intelligence of the modern and scientific variety. And yet the ancient cultures, which he so much admires, were, from any modern viewpoint, hatched in barbarism and superstition. One is entitled to the suspicion that Mr. Pound prefers barbarism, and that by taking up the role of revolution against it he has bitten off his nose to spite his face. He is the confirmed enemy of provincialism, never suspecting that his favorite, Lorenzo the Magnificent, for example, was provincial to the roots of his hair.

The confusion runs through the *Cantos*. It makes the irony that I have spoken of partly unconscious. For as the apostle of humane culture, he constantly discredits it by crying up a rationalistic enlightenment. It would appear from this that his philosophical tact is somewhat feminine, and that, as intelligence, it does not exist. His poetic intelligence is of the finest: and if he doesn't know what liberty is, he understands poetry, and how to write it. This is enough for one man to know. And the first thirty *Cantos* are enough to occupy a loving and ceaseless study—say a canto a year for thirty years, all thirty to be read every few weeks just for the tone.

1931

EZRA POUND AND THE BOLLINGEN PRIZE

What I shall say here is not in further commentary on Mr. William Barrett's article in the April 1949 issue of *Partisan Review;* nor is it the "rational, impersonal, and calm justification" of the award of the Bollingen Prize to Ezra Pound which Mr. Barrett was kind enough to expect from me. I intend rather to set down my own reasons for voting for *The Pisan Cantos.* I shall have in mind the *Partisan* symposium on the award without, I hope, being influenced by it in reconstructing my views of last November.[1]

From the time I first read Pound's verse more than thirty years ago I have considered him a mixed poet. In an essay written in 1931,[2] on the first thirty Cantos, I expressed views which the later accretions to the work have not changed: the work to which I helped to give the Bollingen Prize is formless, eccentric, and personal. The Cantos are now, as I said then, "about nothing at all." They have a voice but no subject. As one of the commentators on Mr. Barrett's article put it, they have no beginning, middle, or end. I used similar language in 1931. It is a striking fact that in talking about this work one must say "Canto XX of the *Cantos";* there is always a Canto of Cantos, not a Canto of a substantive work with a title like Canto XX of the *Purgatorio* of the *Divina Commedia.*

Mr. Pound is incapable of sustained thought in either prose or verse. His acute verbal sensibility is thus at the mercy of random flights of "angelic insight," Icarian self-indulgences of prejudice which are not checked by a total view to which they could be subordinated. Thus his anti-Semitism—which, as Mr. Auden has said, all Gentiles have felt (I have felt it, and felt humiliated by it)—his anti-Semitism is not disciplined by an awareness of its sinister
264

implications in the real world of men. Neither Mr. Pound nor any other man is to be censured for his private feelings; but every man must answer for what he does with his feelings. It has been often observed that Pound fails to get into his verse any sort of full concrete reality. In so far as the *Cantos* have a subject it is made up of historical materials. But if there is any poetry of our age which may be said to be totally lacking in the historical sense, the sense of how ideas move in history, it is Pound's *Cantos*. His verse is an anomaly in an age of acute historical awareness.

I do not know what reasons, motives, or prejudices prompted the other affirmative votes. There has been some public conjecture upon this subject, but I consider it a gross impropriety. I shall do well if I am able to speak honestly for myself. I have little sympathy with the view that holds that Pound's irresponsible opinions merely lie alongside the poetry, which thus remains uncontaminated. The disagreeable opinions are right in the middle of the poetry. And they have got to be seen for what they are: they are personal, wilful, and unrelated; and they are not brought together under a mature conception of life as it is now or ever was. I infer the absence of such a mature view in the man from the incoherence of the form; but it is only the latter that concerns me. Apart from specific objections to his anti-Semitism and fascism, there is a formal principle which, if severely applied, would have been a good enough reason for voting against *The Pisan Cantos*. Not only the anti-Semitism but all the other "insights" remain unassimilated to a coherent form. The assumption of many persons, that a vote for *The Pisan Cantos* was a vote for "formalism" and a vote against "vitality" in poetry, makes no sense at all to me.

There is nothing mysterious about coherent form. It is the presence of an order in a literary work which permits us to understand one part in relation to all the other parts. What should concern us in looking *at* the *Cantos* is the formal irresponsibility; in looking *beyond* the work, the possible effects of this irresponsibility upon society. (If Pound's *Cantos* expressed *anti*-fascist opinions, my formal objections would be the same; but I should think that the formlessness would make him a good Communist party-line poet.) But just as Pound's broadcasts over Radio Rome never influenced anybody in this country, and were chiefly an indignity perpetrated upon himself, I cannot suppose that the anti-Semitism of the *Cantos* will be taken seriously by anybody but liberal intellectuals. Anti-Semites will not "use" it. It is too innocent. I take it seriously in the sense of disliking it, and I cannot "honor the man" for it, as the Fellows of the Library were charged with doing; but I cannot think that it will strengthen anti-Semitism.

I respect differences of opinion on this question, about which I am not well-informed. What I have already said is enough to indicate that my vote for *The Pisan Cantos* was not an easy step to take: I could have voted against it. But this is not all. I had, as many men of my generation might have had, personal reasons for not voting for Mr. Pound. In so far as he has noticed my writings at all, in conversation and correspondence—which the international literary grapevine always reports—he has noticed them with contempt.

Nevertheless I voted for him, for the following reason: the health of literature depends upon the health of society, and conversely; there must be constant vigilance for both ends of the process. The specific task of the man of letters is to attend to the health of society *not at large* but through literature—that is, he must be constantly aware of the condition of language in his age. As a result of observing Pound's use of language in the past thirty years I had become convinced that he had done more than any other man to regenerate the language, if not the imaginative forms, of English verse. I had to face the disagreeable fact that he had done this even in passages of verse in which the opinions expressed ranged from the childish to the detestable.

In literature as in life nothing reaches us pure. The task of the civilized intelligence is one of perpetual salvage. We cannot decide that our daily experience must be either aesthetic or practical—art or life; it is never, as it comes to us, either/or; it is always both/and. But as persons of a particular *ethos*, of a certain habit and character, we discharge

our responsibilities to society from the point of view of the
labors in which we are placed. We are placed in the profession of letters. We cannot expect the businessman and the
politician, the men who run the state, to know that our particular responsibility exists; we cannot ask them to understand the more difficult fact that our responsibility to them
is for the language which they themselves use for the general welfare. They are scarcely aware of language at all;
what one is not aware of one almost inevitably abuses. But
the medium cannot be extricated from the material, the
how from the what: part of our responsibility is to correct
the monism of the statesman who imagines that what he
says is scarcely said in language at all, that it exists apart
from the medium in a "purity" of action which he thinks of
as "practicality." If men of letters do not look after the
medium, nobody else will. We need never fear that the practical man will fail to ignore our concern for the health of
language: this he has already done by indicting Pound as if
Pound, like himself, were a monist of action. Pound's language remains our particular concern. If he were a convicted
traitor, I should still think that, in another direction which
complicates the problem ultimately beyond our comprehension, he had performed an indispensable duty to society.

1949

JOHN PEALE BISHOP

Of the American poets whose first books were published between 1918 and 1929, not more than six or seven are likely to keep their reputations until the end of the present decade. Eliot and Pound are pre-war. Crane, Marianne Moore, Stevens, MacLeish, and Ransom are among the slightly more than half a dozen. The two or three other places may be disputed; but I take it that since 1929 there has been no new name unless it be that of a young man, James Agee, whose first volume appeared in 1934. John Peale Bishop, whose first poetry goes back to the war period, but whose first book, *Now with His Love*,[1] came out in 1932, will, I believe, rank among the best poets of the last decade.

His position has been anomalous. His contemporaries made their reputations in a congenial critical atmosphere, and they have been able to carry over a certain prestige into virtually a new age. (Ages crowd upon one another in a country that has never been young.) But Bishop has lacked that advantage. The first criticism accorded him was largely of the Marxist school. Mr. Horace Gregory, shrewdly discerning the poet's technical skill, became quickly concerned about the sincerity of a man who ignored the "class struggle." Bishop was not, in fact, asked whether he was a poet but whether he expected to survive capitalism: whether, given his roots in the war-generation and the prejudices of the "ruling class," he could hope to achieve the portage over to the "main stream" of American letters recently discovered by Mr. Granville Hicks.

The problems of poetry must necessarily be the same in all ages, but no two ages come to the same solutions. Happiest is that age which, like the age of Sidney and Spenser, felt no need to reduce the problems to ultimate philosophical terms: our critical apparatus is immeasurably more thorough than theirs, our poetic performance appreciably looser. But our problems are inevitably theirs. They are the problem of language and the problem of form. The Elizabethan solution was practical, not speculative. The simple didacticism of the neo-classical Renaissance was as far as the sixteenth century got philosophically. The poets wrote better than they knew. Our knowledge is better than our performance.

In ages weak in form, such as our own age, theory will concentrate upon form, but practice upon the ultimate possibilities of language. Ages that create great varieties of forms, as the Elizabethans did in every branch of poetry, talk about language but actually take it for granted, and score their greatest triumphs with form. The powers of the language were not in the long run determined by theory, but instinctively by poets whose dominating passion was form: the language was determined by the demands of the subject. The more comprehensive the subject, the broader the symbolism, and the more profoundly relevant the scheme of reference to the whole human experience, the richer the language became. The experiment with language as such is *The Shepherd's Calendar,* and it is a failure; but even there the poet attempts only to enlarge his vocabulary with archaic words for "poetical" effect. There is no trace of that forcing of language beyond its natural limits that we find in modern verse. Propriety of diction was the problem, and it was ably discussed by Puttenham in his long *Arte of English Poesie,* a work in some respects comparable to *The Principles of Literary Criticism* by Mr. I. A. Richards, who talks not about the propriety of language but about its ultimate meaning. He thus leaves behind him language as an instrument and, by going into the *kinds* of meaning, converts the discussion into the peculiarly modern problem of form. For form is meaning and nothing but meaning: scheme of reference, supporting symbolism that ceases to support as soon as it is recognized as merely that.

Metrics as a phase of the problem of form needs attention from modern critics. It is a subject poorly understood. It is usually treated as an air-tight compartment of technical speculation. Yet surely a metrical pattern is usable only so long as it is attached to some usable form. It is a curious fact that modern metrics reflects the uncertainty of modern poets in the realm of forms. So the modern poet, struggling to get hold of some kind of meaning, breaks his head against the *impasse* of form, and when he finds no usable form he finds that he has available no metrical system either. For those fixed and, to us, external properties of poetry, rhyme and metrical pattern, are, in the ages of their invention, indeed fixed but not external. It is probable that there is an intimate relation between a generally accepted "picture of the world" and the general acceptance of a metrical system and its differentiations into patterns.

This is to say that the separate arts achieve their special formalisms out of a common center of experience. And from this center of experience, this reference of meaning, any single art will make differentiations within itself: epic, lyric, tragedy, comedy, each with its appropriate pattern of development. When the center of life disappears, the arts of poetry become the art of poetry. And in an advanced stage of the evil, in the nineteenth century and today, we get the *mélange des genres,* one art living off another, which the late Irving Babbitt so valiantly combated without having understood the influences that had brought it about. Painting tries to be music; poetry leans upon painting; all the arts "strive toward the condition of music"; till at last seeing the mathematical structure of music, the arts become geometrical and abstract, and destroy themselves.

The specialization of scientific techniques supplanting a central view of life has, as Mr. John Crowe Ransom showed in a recent essay,[2] tended to destroy the formal arts: poetry has in turn become a specialization of aesthetic effects without formal limitations. And, as Mr. Edmund Wilson has argued,[3] the novel now does the work formerly done by epic and tragedy, forms too "limited" and "artificial" for modern minds. The novel is the least formal of the literary arts; it rose, in fact, upon the debris of the *genres;* and it has been able to drive the formal literary arts from the public interest because, appealing to the ordinary sense of reality fostered by information, science, and journalism, the novelist neither sets forth symbolic fictions nor asks the reader to observe formal limitations.

The poet then at this time must ask, not what limitations he will be pleased, after the manner of the young Milton, to accept, but whether there are any that he can get. I assume that a poet is a man eager to come under the bondage of limitations if he can find them. As I understand John Peale Bishop's poetry, he is that eager man. It is a moral problem, but that phase I cannot touch here. Bishop has no settled metrics; but that too is an aspect of the formal problem that cannot be discussed in the limited space of a note.

It has been said that Bishop has imitated all the chief modern poets. He has virtually conducted his poetical education in public. But the observation is double-edged. In our age of personal expression the poet gets credit for what is "his own": the art is not the thing, but rather the information conveyed about a unique personality. Applauding a poet only for what is uniquely his own, we lose thereby much that is good. If a poem in Yeats' manner appears in Bishop's book—and is as good as Yeats'—it is as good there as it is anywhere else.

More than most living poets Bishop has felt the lack of a central source of form. He is not the poet of personal moods and idle sensation. He constantly strives for formal structure. He has studied closely the poets of his time who, like Yeats, seem to have achieved, out of a revived or invented mythology or by means of a consciously restricted point of view, a working substitute for the supernatural myth and the concentration that myth makes possible. It is, I think, interesting to observe that in Bishop two contemporary influences, Yeats and Eliot, meet strongly, and meet only in him of all the contemporary poets whom I know anything about: Yeats for form, Eliot for the experiment in language. Only the best Yeats is better than this:

> *And Mooch of the bull-red*
> *Hair who had so many dears*
> *Enjoyed to the core*
> *And Newlin who hadn't one*

> *To answer his shy desire*
> *Are blanketed in the mould*
> *Dead in the long war.*
> *And I who have most reason*
> *Remember them only when the sun*
> *Is at his dullest season.*

It is not necessary to illustrate the early influence of Eliot, for it appears everywhere in *Now with His Love*. I will quote two poems that are harder to "place." To critics interested in poetry as private property it may be said that they are evidently his own. The poems—they must be read as carefully climaxed wholes—seem to me to be among the most successful in modern verse:

THE RETURN

Night and we heard heavy and cadenced hoofbeats
Of troops departing: the last cohorts left
By the North Gate. That night some listened late
Leaning their eyelids toward Septentrion.

Morning flared and the young tore down the trophies
And warring ornaments: arches were strong
And in the sun but stone; no longer conquests
Circled our columns; all our state was down

In fragments. In the dust, old men with tufted
Eyebrows whiter than sunbaked faces, gulped
As it fell. But they no more than we remembered
The old sea-fights, the soldiers' names and sculptors'

We did not know the end was coming: nor why
It came; only that long before the end
Were many wanted to die. Then vultures starved
And sailed more slowly in the sky.

We still had taxes. Salt was high. The soldiers
Gone. Now there was much drinking and lewd
Houses all night loud with riot. But only
For a time. Soon the taverns had no roofs.

Strangely it was the young the almost boys
Who first abandoned hope; the old still lived
A little, at last a little lived in eyes.
It was the young whose child did not survive.

Some slept beneath the simulacra, until
The gods' faces froze. Then was fear.
Some had response in dreams, but morning restored
Interrogation. Then O then, O ruins!

Temples of Neptune invaded by the sea
And dolphins streaked like streams sportive
As sunlight rode and over the rushing floors
The sea unfurled and what was blue raced silver.

The poem avoids the difficulty of form by leaning upon a certain violence of language. The form of "The Return" is a very general idea about the fall of Rome. The implications of the form are not wide; and it is a typical modern form in that it offers a rough parallelism with the real subject—which in this poem is modern civilization—and not a direct approach to the subject. Where shall the poet get a form that will permit him to make direct, comprehensive statements about modern civilization? Doubtless nowhere. As a feat of historical insight the "form" of "The Return" is commonplace; yet the poem is distinguished. The poet has manipulated language into painting. The line "Temples of Neptune invaded by the sea" is by no means the same as its prose paraphrase: civilizations die of an excess of the quality that made them great; we, too, shall perish when we no longer have the temple of Neptune, the form, to preserve us from the limitless energy of the sea, which the form held in check. But "Rome" is here not a symbol of anything; our inferences about modern civilization are obvious, but they are not authorized by the poem. "The poem," writes Bishop, "is a simile in which one term of the comparison is omitted." It is rather that by means of a new grasp of language, very different from the "word-painting" of eighteenth-century nature poetry, the poet achieves a plastic objectivity that to some degree liberates him from the problem of finding a structural background of idea.

What I have said about "The Return" applies with even greater force to "Perspectives Are Precipices":

> Sister Anne, Sister Anne,
> Do you see anybody coming?
>
> > *I see a distance of black yews*
> > *Long as the history of the Jews*
> >
> > *I see a road sunned with white sand*
> > *Wide plains surrounding silence. And*
> >
> > *Far off, a broken colonnade*
> > *That overthrows the sun in shade.*
>
> Sister Anne, Sister Anne,
> Do you see nobody coming?
>
> > *A man*
> > *Upon that road a man who goes*
> > *Dragging a shadow by its toes.*
> >
> > *Diminishing he goes, head bare*
> > *Of any covering even hair.*
> >
> > *A pitcher depending from one hand*
> > *Goes mouth down. And dry is sand*
>
> Sister Anne, Sister Anne,
> What do you see?
>
> > *His dwindling stride. And he seems blind*
> > *Or worse to the prone man behind.*
>
> Sister Anne! Sister Anne!
>
> > *I see a road. Beyond nowhere*
> > *Defined by cirrus and blue air.*
> >
> > *I saw a man but he is gone*
> > *His shadow gone into the sun.*

This poem I would cite as the perfect example of certain effects of painting achieved in poetry. Criticism of this kind of poetry must necessarily be tentative. Yet I think it is plain that this particular poem has not only the immediate effect of a modern abstract painting; it gives the illusion of perspective, of objects-in-the-round. Take the "road sunned with white sand"—instead of "sunlight on a sandy road," the normal word-structure for this image. Even more striking is "Wide plains surrounding silence." I leave it to the schoolmen, wherever they are, to decide whether "silence" is commonly abstract or concrete; yet it is certain that in Bishop's phrase it acquires a spatial, indeed almost sensory, value that would have been sacrificed had he written: "silence over the surrounding plains."

It is worth remarking here that the line "Long as the history of the Jews" is the only clear example of "metaphysical wit" that I have been able to find in Bishop's verse. It is possibly a direct adaptation of a passage from Marvell:

> *And you should if you please refuse*
> *Till the conversion of the Jews.*

Bishop's line is the more striking for its isolation in his work, but I think it is clearly a violation of the plastic technique of the poem, and a minor blemish. The influence of Eliot, which could lead two ways, to the metaphysicals and to the Symbolists, led Bishop almost exclusively to the latter. And he has perfected this kind of poetry in English perhaps more than any other writer.

It is an obscure subject: the Horatian formula *ut pictura poesis* bore fruit long before Hérédia and Gautier—as early, in English verse, as Milton. But the mixtures of the *genres* acquired a new significance after the late nineteenth-century French poets began to push the borders of one sense over into another. It was not merely that the poet should be allowed to paint pictures with words—that much the Horatian phrase allowed. It was rather that the new "correspondences" among the five senses multiplied the senses and extended the medium of one art into the medium of another. Rimbaud's absurd sonnet on the colors of the vowels was the extreme statement of an experiment that achieved, in other poets and in Rimbaud's own "Bateau Ivre," brilliant results. But the process cannot go on beyond our generation unless we are willing to accept the eventual destruction of the arts. There is no satisfactory substitute in poetry for the form-symbol.

It is on this dilemma of symbolic form or plastic form that Bishop is intelligent and instructive. He has recently written: "I am trying to make more and more *statements,* without giving up all that we have gained since Rimbaud." The difficulty could not be more neatly put. Two recent poems, "The Saints" and "Holy Nativity," are the result of this effort. The statement is form, the fixed point of reference; "all that we have gained since Rimbaud" is the enrichment of language that we have gained to offset our weakness in form.

The new experiment of Bishop's is not complete. In "Holy Nativity" the attempt to use the Christian myth collapses with a final glance at anthropology:

> *Eagle, swan or dove*
> *White bull or cloud . . .*

His treatment of the supernatural, the attempt to replace our secular philosophy, in which he does not believe, with a vision of the divine, in which he tries to believe, is an instance of our modern unbelieving belief. We are so constituted as to see our experience in two ways. We are not so constituted as to see it two ways indefinitely without peril. Until we can see it in one way we shall not see it as a whole, and until we see it as a whole we shall not see it as poets. Every road is long, and all roads lead to the problem of form.

1935

EDWIN ARLINGTON ROBINSON

Edwin Arlington Robinson, most famous of living American poets, was born at Head Tide, Maine, on December 22, 1869.[1] He attended Harvard from 1891 to 1893, but left college without taking a degree. In 1896 he printed privately his first book of verse, *The Torrent and the Night Before,* which was followed a year later by *The Children of the Night,* a volume little noticed at the time, but one which marks the beginning of a new era in American poetry. In the next fourteen years he published two more books, *Captain Craig* (1902) and *The Town Down the River* (1910). But it was not until 1916 that he attracted wide attention and won a notable fame. For with *The Man Against the Sky* Mr. Robinson stepped quickly into the front rank of American poetry. In his early years he wrote some of the finest lyrics of modern times: these are likely to be his permanent claim to fame.

Able critics have thought otherwise. Not only, they say, are Mr. Robinson's long narrative poems his best work; they are the perfect realization of a "tragic vision." But hear Mr. Mark Van Doren, a distinguished critic whom I do not like to disagree with:

His vision is essentially tragic in that it stresses the degeneration of ideas, the dimming of the light, when these become implicated in the rough action of the world. (Edwin Arlington Robinson [*New York, 1927*], p. 34.)

Passion has its victories no less than reason. The tragic picture would be incomplete without either of these. It is because Mr. Robinson's picture is fairly complete that he deserves the rare title of major American poet. (Ibid., p. 90.)

I should be the last person, I hope, to dispute Mr. Robinson's right to that title. Nor should I contend for a moment that Mr. Robinson lacks the "tragic vision," but I am convinced that Mr. Van Doren's qualifying word, *essentially,* is accurate. For Mr. Robinson writes, I believe, less from the tragic vision than from the tragic sentiment; and the result is the pathetic tale of obscure ambition or thwarted passion; not tragedy.

It is true that he deals with the degeneration of ideas. The question that Mr. Van Doren does not ask, it seems to me, is this: What is the exact significance of the ideas? Is their ultimate reference to a religious or philosophical background, a realm of ideas possessing at least for their time and place the compulsion of absolute truth? Or are they the private ideas of modern persons, the personal forms of some egoistic thrust of the will? In other words, is Mr. Robinson a true tragic poet, or is he a modern poet like other modern poets, whose distinguished gifts are not enough to give him more than the romantic ego with which to work?

Talifer[2] is a psychological narrative of the order of *The Man Against the Sky.* It is the eighth or ninth specimen of this kind of poem that Mr. Robinson has given us. Because the type has grown thinner with each example, the new narrative being, I believe, the least satisfactory of them all, it is the occasion of some inquiry into the causes of Mr. Robinson's preference for this particular form. It is a form that includes the three Arthurian poems, *Merlin, Lancelot,* and *Tristram,* psychological stories that are in all respects similar to the New England tales of Nightingale, Cavender, Bartholow. All is the same but time and place; for the characters are the same.

In *Talifer* there are four characters, two men and two women. The woman Althea—the name is a dry piece of irony —is in love with Talifer; she is woman domestic, sensitive, but commonplace and child-bearing. Talifer himself is an ordinary person, but he talks of his "tradition," carries himself well, and expects of life more than his inner quality entitles him to: so he imagines that he is in love with the other woman, Karen, who is beautiful, treacherous, cold, and erudite, dividing her time between inscrutable moods and incredible reading in the ancients. But she is vaguely conceived by the poet, and the motivation of the hero's action remains obscure.

Talifer has been fatuous enough to say that with Karen

he expects to find Peace. Life becomes, after a year or two
with her, intolerable. Then, one day in his ancestral forest,
he meets Althea, who still loves him, and he decides to leave
Karen. Now all this time, the other man, Doctor Quick, could
have been in love with either of the women; he is too skeptical to push his desires; and his place in the story is that of
commentator. He explains the confusion to the other characters, and affords to the poet a device by which the real actors
become articulate. The story ends with the reappearance,
after a couple of years, of Quick: in the meantime Talifer
has married Althea, who has by him a child. Although Quick
himself has tried to participate in life by taking Karen off
to a "cottage in Wales," his return witnesses his failure. But
he is not much affected by it. He proceeds to analyze for
Althea and Talifer the true basis of their love, which is
thoroughly commonplace after a good deal of romantic pre-
tense.

Mr. Robinson's style in the new poem is uniform with the
style of its predecessors; it is neither better nor worse than the
style of *The Glory of the Nightingales* or of *Cavender's
House*. It requires constant reviewing by Mr. Robinson's admirers to keep these poems distinct; at a distance they lose
outline; blur into one another. They constitute a single complete poem that the poet has not succeeded in writing, a
poem around which these indistinct narratives have been written.

We get, in them all, a character doomed to defeat, or a
character who, when the tale opens, is a failure in the eyes
of his town, but who wins a secret moral victory, as in *The
Man Who Died Twice*. But Talifer, whose ego betrays him
into an emotional life that he cannot understand, is not quite
defeated. The tragic solution of his problem being thus rejected by Mr. Robinson, and replaced by a somewhat awkward
bit of domestic irony, Talifer at first sight appears to be a
new kind of Robinsonian character. Yet the novelty, I think,
lies in the appearance. For Talifer is the standard Robinsonian character grown weary of the tragic sentiment, accepting
at last the fact that his tilt at fate had less intensity than he
supposed, and

> *with grateful ears*
> *That were attuned again to pleasant music*
> *Heard nothing but the mellow bells of peace.*

That is the Tennysonian end of the poem.

I have remarked that the character of Karen is vaguely conceived, with the result that Talifer's relation to her is incomprehensible. Those mellow bells of peace are therefore a little hollow in sound, for their ring is as inexplicable as the noisy chaos of the erudite Karen, upon whose prior significance they entirely depend. The plot, in brief, lacks internal necessity. And the domestic peace of the conclusion remains arbitrary, in spite of Mr. Robinson's efforts through his mouthpiece, Doctor Quick, to point it up with some sly irony at the end. The irony is external—as if Mr. Robinson had not been able to tell the story for what it was, and had to say: This is what life is really like, a simple wife and a child—while ring those bells of peace that would be romantically tiresome if one had tragic dignity.

Mr. Robinson's genius is primarily lyrical; that is to say, he seldom achieves a success in a poem where the idea exceeds the span of a single emotion. It is, I think, significant that in his magnificent "The Mill" the tragic reference sustains the emotion of the poem: his narrative verse yields but a few moments of drama that are swiftly dispersed by the dry casuistry of the commentary. The early "Richard Cory" is a perfect specimen of Mr. Robinson's dramatic powers—when those powers are lyrically expressed; similarly "Luke Havergal," a poem in which the hard images glow in a fierce intensity of light, is one of the great recent lyrics:

> *No, there is not a dawn in eastern skies*
> *To rift the fiery night that's in your eyes;*
> *But there, where western glooms are gathering*
> *The dark will end the dark, if anything . . .*

Mr. Van Doren is the first critic to appreciate this peculiarly Robinsonian legerdemain with figures of light.

It is probable that the explanation of the popular success of *Tristram*, and of most of Mr. Robinson's narratives, lies in our loss of the dramatic instinct. It is a loss increasingly great since the rise of middle-class comedy in the eighteenth century. Since then, in the serious play, instead of the tragic hero whose downfall is deeply involved with his suprahuman relations, we get the romantic, sentimental hero whose problem is chiefly one of adjustment to society, on the one hand, and, on the other, one of futile self-assertion in the realm of the personal ego. Mr. Robinson's Talifer exhibits both these phases of the modern sensibility: he plays with his ego in the irrational marriage with Karen, and he later sees his difficulty strictly in terms of a social institution, or of social adjustment, in the marriage with Althea, who, of course, represents "truth."

The dramatic treatment of the situation Mr. Robinson permits himself to neglect; for the dramatic approach would have demanded the possession, by the hero, of a comprehensive moral scheme. He would have rigorously applied the scheme to his total conduct, with the result that it would have broken somewhere and thrown the hero into a tragic dilemma, from which it had been impossible for him to escape. The story as it is told is hardly more than anecdotal; Mr. Robinson turns his plot, at the end, into an easy joke about the deliquescent effects of marriage upon the pretensions of human nature.

It is one of the anomalies of contemporary literature that Mr. Robinson, who has given us a score of great lyrics, should continue to produce these long narrative poems, one after another, until the reader can scarcely tell them apart. We may only guess the reason for this. Our age provides for the poet no epos or myth, no pattern of well-understood behavior, which the poet may examine in the strong light of his own experience. For it is chiefly those times that prefer one kind of conduct to another, times that offer to the poet a seasoned code, which have produced the greatest dramatic literature. Drama depends for clarity and form upon the existence of such a code. It matters little whether it is a code for the realization of good, like Antigone's; or a code for evil like Macbeth's. The important thing is that it shall tell the poet how people try to behave, and that it shall be too perfect, whether in good or in evil, for human nature. The poet seizes one set of terms within the code—for example, feudal ambition in Macbeth—and shows that the hero's faulty application of the perfect code to his own conduct is doomed to failure. By adhering strictly to the code, the poet exhibits a typical action. The tension between the code and the hero makes the action specific, unique; the code is at once broken up and affirmed, the hero's resistance at once clarified and defined by the limits thus set to his conduct. Macbeth asserts his ego in terms of the code before him, not in terms of courtly love or of the idealism of the age of Werther: he has no choice of code. The modern character has the liberty of indefinite choice, but not the good fortune to be chosen, as Macbeth and Antigone were.

Mr. Robinson has no epos, myth, or code, no suprahuman truth, to tell him what the terminal points of human conduct are, in this age; so he goes over the same ground, again and again, writing a poem that will not be written.

It has been said by T. S. Eliot that the best lyric poetry of our time is dramatic, that it is good because it is dramatic. It is at least a tenable notion that the dramatic instinct, after the Restoration and down to our own time, survived best in the lyric poets. With the disappearance of general patterns of conduct, the power to depict action that is both single and complete also disappears. The dramatic genius of the poet is held to short flights, and the dramatic lyric is a fragment of a total action which the poet lacks the means to sustain.

It is to be hoped that Mr. Robinson will again exercise his dramatic genius where it has a chance for success: in lyrics. Meanwhile it would be no less disastrous to Mr. Robinson's later fame than to our critical standards, should we admire him too abjectly to examine him. Let him then escape the indignity of Hardy's later years when such a piece of bad verse as "Any Little Old Song" won egregious applause all over the British Isles. That Mr. Robinson is unable to write badly will not excuse us to posterity.

1933

HART CRANE

The career of Hart Crane will be written by future critics as a chapter in the neo-Symbolist movement. An historical view of his poetry at this time would be misleading and incomplete. Like most poets of his age in America, Crane discovered Rimbaud through Eliot and the Imagists; it is certain that long before he had done any of his best work he had come to believe himself the spiritual heir of the French poet. He had an instinctive mastery of the fused metaphor of Symbolism, but it is not likely that he ever knew more of the Symbolist poets than he had got out of Pound's *Pavannes and Divisions*. Whether Crane's style is symbolistic, or should, in many instances, like the first six or seven stanzas of "The River," be called Elizabethan, is a question that need not concern us now.

Between "The Bridge" and "Une Saison d'Enfer" there is little essential affinity. Rimbaud achieved "disorder" out of implicit order, after a deliberate cultivation of "derangement," but in our age the disintegration of our intellectual systems is accomplished. With Crane the disorder is original and fundamental. That is the special quality of his mind that belongs peculiarly to our own time. His aesthetic problem, however, was more general; it was the historic problem of Romanticism.

Harold Hart Crane, one of the great masters of the Romantic movement, was born in Garrettsville, Ohio, on July 21, 1899. His birthplace is a small town near Cleveland, in the old Western Reserve, a region which, as distinguished from the lower portions of the state, where people from the Southern up-country settled, was populated largely by New England stock. He seems to have known little of his ancestry, but he frequently said that his maternal forbears had given Hartford, Connecticut, its name, and that they went "back to Stratford-on-Avon"—a fiction surely, but one that gave him distinct pleasure. His formal education was slight. After the third year at high school, when he was fifteen, it ended, and he worked in his father's candy factory in Cleveland, where the family had removed in his childhood. He repeatedly told me that money had been set aside for his education at college, but that it had been used for other purposes. With the instinct of genius he read the great poets, but he never acquired an objective mastery of any literature, or even of the history of his country—a defect of considerable interest in a poet whose most ambitious work is an American epic.

In any ordinary sense Crane was not an educated man; in many respects he was an ignorant man. There is already a Crane legend, like the Poe legend—it should be fostered because it will help to make his poetry generally known—and the scholars will decide it was a pity that so great a talent lacked early advantages. It is probable that he was incapable of the formal discipline of a classical education, and probable, too, that the eclectic education of his time would have scattered and killed his talent. His poetry not only has defects of the surface, it has a defect of vision; but its great and peculiar value cannot be separated from its limitations. Its qualities are bound up with a special focus of the intellect and sensibility, and it would be folly to wish that his mind had been better trained or differently organized.

The story of his suicide is well known. The information that I have seems authentic, but it is incomplete and subject to excessive interpretation. Toward the end of April, 1932, he embarked on the S.S. *Orizaba* bound from Vera Cruz to New York. On the night of April 26 he got into a brawl with some sailors; he was severely beaten and robbed. At noon the next day, the ship being in the Caribbean a few hours out of Havana, he rushed from his stateroom clad in pajamas and overcoat, walked through the smoking-room out onto the deck, and then the length of the ship to the stern. There without hesitation he made a perfect dive into the sea. It is said that a life-preserver was thrown to him; he either did not see it or did not want it. By the time the ship had turned back he had disappeared. Whether he forced himself down

—for a moment he was seen swimming—or was seized by a shark, as the captain believed, cannot be known. After a search of thirty-five minutes his body was not found, and the *Orizaba* put back into her course.

In the summer of 1930 he had written to me that he feared his most ambitious work, *The Bridge*, was not quite perfectly "realized," that probably his soundest work was in the shorter pieces of *White Buildings*, but that his mind, being once committed to the larger undertaking, could never return to the lyrical and more limited form. He had an extraordinary insight into the foundations of his work, and I think this judgment of it will not be refuted.

From 1922 to 1928—after that year I saw him and heard from him irregularly until his death—I could observe the development of his style from poem to poem; and his letters —written always in a pure and lucid prose—provide a valuable commentary on his career. This is not the place to bring all this material together for judgment. As I look back upon his work and its relation to the life he lived, a general statement about it comes to my mind that may throw some light on the dissatisfaction that he felt with his career. It will be a judgment upon the life and works of a man whom I knew affectionately for ten years as a friend.

Suicide was the sole act of will left to him short of a profound alteration of his character. I think the evidence of this is the locked-in sensibility, the insulated egoism, of his poetry —a subject that I shall return to. The background of his death was dramatically perfect: a large portion of his finest imagery was of the sea, chiefly the Caribbean:

> *O minstrel galleons of Carib fire,*
> *Bequeath us to no earthly shore until*
> *Is answered in the vortex of our grave*
> *The seal's wide spindrift gaze towards paradise.*

His verse is full of splendid images of this order, a rich symbolism for an implicit pantheism that, whatever may be its intrinsic merit, he had the courage to vindicate with death in the end.

His pantheism was not passive and contemplative; it rose

out of the collision between his own locked-in sensibility and the ordinary forms of experience. Every poem is a thrust of that sensibility into the world: his defect lay in his inability to face out the moral criticism implied in the failure to impose his will upon experience.

The Bridge is presumably an epic. How early he had conceived the idea of the poem and the leading symbolism, it is difficult to know; certainly as early as February, 1923. Up to that time, with the exception of "For the Marriage of Faustus and Helen" (1922), he had written only short poems, but most of them, "Praise for an Urn," "Black Tambourine," "Paraphrase," and "Emblems of Conduct," [1] are among his finest work. It is a mistake then to suppose that all of *White Buildings* is early experimental writing; a large portion of that volume, and perhaps the least successful part of it, is made up of poems written after *The Bridge* was begun. "Praise for an Urn" was written in the spring of 1922—one of the finest elegies by an American poet—and although his later development gave us a poetry that the period would be much the less rich for not having, he never again had such perfect mastery of his subject—because he never again quite knew what his subject was.

Readers familiar with "For the Marriage of Faustus and Helen" admire it by passages, but the form of the poem, in its framework of symbol, is an abstraction empty of any knowable experience. The originality of the poem is in its rhythms, but it has the conventional diction that a young poet picks up in his first reading. Crane, I believe, felt that this was so; and he became so dissatisfied, not only with the style of the poem, which is heavily influenced by Eliot and Laforgue, but with the "literary" character of the symbolism, that he set about the greater task of writing *The Bridge*. He had looked upon his "Faustus and Helen" as an answer to the pessimism of the school of Eliot, and *The Bridge* was to be an even more complete answer.

There was a fundamental mistake in Crane's diagnosis of Eliot's problem. Eliot's "pessimism" grows out of an awareness of the decay of the individual consciousness and its fixed relations to the world; but Crane thought that it was due to something like pure "orneryness," an unwillingness "to share with us the breath released," the breath being a new kind of freedom that he identified emotionally with the age of the machine. This vagueness of purpose, in spite of the apparently concrete character of the Brooklyn Bridge, which became the symbol of his epic, he never succeeded in correcting. The "bridge" stands for no well-defined experience; it differs from the Helen and Faust symbols only in its un-literary origin. I think Crane was deceived by this difference, and by the fact that Brooklyn Bridge is "modern" and a fine piece of "mechanics." His more ambitious later project permitted him no greater mastery of formal structure than the more literary symbolism of his youth.

The fifteen parts of *The Bridge* taken as one poem suffer from the lack of a coherent structure, whether symbolic or narrative: the coherence of the work consists in the personal quality of the writing—in mood, feeling, and tone. In the best passages Crane has perfect mastery over the quality of his style; but the style lacks an objective pattern of ideas elaborate enough to carry it through an epic or heroic work. The single symbolic image, in which the whole poem centers, is at one moment the actual Brooklyn Bridge; at another, it is any bridge or "connection"; at still another, it is a philosophical pun and becomes the basis of a series of analogies.

In "Cape Hatteras," the airplane and Walt Whitman are analogous "bridges" to some transcendental truth. Because the idea is variously metaphor, symbol, and analogy, it tends to make the poem static. The poet takes it up, only to be forced to put it down again *when the poetic image of the moment is exhausted.* The idea does not, in short, fill the poet's mind; it is the starting point for a series of short flights, or inventions connected only in analogy—which explains the merely personal passages, which are obscure, and the lapses into sentimentality. For poetic sentimentality is emotion undisciplined by the structure of events or ideas of which it is ostensibly a part. The idea is not objective and articulate in itself; it lags after the poet's vision; it appears and disappears; and in the intervals Crane improvises, often beautifully, as in the flight of the airplane, sometimes badly, as in the passage of Whitman in the same poem.

In the great epic and philosophical works of the past, notably *The Divine Comedy,* the intellectual groundwork is not only simple philosophically; we not only know that the subject is personal salvation, just as we know that Crane's is the greatness of America: we are given also the complete articulation of the idea down to the slightest detail, and we are given it objectively apart from anything that the poet is going to say about it. When the poet extends his perception, there is a further extension of the groundwork ready to meet it and discipline it, and to compel the sensibility of the poet to stick to the subject. It is a game of chess; neither side can move without consulting the other. Crane's difficulty is that of modern poets generally: they play the game with half of the men, the men of sensibility, and because sensibility can make any move, the significance of all moves is obscure.

If we subtract from Crane's idea its periphery of sensation, we have left only the dead abstraction, the Greatness of America, which is capable of elucidation neither on the logical plane nor in terms of a generally known idea of America.

The theme of *The Bridge* is, in fact, an emotional oversimplification of a subject-matter that Crane did not, on the plane of narrative and idea, simplify at all. The poem is emotionally homogeneous and simple—it contains a single purpose; but because it is not structurally clarified it is emotionally confused. America stands for a passage into new truths. Is this the meaning of American history? The poet has every right to answer yes, and this he has done. But just what in America or about America stands for this? Which American history? The historical plot of the poem, which is the groundwork on which the symbolic bridge stands, is arbitrary and broken, where the poet would have gained an overwhelming advantage by choosing a single period or episode, a concrete event with all its dramatic causes, and by following it up minutely, and being bound to it. In short, he would have gained an advantage could he have found a subject to stick to.

Does American culture afford such a subject? It probably does not. After the seventeenth century the sophisticated history of the scholars came into fashion; our popular, legendary chronicles come down only from the remoter European past. It was a sound impulse on Crane's part to look for an American myth, some simple version of our past that lies near the center of the American consciousness; an heroic tale with just enough symbolism to give his mind both direction and play. The soundness of his purpose is witnessed also by the kind of history in the poem: it is inaccurate, and it will not at all satisfy the sticklers for historical fact. It is the history of the motion picture, of naïve patriotism. This is sound; for it ignores the scientific ideal of historical truth-in-itself, and looks for a cultural truth which might win the spontaneous allegiance of the people. It is on such simple integers of truth, not truth of fact but of religious necessity, that men unite. The American mind was formed by the eighteenth-century Enlightenment, which broke down the European "truths" and gave us a temper deeply hostile to the making of new religious truths of our own.

The impulse in *The Bridge* is religious, but the soundness of an impulse is no warrant that it will create a sound art form. The form depends on too many factors beyond the control of the poet. The age is scientific and pseudo-scientific, and our philosophy is Dewey's instrumentalism. And it is possibly this circumstance that has driven the religious attitude into a corner where it lacks the right instruments for its defense and growth, and where it is in a vast muddle about just what these instruments are. Perhaps this disunity of the intellect is responsible for Crane's unphilosophical belief that the poet, unaided and isolated from the people, can create a myth.

If anthropology has helped to destroy the credibility of myths, it has shown us how they rise: their growth is mysterious from the people as a whole. It is probable that no one man ever put myth into history. It is still a nice problem among higher critics, whether the authors of the Gospels

were deliberate myth-makers, or whether their minds were
simply constructed that way; but the evidence favors the
latter. Crane was a myth-maker, and in an age favorable to
myths he would have written a mythical poem in the act of
writing an historical one.

It is difficult to agree with those critics who find his epic
a single poem and as such an artistic success. It is a collection of lyrics, the best of which are not surpassed by anything
in American literature. The writing is most distinguished
when Crane is least philosophical, *when he writes from
sensation.* "The River" has some blemishes towards the end,
but by and large it is a masterpiece of order and style; it
alone is enough to place Crane in the first rank of American
poets, living or dead. Equally good but less ambitious are the
"Proem: To Brooklyn Bridge," and "Harbor Dawn," and
"The Dance" from the section called "Powhatan's Daughter."

These poems bear only the loosest relation to the symbolic
demands of the theme; they contain allusions to the historical pattern or extend the slender structure of analogy running through the poem. They are primarily lyrical, and each
has its complete form. The poem "Indiana," written presumably to complete the pattern of "Powhatan's Daughter,"
does not stand alone, and it is one of the most astonishing
failures ever made by a poet of Crane's genius. "The Dance"
gives us the American background for the coming white
man, and "Indiana" carries the stream of history to the pio-
neer West. It is a nightmare of sentimentality. Crane is at his
most "philosophical" in a theme in which he feels no poetic
interest whatever.

The structural defect of *The Bridge* is due to this fundamental contradiction of purpose. In one of his best earlier
poems, "The Wine Menagerie," he exclaims: "New thresh-
olds, new anatomies!"—new sensation, but he could not sub-
due the new sensation to a symbolic form.

His pantheism is necessarily a philosophy of sensation without point of view. An epic is a judgment of human action,
an implied evaluation of a civilization, a way of life. In *The
Bridge* the civilization that contains the subway hell of the

section called "The Tunnel" is the same civilization of the airplane that the poet apostrophizes in "Cape Hatteras": there is no reason why the subway should be a fitter symbol of damnation than the airplane: both were produced by the same mentality on the same moral plane. There is a concealed, meaningless analogy between, on the one hand, the height of the plane and the depth of the subway, and, on the other, "higher" and "lower" in the religious sense. At one moment Crane faces his predicament of blindness to any rational order of value, and knows that he is damned; but he cannot face it long, and he tries to rest secure upon the intensity of sensation.

To the vision of the abyss in "The Tunnel," a vision that Dante passed through midway of this mortal life, Crane had no alternative: when it became too harrowing he cried to his Pocahontas, a typically romantic and sentimental symbol:

> *Lie to us—dance us back our tribal morn!*

It is probably the perfect word of Romanticism in this century. When Crane saw that his leading symbol, the bridge, would not hold all the material of his poem, he could not sustain it ironically, in the classical manner, by probing its defects; nor in the personal sections, like "Quaker Hill," does he include himself in his Leopardian denunciation of life. He is the blameless victim of a world whose impurity violates the moment of intensity, which would otherwise be enduring and perfect. He is betrayed, not by a defect of his own nature, but by the external world; he asks of nature, perfection—requiring only of himself, intensity. The persistent, and persistently defeated, pursuit of a natural absolute places Crane at the center of his age.

Alternately he asserts the symbol of the bridge and abandons it, because fundamentally he does not understand it. The idea of bridgeship is an elaborate blur leaving the inner structure of the poem confused.

Yet some of the best poetry of our generation is in *The Bridge*. Its inner confusion is a phase of the inner cross-purposes of the time. Crane was one of those men whom every age seems to select as the spokesmen of its spiritual life; they give the age away. The accidental features of their lives, their place in life, their very heredity, seem to fit them for their role; even their vices contribute to their preparation. Crane's biographer will have to study the early influences that confirmed him in narcissism, and thus made him typical of the rootless spiritual life of our time. The character formed by those influences represents an immense concentration, and becomes almost a symbol, of American life in this age.

Crane's poetry has incalculable moral value: it reveals our defects in their extremity. I have said that he knew little of the history of his country. It was not merely a defect of education, but a defect, in the spiritual sense, of the modern mind. Crane lacked the sort of indispensable understanding of his country that a New England farmer has who has never been out of his township. *The Bridge* attempts to include all American life, but it covers the ground with seven-league boots and, like a sightseer, sees nothing. With reference to its leading symbol, it has no subject-matter. The poem is the effort of a solipsistic sensibility to locate itself in the external world, to establish points of reference.

It seems to me that by testing out his capacity to construct a great objective piece of work, in which his definition of himself should have been articulated, he brought his work to an end. I think he knew that the structure of *The Bridge* was finally incoherent, and for that reason—as I have said—he could no longer believe even in his lyrical powers; he could not return to the early work and take it up where he had left off. Far from "refuting" Eliot, his whole career is a vindication of Eliot's major premise—that the integrity of the individual consciousness has broken down. Crane had, in his later work, no individual consciousness: the hard firm style of "Praise for an Urn," which is based upon a clear-cut perception of moral relations, and upon their ultimate inviolability, begins to disappear when the poet goes out into the world and finds that the simplicity of a child's world has no universal sanction. From then on, instead of the effort to define himself in the midst of almost overwhelming complications—a situation that might have produced a tragic poet—he falls back upon the intensity of consciousness, rather than the clarity, for his center of vision. And that is Romanticism.

His world had no center, and the thrust into sensation is responsible for the fragmentary quality of his most ambitious work. This thrust took two directions—the blind assertion of the will, and the blind desire for self-destruction. The poet did not face his first problem, which is to define the limits of his personality and to objectify its moral implications in an appropriate symbolism. Crane could only assert a quality of will against the world, and at each successive failure of the will he turned upon himself. In the failure of understanding —and understanding, for Dante, was a way of love—the Romantic modern poet of the age of science attempts to impose his will upon experience and to possess the world.

It is this impulse of the modern period that has given us the greatest Romantic poetry: Crane instinctively continued the conception of the will that was the deliberate discovery of Rimbaud. A poetry of the will is a poetry of sensation, for the poet surrenders to his sensations of the object in his effort to identify himself with it, and to own it. Some of Crane's finest lyrics—those written in the period of *The Bridge*—carry the modern impulse as far as you will find it anywhere in the French Romantics. "Lachrymae Christi" and "Passage," though on the surface made up of pure images without philosophical meaning of the explicit sort in *The Bridge,* are the lyrical equivalents of the epic: the same kind of sensibility is at work. The implicit grasp of his materal that we find in "Praise for an Urn," the poet has exchanged for an external, random symbol of which there is no possibility of realization. *The Bridge* is an irrational symbol of the will, of conquest, of blind achievement in space; its obverse is "Passage," whose lack of external symbolism exhibits the poetry of the will on the plane of sensation; and this is the self-destructive return of the will upon itself.

Criticism may well set about isolating the principle upon which Crane's poetry is organized. Powerful verse overwhelms its admirers, and betrays them into more than technical imitation. That is one of the arguments of Platonism against literature; it is the immediate quality of an art rather than its whole significance that sets up schools and traditions. Crane not only ends the Romantic era in his own person; he ends it logically and morally. Beyond Crane no future poet can go. (This does not mean that the Romantic impulse may not rise and flourish again.) The finest passages in his work are single moments in the stream of sensation; beyond the moment he goes at his peril; for beyond it lies the discrepancy between the sensuous fact, the perception, and its organizing symbol— a discrepancy that plunges him into sentimentality and chaos. But the "bridge" is empty and static, it has no inherent content, and the poet's attribution to it of the qualities of his own moral predicament is arbitrary. That explains the fragmentary and often unintelligible framework of the poem. There was neither complete action nor ordered symbolism in terms of which the distinct moments of perception could be clarified.

This was partly the problem of Rimbaud. But Crane's problem was nearer to the problem of Keats, and *The Bridge* is a failure in the sense that "Hyperion" is a failure, and with comparable magnificence. Crane's problem, being farther removed from the epic tradition, was actually more difficult than Keats', and his treatment of it was doubtless the most satisfactory possible in our time. Beyond the quest of pure sensation and its ordering symbolism lies the total destruction of art. By attempting an extreme solution of the Romantic problem Crane proved that it cannot be solved.

1932–1937

CRANE: THE POET AS HERO

An Encomium Twenty Years Later

Anybody who knew Hart Crane will come away from his letters both depressed and relieved. I confess that I hope I shall not have to follow again the melancholy course of this desperate life. I prefer to cherish, after the violence and final frustration of a great lyric poet, an image of Crane the poet as hero. What at last destroyed him one cannot quite say, even after the copious evidence that Mr. Weber's ably edited volume[1] puts before us. The clue to the mystery is not here: it seems to lie far back of the written testimony of the letters, in his boyhood, when at eleven he became the "bloody battleground" of his father's and mother's "sex lives and troubles," which ended not only in divorce but in such disorder that the boy was set adrift. The family was by no means poor, but he was not sent to college; he was turned loose in New York when he was seventeen.

What astonishes me in the early letters—and what I had not got from Crane himself or from Mr. Philip Horton's excellent biography[2]—is not only the intellectual precocity but the precocity of moral insight. He was seventeen when he wrote to his father from New York:

When I perceive one emotion overpowering to a fact, or a statement of reason, then the only manly, worthy, sensible thing to do, is build up the logical side, and attain balance, and in art—formal expression.

In 1926, nine years later, he wrote to an anonymous friend:

. . . with the sailor no faith or such is properly expected, *and how jolly and cordial and warm. . . . Let my lusts be my ruin, then, since all else is fake and mockery.*

295

The intellectual deterioration came more slowly. What had happened to him morally between 1917 and 1926? The letters definitely answer this question. He had been confirmed in his homosexuality and cut off finally from any relationship, short of a religious conversion, in which the security necessary to mutual love was possible. I was surprised, after two years of correspondence with him, when in 1924 I met him and learned a little later that he was a homosexual: he had none of the characteristics popularly attributed to homosexuality. The violence of his obscenity (particularly about women) and his intense emotional attachments to women his own age (not to middle-aged women) convinced me even then that he was an extreme example of the *unwilling* homosexual. It is significant that his last love affair, quite real if not wholly "committed," was with a woman; his letters to her are in every sense the letters of a man to a woman down to the full implications of physical love.

I dwell upon this part of the record because beneath it lies the mystery of the disintegration, at the age of thirty-two, of the most gifted poet of his generation. The "causes" of homosexuality are no doubt as various as the causes of other neuroses. But the effect on the lives of its victims seems to be uniform: they are convinced that they cannot be loved, and they become incapable of loving. This is not to say that they are incapable of strong affection: they are incapable of sustaining it in a sexual relationship. They may have affection *or* sex, but not both; or if both, both are diluted and remote. Crane's intensity excluded this compromise. Incidents of the "bloody battleground" that he told me and other friends about in the late twenties have never appeared in print, and this is not the occasion to recite them. Is it not reasonable to assume that the hatred and suffering that accompanied the violent sex-life of his parents were the decisive force that gave him eventually the homosexual neurosis? Was it possible for an eleven-year-old boy, or for the man later, to dissociate hate from the sexual relation with a woman? Possible for most men, but not, under all the conditions of his childhood, for Crane. Almost to the end of his life he was still trying to "explain" himself to his mother and to force from a peculiarly stupid and selfish woman the recognition and love of what he was. He could still love her because he could not be her lover.

It has always seemed to me that the defection of his mother precipitated the final disaster. He had been endowed with powerful family affections that were progressively frustrated. His letters to his divorced parents are among the most considerate, tender, and moving in literary history. He turned to his friends for the totally committed love, the disinterested *caritas,* that only one's family can sustain and that alone will condone repeatedly violent and aggressive conduct. None of us was capable in the end of taking the place of his family— and that was what he demanded of us; our failure—and I speak now not only for myself but, not improperly, I think, for his entire intimate circle—also contributed to the final disaster. But there was for us no other way: we also had families and our own lives.

Out of these conflicts, which in the end became one conflict, emerged a peculiar focus of the intelligence and sensibility that represents "modernism" in its extreme development. (Towards the end he speaks of himself as the "last Romantic.") He had an abnormally acute response to the physical world, an exacerbation of the nerve-ends, along with an incapacity to live within the limitations of the human condition. It has become commonplace to describe this as the mentality of "alienation." But the point to be borne in mind—and it is amply confirmed by the letters—is that Crane was never *alienated.* He did not reject, he simply could not achieve, in his own life, the full human condition: he did not for a moment suppose that there was a substitute for it. This is borne out not only by his poetry—for example, *The Bridge* is not in intention a poem of "rejection," in the tradition of Rimbaud, but of "acceptance," an attempt to assimilate a central tradition; it is confirmed also by his life, reflected day by day, year after year, in the letters. His deepest friendships were not with homosexuals; they were with Malcolm Cowley, Slater Brown, Kenneth Burke, Gorham Munson, Waldo Frank, and myself; it was with these men that he lived the life of the mind and the imagination. He could not pretend that the alienated society of the committed homosexual was complete; for this unhappy person—for his epicene manners and for his irresponsibility—he felt compassion and contempt. There is a Christian commonplace which says that God does not despise conditions. Out of the desperate conditions of his life—which included almost unimaginable horrors of depravity and perversity of will—he produced in the end a shining *exemplum* of uncompromising human dignity: his poetry.

He came to New York at seventeen equipped with an hysterical and disorderly family, almost no formal education, and the cultural inheritance of a middle-western small town; his religious training had been in Christian Science. By the time he was twenty-five, before *The Bridge* had scarcely been conceived, he had written a body of lyric poetry which for originality, distinction, and power, remains the great poetic achievement of his generation. If he is not our twentieth-century poet as hero, I do not know where else to look for him.

1952

MacLEISH'S CONQUISTADOR

Archibald MacLeish has been up to this time a poet like most of his contemporaries, limited to the short flight. There is, in his earlier work, no premonitory sounding of the finely sustained tone of *Conquistador*. For modern poetry the poem is long. It is an epic in miniature of about two thousand lines. In versification and style, and with respect to the narrational "point of view," there is no other poem in English with which as a whole it may be compared. It is evident, of course, that MacLeish has studied Ezra Pound; but this is no disparagement of Pound's pupil. The *Cantos* are full of technical instruction for the poet who knows what he needs to learn. The followers of Eliot take his "philosophy" as well as his style, and give us work of "lower intensity" than the original. Pound's disciples are either less plausible or more independent. They exercise thinly with Mr. Dudley Fitts or practice the admirable craft of *Conquistador*.

The background of the poem is the conquest of Mexico. For a complete history of the conquest one will have to go to the historians. The poem is a reconstruction of the part played by one of the lesser heroes, Bernal Diaz del Castillo, who as an old man wrote his own story in resentment against the official histories by Gomara and others—

The quilled professors: the taught tongues of fame:
What have they written of us: the poor soldiers . . .

They call the towns for the kings that bear no scars:
They keep the names of the great for time to stare at—
The bishops rich men generals cocks-at-arms . . .

Bernal tells the story in flashes of recollection that have just enough narrative progression to give to the narrator a constantly new field of imagery. But the historical pattern of the conquest is never explicit, never obtrusive enough to take the reader's attention from the personality of Bernal and the quality of his character. For the personality of Bernal is the subject of the poem.

Thus narrowing the action down to the focus of a single mind and what it saw, MacLeish disposes of two enormous difficulties of epic poetry: he eliminates the objective detail of the total scene, at once the conventional privilege and the burden of the classical poet; and he dispenses with the need of cosmic machinery. There is no external "idea"; there is no theme; there is no "typical action."

We get the peculiarly modern situation: the personality of one man is dramatized against an historical setting. "What have they written of us: the poor soldiers"—what can the private sensibility get out of history to sustain it? What can Bernal get out of his past? Nothing appears in the story that Bernal did not see; it is all enriched by memory. Although Bernal announces his subject as "That which I have myself seen and the fighting," there is little fighting; there is little action; for the dramatic tension of the poem grows out of the narrator-hero's fear of death upon the gradual disappearance of sensation. The dramatic quality of the poem—a quality that has little to do with the story as such—lies thus in the hero's anxiety to recover his sensuous early years, upon which his identity as a person, and hence his life, depends.

This is the subject of the poem. The "meaning" of the poem is an implicit quality of Bernal's mind, but only a little logical violence will isolate it. It is the futility of individual action. For unless the hero, in his old age, can recapture the sensation of action, the action itself must fade into the obscure shuffle of abstract history. We have seen that Bernal cannot accept the public versions of the conquest. (Is Bernal, then, a soldier of the sixteenth century or of the First World War?) He cannot identify the moment of action with the ostensible common purpose for which the whole series of events took place. He is confined to memories, to the mechanism of sensation.

I dwell upon this "meaning" of *Conquistador* for two reasons. It obviously, in the first place, explains the form in which MacLeish found it necessary to cast his narrative, a form that I have briefly described; the necessity of this form explains the presence, I believe, of those features of the style that MacLeish borrowed from Pound and perfected. And, secondly, the meaning of this distinguished poem, as I apprehend it, may lead some of the younger critics to reconsider, not their enthusiasm for the workmanship, which it richly deserves, but their hasty acceptance of its "philosophy." It is a mistake to suppose that MacLeish has offered a "way out" of the introspective indecision of the school of T. S. Eliot, affirming a faith in heroic action against the moral paralysis presumably suffered by the best minds of that older generation. Not only is there, in the poem, a lack of belief in any kind of action that we might imitate; the poet does not feel much interest in the action implied by the reminiscences that support the narrative.

There is not one moment of action rendered objectively in the entire poem. There is constantly and solely the pattern of sensation that surrounded the moment of action—the fringe of the physical shock and awareness that survive in memory. The technique of rendering this special quality of memory is MacLeish's contribution to poetic style:

> *Gold there on that shore on the evening sand—*
> *"Colua" they said: pointing on toward the sunset:*
> *They made a sign on the air with their solemn hands . . .*

> *And that voyage it was we came to the Island:*
> *Well I remember the shore and the sound of that place*
> *And the smoke smell on the dunes and the wind dying.*

> *Well I remember the walls and the rusty taste of the*
> *New-spilled blood in the air: many among us*
> *Seeing the priests with their small arrogant faces . . .*

> *Ah how the throat of a girl and girl's arms are*
> *Bright in the riding sun and the young sky*
> *And the green year of our lives where the willows are!*

This clarity of sensuous reminiscence that suffuses the poem is a new quality in American verse. The images are not imbedded in metaphor; they exist spatially in the round. Pound supplied the model:

> *Eyes brown topaz,*
> *Brookwater over brown sand,*
> *The white hounds on the slope,*
> *Glide of water, lights on the prore,*
> *Silver beaks out of night,*
> *Stone, bough over bough, lamps fluid in water,*
> *Pine by the black trunk of its shadow*
> *The trees melted in air.*

The images are impersonal, objective, and timeless, detached from Pound's moral position. The focus of MacLeish's imagery is personal: the image exists in terms of Bernal's recovery of memory, of his struggle for personal identity. Its precision has been disciplined in the workshop of Ezra Pound, whose quality of floating clarity is localized by MacLeish in a Browning-esque monologue, where the casuistry gives way to a sophisticated version of the *chanson de geste.*

Poets in this age cannot set forth with security a conscious philosophical system. Reasons for this I have mentioned in another place. When there is no systematic philosophy at hand, the poet is likely to slip into an unsystematic one of his own: this, perhaps, is better than an elaborate system that he cannot assimilate and understand. MacLeish's philosophy is personal and unarticulated. It may be stated in moral terms. We cannot linger over even the finest passages of *Conquistador* without becoming aware that we are in the presence of a sentimental view of experience. I have said that there is no objective design to uphold the sensibility of the narrator-hero. Perhaps, in this poem, MacLeish is no less able a poet than the young Milton of *Lycidas;* but Milton had an objective convention that absorbed every implication of his personal feeling. I use the term sentimental, then, in a strict, not a pejorative, sense. The melancholy of the hero's disgust with the "taught tongues of fame" is personal, sentimental; it is necessarily meaningless and obscure.

The disgust of Bernal does not rise to the level of rational criticism. It would serve as a rational evaluation of the "conquest" if there were a full stream of objective action in the light of which it could acquire significance. To have set off the private experience of the soldier against the grandiose avowals of purpose by the conquerors, might possibly have provided the poet with the situation of tragic irony. But there is no conflict of this order in the poem. The emotion is pathos. We get Bernal's sentimental regret; his anger rises at the failure of the official historians to re-create the sensuous correspondence to his own part in the campaign. He says in effect not *quorum pars magna fui* but rather *solus quorum omnis fui*—alone in his perceptions. The poem recovers the perceptions but it does not place them against a coherent stream of events. The hero is concerned with his personal survival. He is modern and sentimental; not tragic and ironic. The motivation of his story is the fear of death.

I am ungrateful to MacLeish; I have dwelt upon a philosophical limitation that is not peculiar to this poet, but is deeply rooted in the age. The technical perfection of *Conquistador* is, of course, not merely a technical feat. The poem is one of the examples of our modern sensibility at its best; it has the defect of its qualities.

The verse is *terza rima,* a metrical form enormously difficult in English. The paucity of English rhymes leaves it clumsy and monotonous in all but the hands of a master. Shelley tried it once with moderate success; Wyat adapted it to an epistolary style that doubtless should have been but never was a model for later poets. But MacLeish, foreseeing in a long poem the monotony of conventionally rhymed *terza rima,* varies rhyme with terminal assonance that is usually hidden and always cunningly placed. He achieves something of the fluent ease of the Italian, which is rich in rhyme-words, and gives us the first successful example of *terza rima* in a long English poem.

It is the only considerable metrical achievement by a poet of this generation. Yet the perfection of the experiment will make future use of *terza rima* dangerous. The technique of the verse is a quality of MacLeish's mind, and is inimitable.

"Waller refined our numbers"—but this time Waller is a hard-pressed modern whose brilliance, once flashed, burns out before it can be passed to other hands. It is the present fate of poetry to be always beginning over again. The kind of "culture" in *Conquistador* is purely literary; the kind of experience in it is the sentimentality of moral isolation. The refinement of the craftsmanship hovers over a void.

1932

THE PROFESSION OF LETTERS IN THE SOUTH

The profession of letters in France dates, I believe, from the famous manifesto of Du Bellay and the Pléiade in 1549. It is a French habit to assume that France has supported a profession of letters ever since. There is no other country where the writer is so much honored as in France, no other people in western culture who understand so well as the French the value of literature to the state. The national respect for letters begins far down in society. In a French village where I was unknown I was able to use a letter-of-credit without identification upon my word that I was a man of letters. The French have no illusions; we are not asked to believe that all French writers are respectable. The generation of Rimbaud and Verlaine was notoriously dissolute. French letters are a profession, as law, medicine, and the army are professions. Good writers starve and lead sordid lives in France as elsewhere; yet the audience for high literature is larger in France than in any other country; and a sufficient number of the best writers find a public large enough to sustain them as a class.

It goes somewhat differently with us. The American public sees the writer as a businessman because it cannot see any other kind of man, and respects him according to his income. And, alas, most writers themselves respect chiefly and fear only their competitors' sales. A big sale is a "success." How could it be otherwise? Our books are sold on a competitive market; it is a book market, but it is a luxury market; and luxury markets must be fiercely competitive. It is not that the natural depravity of the writer as fallen man betrays him into imitating the tone and standards of his market; actually he cannot find a public at all, even for the most lost of lost causes, the *succès d'estime,* unless he is willing to enter the competitive racket of publishing. This racket, our society being what it is, is a purely economic process, and literary opinion is necessarily manufactured for its needs. Its prime need is shoddy goods, because it must have a big, quick turnover. The overhead in the system is so high that the author gets only 10 to 15 per cent of the gross. It is the smallest return that any producer gets in our whole economic system. To live even frugally, a novelist, if he does not do odd jobs on the side, must have a sale of about 30,000 copies every two years. Not only the publisher's but his turnover, too, must be quick. He has his own self-sweatshop. One must agree with Mr. Herbert Read, in the February, 1935, London *Mercury,* that authors under modern capitalism are a sweated class.

We have heard for years, we began hearing it as early as Jeffrey's review of the first "Hyperion," that science is driving poetry to cover. I suppose it is; and we have the weight of Mr. I. A. Richards' arguments to prove it, and Mr. Max Eastman's weight, which is fairly light. Nineteenth-century science produced a race of "problem" critics and novelists. The new "social" point of view has multiplied the race. Literature needs no depth of background or experience to deal with problems; it needs chiefly the statistical survey and the conviction that society lives by formula, if not by bread alone. The nineteenth century began this genre, which has become the standard mode. I confess that I cannot decide whether "science" or the mass production of books, or the Spirit that made them both, has given us shoddy in literature. We were given, for example, Bennett and Wells; Millay and Masefield. And I surmise that not pure science but shoddy has driven the poets into exile, where, according to Eastman, they are "talking to themselves."

I shall not multiply instances. The trouble ultimately goes back to the beginnings of finance-capitalism and its creature, machine-production. Under feudalism the artist was a member of an organic society. The writer's loss of professional standing, however, set in before the machine, by which I mean the machine-age as we know it, appeared. It began with the rise of mercantile aristocracy in the eighteenth century. The total loss of professionalism in letters may be seen in our age—an age that remembers the extinction of aristocracy and witnesses the triumph of a more inimical plutocratic society.

If my history is not wholly incorrect, it must follow that our unlimited pioneering, the pretext of the newness of the country, and our low standards of education, do not explain the decline of the professional author. Pioneering became our way of industrial expansion, a method of production not special to us; we are a new country in so far as our industrialism gave to the latent vices of the European mind a new opportunity; and our standards of education get lower with the increasing amount of money spent upon them. For my purposes, then, it is sufficient that we should look at the history of professionalism in letters in terms of the kinds of rule that European society, which includes American society, has had.

The South once had aristocratic rule; the planter class was about one fifth of the population; but the majority followed its lead. And so, by glancing at the South, we shall see in American history an important phase of the decline of the literary profession. There was, perhaps, in and around Boston, for a brief period, a group of professional writers. But not all of them, not even most of them, made their livings by writing. Even if they had, we should still have to explain why they were second-rate, and why the greatest of the Easterners, Hawthorne, Melville, Dickinson, had nothing to do with them or with the rising plutocracy of the East. But it is a sadder story still in the South. We had no Hawthorne, no Melville, no Emily Dickinson. We had William Gilmore Simms. We made it impossible for Poe to live south of the Potomac. Aristocracy drove him out. Plutocracy, in the East, starved him to death. I prefer the procedure of the South; it knew its own mind, knew what kind of society it wanted. The East, bent upon making money, could tolerate, as it still tolerates, any kind of disorder on the fringe of society as long as the disorder does not interfere with money-making. It did not know its own social mind; it was, and still is, plutocracy.

But let us look a little at the backgrounds of Southern literature. I say backgrounds, for the South is an immensely complicated region. It begins in the Northeast with southern Maryland; it ends with eastern Texas; it includes to the

north a little of Missouri. But that the people in this vast
expanse of country have enough in common to bind them in
a single culture cannot be denied. They often deny it themselves—writers who want to have something to jabber about;
or other writers who want to offset the commercial handicap
of being Southern; or newly rich persons in cities that would
rather be like Pittsburgh than like New Orleans. It must be
confessed that the Southern tradition has left no cultural
landmark so conspicuous that the people may be reminded by
it constantly of what they are. We lack a tradition in the
arts; more to the point, we lack a literary tradition. We lack
even a literature. We have just enough literary remains from
the old regime to prove to us that, had a great literature
risen, it would have been unique in modern times.

The South was settled by the same European strains as
originally settled the North. Yet, in spite of war, reconstruction, and industrialism, the South to this day finds its most
perfect contrast in the North. In religious and social feeling
I should stake everything on the greater resemblance to
France. The South clings blindly to forms of European feeling and conduct that were crushed by the French Revolution
and that, in England at any rate, are barely memories. How
many Englishmen have told us that we still have the
eighteenth-century amiability and consideration of manners,
supplanted in their country by middle-class reticence and suspicion? And where, outside the South, is there a society that
believes even covertly in the Code of Honor? This is not
idle talk; we are assured of it by Professor H. C. Brearley,
who, I believe, is one of the most detached students of Southern life. Where else in the modern world is the patriarchal
family still innocent of the rise and power of other forms of
society? Possibly in France; probably in the peasant countries
of the Balkans and of Central Europe. Yet the "orientation"—
let us concede the word to the University of North Carolina
—the rise of new Southern points of view, even now in the
towns, is tied still to the image of the family on the land.
Where else does so much of the reality of the ancient land-
society endure, along with the infatuated avowal of beliefs
that are hostile to it? Where in the world today is there a

more supine enthusiasm for being amiable to forces under-
mining the life that supports the amiability? The anomalous
structure of the South is, I think, finally witnessed by its
religion. Doctor Poteat of South Carolina deplores a fact
which he does not question, that only in the South does one
find a convinced supernaturalism: it is nearer to Aquinas than
to Calvin, Wesley, or Knox. Nor do we doubt that the conflict between modernism and fundamentalism is chiefly the
impact of the new middle-class civilization upon the rural
society; nor, moreover, should we allow ourselves to forget
that philosophers of the State, from Sir Thomas More to
John C. Calhoun, were political defenders of the older religious community.

The key to unlock the Southern mind is, fortunately, like
Bluebeard's, bloody and perilous; there is not the easy sesame
to the cavern of gaping success. The South has had reverses
that permit her people to imagine what they might have been.
(And only thus can people discover what they *are*.) Given
the one great fact of the expanding plantation system at the
dawn of the last century, which voice should the South have
listened to? Jefferson, or Marshall, or Calhoun? I mean,
which voice had the deepest moral and spiritual implications
for the permanence of Southern civilization?

There was not time to listen to any voice very long. The
great Southern ideas were strangled in the cradle, either by
the South herself (for example, by too much quick cotton
money in the Southwest) or by the Union armies. It is plain
to modern historians of culture that peoples do not make,
much less buy, a culture overnight; it takes time. Which view
would have given the South a unified sense of its own destiny? Our modern "standard of living" is not a point of view,
and it is necessary that a people should gather its experience
round some seasoned point of view before it may boast a high
culture. It must be able to illuminate from a fixed position all
its experience; it must bring to full realization the high forms
as well as the contradictions and miseries inherent in human
society.

The miseries and contradictions bemuse and alarm us now.
I hope I shall not be called flint-hearted if I dare to believe

that the humanitarian spirit can never remove them. So long as society is committed to a class-system—and it will probably never be committed to a classless system—the hard-hearted will keep on believing that the high forms are as necessary to the whole of society as bread to the major fraction to whom it is now denied. If man does not live by bread alone, he lives thinly upon bread and sentiment; for sentiment and bread will nourish him but little unless they partake of the peculiarly elevating virtues of form. I might even quote Shelley, whom it is becoming fashionable again to quote: "Our calculations have outrun conception; we have eaten more than we can digest." I am willing to take the sentence in full literalness, if I may read form for conception, and produced for eaten. For the concrete forms of the social and religious life are the assimilating structure of society.

Where, as in the Old South, there were high forms, but no deep realization of the spirit was achieved, we must ask questions. (The right questions: not why the South refused to believe in Progress, or why it did not experiment with "ideas.") Was the structure of society favorable to a great literature? Suppose it to have been favorable: Was there something wrong with the intellectual life for which the social order cannot be blamed?

The answer is both yes and no to the first question. It is emphatically yes and no to the second. So our answers are confused. At a glance one would expect the rich leisured class, well-educated as the Southern aristocracy was—for the South of the fifties had proportionately a larger educated minority than Massachusetts—to devote a great part of its vitality to the arts, the high and conscious arts. As for the arts otherwise, even peasant societies achieve the less conscious variety—manners, ritual, charming domestic architecture.

Assuming, as I do not think I am allowed to assume very confidently, that this society was a good soil for the high arts, there was yet a grave fault in the intellectual life. It was hag-ridden with politics. We like to think that Archimago sent the nightmare down from the North. He did. But it was partly rooted in the kind of rule that the South had, which was aristocratic rule. All aristocracies are obsessed po-

litically. (Witness *Henry IV*, Parts One and Two; *Henry V*.)
The best intellectual energy goes into politics and goes of
necessity; aristocracy is class-rule; and the class must fight for
interest and power. Under the special conditions of the nineteenth century, the South had less excess of vitality for the
disinterested arts of literature than it might have had ordinarily. There are no simple answers to the questions that I
have asked. The South was a fairly good place for the arts,
as good possibly as any other aristocratic country; only its inherent passion for politics was inflamed by the furious contentions that threatened its life. Every gifted person went into
politics, not merely the majority.

The furious contentions themselves provided later answers
to the problem of the arts in the South. At the end of the
century one of the popular answers was that of the distinguished William Peterfield Trent, who laid bare all the
Southern defects with the black magic talisman, Slavery.
The defects could be whisked away, he argued in his life of
Simms, with "essential faith in American democracy." The
Northern people, at that time, may be forgiven this faith; it
was the stuffed shirt of plutocracy and it was making them
money; they had a right to believe in it. I cannot decide between credulity and venality as the reason for its being believed in the South. I am certain that in Trent's case it was
credulity. If slavery was the cause of war, then slavery explained the political mania of the Old South; and the political mania stunted the arts. Partly true; partly false. Such
an answer is more dangerous than an answer wholly false.
In this instance it led the people to believe that their sole
obstacle to perfection, slavery, had been removed. There was
no need to be critical of anything else, least of all of the society that had come down and removed the blight: a society
that by some syllogistic process unknown to me was accepted
as perfect by the new Southern Liberals.

But the abolition of slavery did not make for a distinctively
Southern literature. We must seek the cause of our limitations
elsewhere. It is worth remarking, for the sake of argument,
that chattel slavery is not demonstrably a worse form of
slavery than any other upon which an aristocracy may base its

power and wealth. That *African* chattel slavery was the worst groundwork conceivable for the growth of a great culture of European pattern, is scarcely at this day arguable. Still, as a favorable "cultural situation" it was probably worse than white-chattel, agricultural slavery only in degree. The distance between white master and black slave was unalterably greater than that between white master and white serf after the destruction of feudalism. The peasant *is* the soil. The Negro slave was a barrier between the ruling class and the soil. If we look at aristocracies in Europe, say in eighteenth-century England, we find at least genuine social classes, each carrying on a different level of the common culture. But in the Old South, and under the worse form of slavery that afflicts both races today, genuine social classes could not exist. The enormous "difference" of the Negro doomed him from the beginning to an economic status purely: he has had much the same thinning influence upon the class above him as the anonymous city proletariat has had upon the culture of industrial capitalism.

All great cultures have been rooted in peasantries, in free peasantries, I believe, such as the English yeomanry before the fourteenth century: they have been the growth of the soil. What the Southern system might have accomplished we do not know: it would have been, as I have said, something new. Of course, the absence of genuine cultural capitals in the South has been cited as a cause of lassitude in the arts; perhaps it was a cause, as it is today. But it does not wholly explain the vague and feeble literature that was produced. The white man got nothing from the Negro, no profound image of himself in terms of the soil.

I suspect that, in the age of social science, the term "image" is not clear, and this, I suppose, is due to the disappearance, in such an age, of the deep relation between man and a local habitation. An environment is an abstraction, not a place; Natchez is a place but not an environment. The difference will be clear to those who are morally able to see that it exists. The citizen of Natchez lived in a place but he could not deepen his sense of its life through the long series of gradations represented by his dependents, who stood between him and the earth. He instructed his factor to buy good furniture of the Second Empire, and remained a Colonial. But the Negro, who has long been described as a responsibility, got everything from the white man. The history of French culture, I suppose, has been quite different. The high arts have been grafted upon the peasant stock. We could graft no new life upon the Negro; he was too different, too alien.

Doubtless the confirmed if genteel Romanticism of the old Southern imaginative literature (I make exception for the political writers of South Carolina—Hammond, Harper, Calhoun: they are classical and realistic) was in the general stream of Romanticism; yet the special qualities that it produced, the unreal union of formless revery and correct sentiment, the inflated oratory—even in private correspondence you see it witness a feeble hold upon place and time. The roots were not deep enough in the soil. Professor Trent was right; but he was right for the wrong reason. It was not that slavery was corrupt "morally." Societies can bear an amazing amount of corruption and still produce high cultures. Black slavery could not nurture the white man in his own image.

Although the Southern system, in spite of the Negro, was closer to the soil than the mercantile-manufacturing system of the Middle and New England states, its deficiencies in spiritual soil were more serious even than those of the debased feudal society of eighteenth-century rural England. With this society the ante-bellum South had much in common.

The South came from eighteenth-century England, its agricultural half; there were not enough large towns in the South to complete the picture of an England reproduced. The Virginian and the Carolinian, however, imitated the English squire. They held their land, like their British compeer, in absolute, that is to say unfeudal, ownership, as a result of the destruction, first under Henry VIII and then under Cromwell, of the feudal system of land tenure. The landlord might be humane, but he owed no legal obligation to his land (he could wear it out) or to his labor (he could turn it off: called "enclosure" in England, "selling" under Negro slavery). A pure aristocracy, or the benevolent rule of a landed class in the interest of its own wealth and power, had superseded royalty which, in theory at any rate, and often in practice, had tried to balance class interests under protection of the Crown.

It should be borne in mind, against modern egalitarian and Marxian superstition, that royalty and aristocracy are fundamentally opposed systems of rule; that plutocracy, the offspring of democracy, and that Marxism, the child of plutocracy, are essentially of the aristocratic political mode: they all mean class rule. Virginia took the lead in the American Revolution, not to set up democracy, as Jefferson tried to believe, but to increase the power of the tobacco-exporting aristocracy. The planters wished to throw off the yoke of the British merchant and to get access to the free world market.

But the Southern man of letters cannot permit himself to look upon the old system from a purely social point of view, or from the economic view: to him it must seem better than the system that destroyed it, better, too, than any system with which the modern planners, Marxian or other color, wish to replace the present order. Yet the very merits of the Old South tend to confuse the issue: its comparative stability, its realistic limitation of the acquisitive impulse, its preference for human relations compared to relations economic, tempt the historian to defend the poor literature simply because he feels that the old society was a better place to live in than the new. It is a great temptation—if you do not read the literature.

There is, I believe, a nice object-lesson to be drawn from the changed relation of the English writer to society in the eighteenth century; it is a lesson that bears directly upon the attitude of the Old South towards the profession of letters. In the seventeenth century, in the year 1634, a young, finical man, then in seclusion at Horton after taking his degrees at Cambridge, and still unknown, was invited by the Earl of Bridgewater to write a masque for certain revels to be celebrated at Ludlow Castle. The masque was *Comus,* and the revels were in the feudal tradition. The whole celebration was "at home"; it was a part of the community life, the common people were present, and the poet was a spiritual member of the society gathered there. He might not be a gentleman:

had Milton become a member of Egerton's "household" he would have been a sort of upper servant. But he would have been a member of the social and spiritual community.

Now examine the affair of Johnson and the Earl of Chesterfield: it is the eighteenth century. It was conducted in the new "aristocratic" style. For the flattery of a dedication the nobleman was loftily willing to give his patronage, a certain amount of money, to an author who had already completed the work, an author who had faced starvation in isolation from society. There is no great publishing system in question here; there were only booksellers. But there was already the cash nexus between the writer and society. The Earl of Chesterfield was a capitalist, not a feudal noble as Egerton to some extent still was: Chesterfield had lost the community; he required of the arts a compliment to the power of his class.

He was the forerunner of the modern plutocrat who thinks that the arts are thriving so long as he can buy Italian paintings, or so long as he creates "foundations" for the arts, or the sales sheets of the publishers show a large volume of "business." But the plutocrat no less than the artist participates in his society through the cash nexus. I hope I do not convince the reader that this wicked fellow has undertaken a deliberate conspiracy against the artist. The artist as man invariably has the same relation to the society of his time as everybody else has: his misfortune and his great value is his superior awareness of that relation. The "message" of modern art at present is that social man is living, without religion, morality, or art (without the high form that concentrates all three in an organic whole), in a mere system of money references through which neither artist nor plutocrat can perform as an entire person.

Is there anything in common between the Earl of Chesterfield and a dour Scots merchant building a fortune and a place in the society of Richmond, Virginia, in the first third of the nineteenth century? I think that they have something in common. It was not John Allan who drove Poe out of Virginia. The foreigner, trying to better himself, always knows the practical instincts of a society more shrewdly than the society knows them. Allan was, for once, the spokesman of Virginia, of the plantation South. There was no place for Poe in the spiritual community of Virginia; there was no class of professional writers that Poe could join in dedicating their works to the aristocracy under the system of the cash nexus. The promising young men were all in politics bent upon more desperate emergencies. It was obvious, even to John Allan, I suppose, that here was no dabbler who would write pleasant, genteel poems and stories for magazines where other dabbling gentlemen printed their pleasant, genteel stories and poems. Anybody could have looked at Poe and known that he meant business.

And until the desperate men today who mean business can become an independent class, there will be no profession of letters anywhere in America. It remains only to add to the brief history adumbrated in this essay some comment on the present situation of the desperate men of the South in particular. There are too many ladies and gentlemen, too many Congreves whose coxcombry a visit from Voltaire would do a great deal of good. I trust that I do not argue the case too well. Congreve frivolously gave up the honor of his profession when Voltaire asked to see the great dramatist and got the answer that Mr. Congreve was no scribbler but a man of fashion. They were more explicit about those things in those days. I should barely hope that the Southern writer, or the Northern or Western, for that matter, may decide that his gentility, being a quality over which he has no control, may get along as it can. For the genteel tradition has never done anything for letters in the South; yet the Southern writers who are too fastidious to become conscious of their profession have not refused to write best sellers when they could, and to profit by a cash nexus with New York. I would fain believe that matters are otherwise than so: but facts are facts. If there is such a person as a Southern writer, if there could be such a profession as letters in the South, the profession would require the speaking of unpleasant words and the violation of good literary manners.

I wish this were the whole story: only cranks and talents of the quiet, first order maintain themselves against fashion and prosperity. But even these desperate persons must live, and they cannot live in the South without an "independent income." We must respect the source of our income, that is, we ought to; and if we cannot respect it we are likely to fear it. This kind of writer is not luckier than his penniless fellow. (The only man I know who devotes a large income to changing the system that produced it is a New Yorker.) Because there is no city in the South where writers may gather, write, and live, and no Southern publisher to print their books, the Southern writer, of my generation at least, went to New York. There he was influenced not only by the necessity to live but by theories and movements drifting over from Europe.

It was, possibly, a dangerous situation. Mr. John Crowe Ransom has pointed out its implications:

> *If modernism is regarded as nothing but a new technique, what was wrong with the old technique? Principally, perhaps, the fact that it was old; for modernism is apt to assume that tradition is not so much a prop which may be leant upon as a dead burden which must be borne. The substance of modernism is not a technique but an attitude. And a dangerous attitude . . .*
>
> *The Southern artists in going modern offer us their impression of a general decay, and that is not a pleasant thing to think about.*[1]

The Southern writer was perilously near to losing his identity, becoming merely a "modern" writer. He lost the Southern feeling which, in the case of Mr. Young, informs the Southern style: he might retain a Southern subject and write about it as an outsider, with some novelty of technique and in smart, superior detachment. These bad features of the last decade may be deplored, I hope, without asking the Southerner to stay at home and starve. That, it seems to me, is what Mr. Ransom asks the Southern writer to do. It was not an uprooted modern, but the classical Milton who remarked, "Wherever we do well is home": wherever we are allowed best to realize our natures—a realization that, for an artist, presupposes permission to follow his craft—is the proper place to live. The Southern writer should if possible be a Southerner in the South. The sole condition that would make that possible is a profession of letters.

But the arts everywhere spring from a mysterious union of indigenous materials and foreign influences: there is no great art or literature that does not bear the marks of this fusion. So I cannot assume, as Mr. Ransom seems to do, that exposure to the world of modernism (Petrarchism was modernism in the England of 1540) was of itself a demoralizing experience. Isn't it rather that the Southerner before he left home had grown weak in his native allegiance? That his political and social history, and his domestic life, had been severely adulterated no less by his fellow Southerners than by the people in the North to whom he fled? Apart from this menace abroad, who cannot bring himself to wish that Miss Glasgow had studied James and Flaubert in her apprenticeship, and spared herself and us her first three or four novels? Could Mr. Young have written his fiction, to say nothing of his plays and criticism, had he read only Cable and Page? And, lastly, what shall we say of Mr. Ransom's own distinguished and very modern poetry?

Is not Mr. Ransom really deploring the absence, as I deplore it, of a professional spirit and professional opportunities in Southern literature? There is no reason why the Southern writer should not address a large public, but if he does he will learn sooner or later that—but for happy accidents—the market, with what the market implies, dictates the style. To create a profession of literature in the South we should require first an independent machinery of publication. I fall into the mechanical terms. A Southern publishing system would not, I imagine, publish Southern books alone; nor should Southern magazines print only Southern authors. The point of the argument leads to no such comforting simplicity. The literary artist is seldom successful as a colonial; he should be able to enjoy the normal belief that he is at the center of the world. One aid to that feeling would be a congenial medium of communication with his public. Let the world in this fashion sit at his feet; let him not have to seek the world.

The exact degree of immediate satisfaction that Southern publication would bring to its authors I cannot predict. It, too, would be the system of the cash nexus; and the Southern publisher would be a capitalist plutocrat not noticeably different from his colleague in the North. Like his Northern friend he would, for a few years at least, sell the Southern article mostly north of the border. Until he could be backed by a powerful Southern press he would need the support of the New York journals for his authors, if he expected them to be read at home. I suppose the benefits of a Southern system would lie chiefly in this: that the Southern writer would not have to run the New York gauntlet, from which he emerges with a good understanding of what he can and cannot do.

We have exchanged the reasoned indifference of aristocracy for the piratical commercialism of plutocracy. Repudiating the later master, the new profession in the South would have to tell New York, where it had hitherto hawked its wares, that no more wares of the prescribed kind would be produced. For the prescribed ware is the ware that the Southerner also must produce, and it is not heartening to observe that his own Southern public waits for the New York journals to prescribe the kind, before he can get a hearing at home. Can there be a profession of letters in the South? Our best critical writing—and we have critical writing of distinction—can never constitute a Southern criticism so long as it must be trimmed and scattered in Northern magazines, or published in books that will be read as curiously as travel literature, by Northern people alone.

The considerable achievement of Southerners in modern American letters must not beguile us into too much hope for the future. The Southern novelist has left his mark upon the age; but it is of the age. From the peculiarly historical consciousness of the Southern writer has come good work of a special order; but the focus of this consciousness is quite temporary. It has made possible the curious burst of intelligence that we get at a crossing of the ways, not unlike, on an infinitesimal scale, the outburst of poetic genius at the end of the sixteenth century when commercial England had already begun to crush feudal England. The Histories and Tragedies of Shakespeare record the death of the old regime, and Doctor Faustus gives up feudal order for world power.

The prevailing economic passion of the age once more tempts, even commands, the Southern writer to go into politics. Our neo-communism is the new form in which the writer from all sections is to be dominated by capitalism, or "economic society." It is the new political mania. And there is no escape from it. The political mind always finds itself in an emergency. And the emergency, this time real enough, becomes a pretext for ignoring the arts. We live in the sort of age that Abraham Cowley complained of—a good age to write about but a hard age to write in.

1935

THE NEW PROVINCIALISM

With an Epilogue on the Southern Novel

A note written around a subject needs a formidable title to remind the writer where he is going and to make the elusive subject a little clearer to the reader. I confess to feelings of peculiar inadequacy on this occasion;[1] it reminds me of a similar occasion ten years ago, when I was writing an essay for the tenth anniversary number of *The Virginia Quarterly Review*. That essay (as I recall it: I have not been able to bring myself to reread it as I begin to write)—that essay was possibly a little stuffy and more certain of itself than these notes can be. It was written at the height of the Southern literary renascence. That renascence is over; or at any rate that period is over; and I write, we all write, in the time of the greatest war. Will the new literature of the South, or of the United States as a whole, be different from anything that we knew before the war? Will American literature be more alike all over the country? And more like the literature of the world?

An affirmative answer to the last question would make our literary nationalists—Mr. Van Wyck Brooks, Mr. Kazin, and Mr. De Voto—look a little old-fashioned, very much as they have actually been all along as the intellectual contemporaries of Buckle and Taine. Their influence is no longer very much felt by anybody who seriously writes; and it is sufficient here merely to state the paradox that not even literary nationalism could abort a genuine national literature when it is ready to appear; when, in fact, we become a nation. But it is more likely that we may become an internation first. These reflections are set down to prepare for something that I have long wanted the occasion to say: that mere regionalism, as we have heard it talked about in recent years, is not enough.

For this picturesque regionalism of local color is a by-product of nationalism. And it is not informed enough to support a mature literature. But neither is nationalism.

Yet no literature can be mature without the regional consciousness; it can only be senile, with the renewed immaturity of senility. For without regionalism, without locality in the sense of local continuity in tradition and belief, we shall get a whole literature which Mr. John Dos Passos might have written: perhaps a whole literature which, in spite of my admiration for Mr. Dos Passos' novels, I shall not even be able to read. This new literature will probably be personal, sentimentally objective, tough, and "unsocial," and will doubtless achieve its best effects in a new version of the old travel story (like most of Mr. Dos Passos' books, which are travel stories) both abroad and at home: the account of voyages to the South and West, and to the ends of the world. New Crusoes, new Captain Singletons, new Gullivers will appear, but Gullivers who see *with,* not *through* the eye. It will not be a "national" literature, or even an "international"; it may be a provincial literature with world horizons, the horizons of the geographical world, which need not be spiritually larger than Bourbon County, Kentucky: provincialism without regionalism.

II

If regionalism is not enough, is a world provincialism enough? It has been generally supposed in our time that the limitations of the mere regional interest, which are serious, could be corrected by giving them up for a "universal" point of view, a political or social doctrine which would "relate" or "integrate" the local community with the world in the advance of a higher culture. What this higher culture is or might be nobody was ever quite clear about. It looked political, or at any rate "social," and it ranged in imaginative emphasis all the way from the Stalinist party line, upon whose front, in this country, was written the slogan, Defense of Culture (*whose culture?*), to Mr. Wallace's Common Man, whom Mr. Wallace seemed willing to let remain common.

What it never occurred to anybody to ask was this simple question: What happens if you make the entire world into one vast region? This, it seems to me, is the trouble with our world schemes today: they contemplate a large extension of the political and philosophical limitations of the regional principle. "Let's get closer to the Chinese." "Know your fellow men, and you will like them better, and cease to fight them." Are these propositions true? I doubt it. Europeans are fighting one another today not because they didn't "know" one another. It does not, of course, follow that they are fighting because they did know one another; but that proposition makes as good sense as its contrary. For the real end is not physical communication, or parochial neighborliness on a world scale. The real end, as I see it, is *what* you are communicating after you get the physical means of communication. It is possible for men to face one another and not have anything to say. In that case it may occur to them, since they cannot establish a common understanding, to try to take something away from one another; and they may temporarily establish, as they did a generation ago, certain rules of mutual plunder that look for a time like "international cooperation."

All this has a bearing on literature today, the literature of the United States, and of the South, in the recent past and in the near future. For the logical opposite, or the historic complement, of the isolated community or region is not the world community or world region. In our time we have been the victims of a geographical metaphor, or a figure of space: we have tried to compensate for the limitations of the little community by envisaging the big community, which is not necessarily bigger spiritually or culturally than the little community. The complement of the regional principle, the only force which in the past has kept the region (of whatever size) from being provincial, from being committed to the immediate interest, is a non-political or supra-political culture such as held Europe together for six hundred years and kept war to the "limited objective." That is to say, there was sufficient unity, somewhere at the top, to check the drive of mere interest, and to limit war to a few massacres prompted by religious zeal or by the desire of rulers to keep their neighbors from getting out of hand. The small professional army at the top never tried to use and thus to menace the vast, stable energy of the masses, until the age of Louis XIV; and it was not until Napoleon that it was thought possible to make a whole nation fight.

The kind of unity prevailing in the West until the nineteenth century has been well described by Christopher Dawson as a peculiar balance of Greek culture and Christian other-worldliness, both imposed by Rome upon the northern barbarians. It was this special combination that made European civilization, and it was this that men communicated in the act of living together. It was this force which reduced the regional heterogeneity to a manageable unity, or even sublimated it into universal forms. Is not this civilization just about gone? Only men who are committed to perverse illusion or to public oratory believe that we have a Christian civilization today: we still have Christians in every real sense, but in neither politics nor education, by and large, do Christian motives or standards, or even references, have an effective part. We do not ask: Is this right? We ask: Will this work? It is the typical question for men who represent the decadent humanism of the Greek half of our tradition. For that humanism has ended up as the half of a half: it stands for only half of the Greek spirit, the empirical or scientific half which gives us our technology. Technology without Christianity is, I think, barbarism quite simply; but barbarism refined, violent, and decadent, not the vigorous barbarism of the forest and the soil. I do not believe that we could say of our culture what Burke said of the English in 1790, that we have not "subtilized ourselves into savagery."

This is the catastrophic view. I did not originate it. And I suppose it cannot be wholly true. A few men will still somehow evade total efficiency, and live much as they did in the past; many will be bored by machines or, like the retired banker in my community, refuse to use their products by making by hand the articles of daily utility. The individual human being will probably have in the future as in the past a natural economy to which he can occasionally return, if he is not meddled with too much by power at a distance.

This natural economy cannot be an effective check upon the standardizing forces of the outside world without the protection of the regional consciousness. For regionalism is that consciousness or that habit of men in a given locality which influences them to certain patterns of thought and conduct handed to them by their ancestors. Regionalism is thus limited in space but not in time.

The provincial attitude is limited in time but not in space. When the regional man, in his ignorance, often an intensive and creative ignorance, of the world, extends his own immediate necessities into the world, and assumes that the present moment is unique, he becomes the provincial man. He cuts himself off from the past, and without benefit of the fund of traditional wisdom approaches the simplest problems of life as if nobody had ever heard of them before. A society without arts, said Plato, lives by chance. The provincial man, locked in the present, lives by chance.

III

It must be plain from this train of ideas whither I am leading this discussion. For the world today is perhaps more provincial in outlook than it has been at any time since the ninth century, and even that era had, in its primitive agrarian economy, a strong regional basis for individual independence. Industrial capitalism has given us provincialism without regionalism: we are committed to chance solutions of "problems" that seem unique because we have forgotten the nature of man. And having destroyed our regional societies in the West, we are fanatically trying to draw other peoples into our provincial orbit, for the purpose of "saving" them.

Our Utopian politics is provincial. It is all very well to meet at Dumbarton Oaks or on the Black Sea to arrange the world, but unless the protagonists of these dramas of journalism have secret powers the presence of which we have hitherto had no reason to suspect, the results for the world must almost necessarily be power politics, or mere *rules of plunder which look like cooperation*. The desired cooperation is for the physical welfare of man. But it is a curious fact (I have not been able to find any history which denies the fact) that the physical welfare of man, pursued as an end in itself, has seldom prospered. The nineteenth century dream of a secular Utopia produced Marxian socialism, National Socialism, and the two greatest wars of history; and it is perhaps only another sign of our provincialism that we ignore the causation between the dream and the wars, and urge more of the same dream to prevent other wars which the dream will doubtless have its part in causing. Nobody wants to see the Oriental peoples dominated by the Japanese and to go hungry and ill-clad; yet so far in the history of civilization it has been virtually impossible to feed and clothe people with food and clothing. It is my own impression that they get fed and clothed incidentally to some other impulse, a creative power which we sometimes identify with religion and the arts.

It is small game; yet are not the Four Freedoms a typical expression of our world provincialism? Here is a radio fantasy on the secular dream of the nineteenth century. We guarantee to the world freedom of thought—to think about what? (I had supposed we were opposed to freedom of thought for the Germans and the Japanese.) Is it freedom to think *our* thoughts? We guarantee to the world freedom of worship—to worship what? Unless you cut the worship off from everything else that the Javanese, the Hottentots, the Russians, and the Americans may be doing (in our own case we have almost succeeded in this), what is to keep the Javanese, the Hottentots, the Russians, and ourselves from worshiping a war-god and putting this religion to the test of action? We guarantee to the world freedom from want. We had better—or somebody had better guarantee it, even if the guarantee is no good; for nineteenth-century industrial capitalism and our own more advanced technology have made it very difficult for "backward peoples" (to say nothing of ourselves in small units and groups) to make their living independently of somebody else nine thousand miles away. In other words we have destroyed the regional economies, and we offer a provincial remedy for the resulting evils; that is to say, a Utopian remedy which ignores our past experience. We guarantee to the world freedom from fear. On this freedom I confess that I have nothing to say. Provincial arrogance could not go further; and if my own religion had not been destroyed by the same forces that destroyed Mr. Roosevelt's and Mr. Churchill's (I do not deny them or myself feelings of common piety), I should expect the wrath of God to strike them. I infer from the hedging cynicism of their repudiation of the Four Freedoms as an "official document" the casual frivolity with which they must have written it in the first place. There was a radio on the ship. The ease of modern communication compelled these gentlemen to communicate with the world, when there was nothing to communicate.

IV

I am a little embarrassed at having used so many large conceptions, with so little specification. I ought to make plainer, before I go further, certain connections between regionalism and provincialism that I have only implied. The regional society is, with respect to high civilization, the neutral society: it can be primitive or highly cultivated, or any of the steps between. In the West our peculiar civilization was based upon regional autonomy, whose eccentricities were corrected and sublimated by the classical-Christian culture which provided a form for the highest development of man's potentialities *as man*. Man belonged to his village, valley, mountain, or sea-coast; but wherever he was he was a Christian whose Hebraic discipline had tempered his tribal savagery and whose classical humanism had moderated the literal imperative of his Christianity to suicidal other-worldliness.

If this peculiar culture of the West is weakening or is even gone as a creative force, we are left with our diverse regionalisms; or *were* left with them. For the myth of science which undermined this culture and created the modern economic man rooted out the regional economies, and is now creating a world regional economy. Regional economy means interdependence of the citizens of a region, whether the region be an Alpine village or the world. And the world, like the Alpine village, can be neutral with respect to high civilization. Regionalism without civilization—which means, with us, regionalism without the classical-Christian culture—becomes provincialism; and world regionalism becomes world provincialism. For provincialism is that state of mind in which regional men lose their origins in the past and its continuity into the present, and begin every day as if there had been no yesterday.

We are committed to this state of mind. We are so deeply involved in it (I make no exception of myself) that we must participate in its better purposes, however incomplete they may be; for good-will, even towards the Four Freedoms, is better than ill-will; and I am convinced that even the die-hard traditionalist would deny his own shrinking tradition if he refused to act for the remnant of it left because he can't have it all. For this remnant may be useful; there will be a minority with a memory which has not been dimmed by what Christian Gauss has called the Reversal of the Time Sense. We shall not all derive our standards of human nature and of the good society from an unexperienced future imagined by the late H. G. Wells or Mr. Henry Wallace.

v

The brilliant and unexpected renascence of Southern writing between the two wars is perhaps not of the first importance in the literature of the modern world; yet for the first time the South had a literature of considerable maturity which was distinctive enough to call for a special criticism which it failed to get. The provincial ideas of the critics of the North and East (there was no Southern criticism: merely a few Southern critics)—the provincial views of Southern writing of the recent renascence followed a direction somewhat as follows: The South, backward and illiberal, and controlled by white men who cherish a unique moral perversity, does not offer in itself a worthy subject to the novelist or the poet; it follows that the only acceptable literature that the South can produce must be a literature of social agitation, through which the need of reform may be publicized.

There were dozens of Southern novels written to this prescription. (I can think of only one Southern novelist of the period who ignored it and who was continuously popular: the late Elizabeth Madox Roberts.) The formula generally imposed two limitations upon the Southern writer: first, he must ignore the historical background of his subject; and second, he must judge the subject strictly in terms of the material welfare of his characters and of the "injustice" which keeps them from getting enough of it. My testimony is perhaps not wholly disinterested, yet I am convinced that not one distinguished novel was produced in or about the South from this point of view. The novel that came nearest to real distinction was probably Miss Glasgow's *Barren Ground;* but even this excellent novel is written outside the subject, with the result that the frustration of her Virginia farmers is not examined as an instance of the decay of rural culture everywhere, but rather as a simple object-lesson in the lack of standard American "advantages." (Miss Glasgow's other and later books pose other problems, chiefly the problem of the consciously "liberal" writer who draws his knowledge of human nature from a source richer than that of his ideas, and who thus writes somewhat below the level of his historical tradition.) But this is not a roster of all the sociological novels about the South from 1918 to the present. If these notes were a parlor game, I should challenge the "critics" who hailed them in the twenties and thirties to exhibit just one novel of this school which they would be willing to let compete with the best European writing of the period.

There has been some confusion in the South as well as elsewhere about the subjects accessible to Southern writers; this confusion results from the appeal to history: what *is* the structure of Southern society? What *was* it in the eighteen-forties and -fifties? It is not necessary, fortunately, to answer those questions here. To bring these notes to a close I should like to make a few elementary distinctions. If the Southern subject is the destruction by war and the later degradation of the South by carpetbaggers and scalawags, and a consequent lack of moral force and imagination in the cynical materialism of the New South, then the sociologists of fiction and the so-called traditionalists are trying to talk about the same thing. But with this difference—and it is a difference between two worlds: the provincial world of the present, which sees in material welfare and legal justice the whole solution to the human problem; and the classical-Christian world, based upon the regional consciousness, which held that honor, truth, imagination, human dignity, and limited acquisitiveness, could alone justify a social order however rich and efficient it may be; and could do much to redeem an order dilapidated and corrupt, like the South today, if a few people passionately hold those beliefs.

So, in the period of the Southern renascence, our writers, poets as well as novelists, may be put into the two broad groups which I have indicated. Among the traditionalists whose work I believe will last I should name Stark Young, Elizabeth Madox Roberts, Katherine Anne Porter, Robert Penn Warren, Caroline Gordon, Ellen Glasgow (especially in *The Sheltered Life*), and William Faulkner, who is the most powerful and original novelist in the United States and one of the best in the modern world. It ought to be plain that by traditionalist I do not mean a writer who either accepts or rejects the conventional picture of Southern life in the past. By the traditional as opposed to the provincial writer, I mean the writer who takes the South as he knows it today or can find out about it in the past, and who sees it as a region with some special characteristics, but otherwise offering as an imaginative subject the plight of human beings as it has been and will doubtless continue to be, here and in other parts of the world.

But if the provincial outlook, as I have glanced at it here, is to prevail, there is no reason to think that the South will remain immune to it. With the war of 1914-1918, the South re-entered the world—but gave a backward glance as it stepped over the border: that backward glance gave us the Southern renascence, a literature conscious of the past in the present. In the essay to which I referred in the first paragraph of these notes (I have now reread it) I said: "From the peculiarly historical consciousness of the Southern writer has come good work of a special order; but the focus of this consciousness is quite temporary. It has made possible the curious burst of intelligence that we get at a crossing of the ways, not unlike, on an infinitesimal scale, the outburst of poetic genius at the end of the sixteenth century when commercial England had already begun to crush feudal England." I see no reason to change that view.

From now on we are committed to seeing *with,* not *through* the eye: we, as provincials who do not live anywhere.

1945

NARCISSUS AS NARCISSUS

On this first occasion, which will probably be the last, of my writing about my own verse, I could plead in excuse the example of Edgar Allan Poe, who wrote about himself in an essay called "The Philosophy of Composition." But in our age the appeal to authority is weak, and I am of my age. What I happen to know about the poem that I shall discuss is limited. I remember merely my intention in writing it; I do not know whether the poem is good; and I do not know its obscure origins.

How does one happen to write a poem: where does it come from? That is the question asked by the psychologists or the geneticists of poetry. Of late I have not read any of the genetic theories very attentively: years ago I read one by Mr. Conrad Aiken; another, I think, by Mr. Robert Graves; but I have forgotten them. I am not ridiculing verbal mechanisms, dreams, or repressions as origins of poetry; all three of them and more besides may have a great deal to do with it. Other psychological theories say a good deal about compensation. A poem is an indirect effort of a shaky man to justify himself to happier men, or to present a superior account of his relation to a world that allows him but little certainty, and would allow equally little to the happier men if they did not wear blinders—according to the poet. For example, a poet might be a man who could not get enough self-justification out of being an automobile salesman (whose certainty is a fixed quota of cars every month) to rest comfortably upon it. So the poet, who wants to be something that he cannot be, and is a failure in plain life, makes up fictitious versions of his predicament that are interesting even to other persons because nobody is a perfect automobile salesman. Everybody, alas, suffers a little. . . . I constantly read this kind of criticism of my own verse. According to its doctors, my one intransigent desire is to have been a Confederate general, and because I could not or would not become anything else, I set up for poet and began to invent fictions about the personal ambitions that my society has no use for.

Although a theory may not be "true," it may make certain insights available for a while; and I have deemed it proper to notice theories of the genetic variety because a poet talking about himself is often expected, as the best authority, to explain the origins of his poems. But persons interested in origins are seldom quick to use them. Poets, in their way, are practical men; they are interested in results. What is the poem, after it is written? That is the question. Not where it came from, or why. The Why and Where can never get beyond the guessing stage because, in the language of those who think it can, poetry cannot be brought to "laboratory conditions." The only real evidence that any critic may bring before his gaze is the finished poem. For some reason most critics have a hard time fixing their minds directly under their noses, and before they see the object that is there they use a telescope upon the horizon to see where it came from. They are wood cutters who do their job by finding out where the ore came from in the iron of the steel of the blade of the ax that Jack built. I do not say that this procedure is without its own contributory insights; but the insights are merely contributory and should not replace the poem, which is the object upon which they must be focused. A poem may be an instance of morality, of social conditions, of psychological history; it may instance all its qualities, but never one of them alone, nor any two or three; never less than all.

Genetic theories, I gather, have been cherished academically with detachment. Among "critics" they have been useless and not quite disinterested: I have myself found them applicable to the work of poets whom I do not like. That is the easiest way.

I say all this because it seems to me that my verse or anybody else's is merely a way of knowing something: if the poem is a real creation, it is a kind of knowledge that we did not possess before. It is not knowledge "about" something

else; the poem is the fullness of that knowledge. We know
the particular poem, not what it says that we can restate.
In a manner of speaking, the poem is its own knower,
neither poet nor reader knowing anything that the poem says
apart from the words of the poem. I have expressed this
view elsewhere in other terms, and it has been accused of
aestheticism or art for art's sake. But let the reader recall
the historic position of Catholicism: *nulla salus extra ec-
clesiam.* That must be religion*ism.* There is probably nothing
wrong with art for art's sake if we take the phrase seriously,
and not take it to mean the kind of poetry written in England forty years ago. Religion always ought to transcend any
of its particular uses; and likewise the true art-for-art's-sake
view can be held only by persons who are always looking for
things that they can respect apart from use (though they may
be useful), like poems, fly-rods, and formal gardens. . . .
These are negative postulates, and I am going to illustrate
them with some commentary on a poem called "Ode to the
Confederate Dead."

II

That poem is "about" solipsism, a philosophical doctrine
which says that we create the world in the act of perceiving
it; or about Narcissism, or any other *ism* that denotes the
failure of the human personality to function objectively in
nature and society. Society (and "nature" as modern society
constructs it) appears to offer limited fields for the exercise
of the whole man, who wastes his energy piecemeal over
separate functions that ought to come under a unity of being.
(Until the last generation, only certain women were whores,
having been set aside as special instances of sex amid a social scheme that held the general belief that sex must be part
of a whole; now the general belief is that sex must be special.)
Without unity we get the remarkable self-consciousness of
our age. Everybody is talking about this evil, and a great
many persons know what ought to be done to correct it.
As a citizen I have my own prescription, but as a poet I

am concerned with the experience of "solipsism." And an experience *of* it is not quite the same thing as a philosophical statement *about* it.

I should have trouble connecting solipsism and the Confederate dead in a rational argument; I should make a fool of myself in the discussion, because I know no more of the Confederate dead or of solipsism than hundreds of other people. (Possibly less: the dead Confederates may be presumed to have a certain privacy; and as for solipsism, I blush in the presence of philosophers, who know all about Bishop Berkeley; I use the term here in its strict etymology.) And if I call this interest in one's ego Narcissism, I make myself a logical ignoramus, and I take liberties with mythology. I use Narcissism to mean only preoccupation with self; it may be either love or hate. But a good psychiatrist knows that it means self-love only, and otherwise he can talk about it more coherently, knows more about it than I shall ever hope or desire to know. He would look at me professionally if I uttered the remark that the modern squirrel cage of our sensibility, the extreme introspection of our time, has anything whatever to do with the Confederate dead.

But when the doctor looks at literature it is a question whether he sees it: the sea boils and pigs have wings because in poetry all things are possible—if you are man enough. They are possible because in poetry the disparate elements are not combined in logic, which can join things only under certain categories and under the law of contradiction; they are combined in poetry rather as experience, and experience has decided to ignore logic, except perhaps as another field of experience. Experience means conflict, our natures being what they are, and conflict means drama. Dramatic experience is not logical; it may be subdued to the kind of coherence that we indicate when we speak, in criticism, of form. Indeed, as experience, this conflict is always a logical contradiction, or philosophically an antinomy. Serious poetry deals with the fundamental conflicts that cannot be logically resolved: we can state the conflicts rationally, but reason does not relieve us of them. Their only final coherence is the formal re-creation of art, which "freezes" the experience as permanently as a logical formula, but without, like the formula, leaving all but the logic out.

Narcissism and the Confederate dead cannot be connected logically, or even historically; even were the connection an historical fact, they would not stand connected as art, for no one experiences raw history. The proof of the connection must lie, if anywhere, in the experienced conflict which is the poem itself. Since one set of references for the conflict is the historic Confederates, the poem, if it is successful, is a certain section of history made into experience, but only on this occasion, and on these terms: even the author of the poem has no experience of its history apart from the occasion and the terms.

It will be understood that I do not claim even a partial success in the junction of the two "ideas" in the poem that I am about to discuss. I am describing an intention, and the labor of revising the poem—a labor spread over ten years— fairly exposes the lack of confidence that I have felt and still feel in it. All the tests of its success in style and versification would come in the end to a single test, an answer, yes or no, to the question: Assuming that the Confederates and Narcissus are not yoked together by mere violence, has the poet convinced the reader that, on the specific occasion of this poem, there is a necessary yet hitherto undetected relation between them? By necessary I mean dramatically relevant, a relation "discovered" in terms of the particular occasion, not historically argued or philosophically deduced. Should the question that I have just asked be answered yes, then this poem or any other with its specific problem could be said to have form: what was previously a merely felt quality of life has been raised to the level of experience—it has become specific, local, dramatic, "formal"—that is to say, *in*-formed.

III

The structure of the Ode is simple. Figure to yourself a man stopping at the gate of a Confederate graveyard on a late autumn afternoon. The leaves are falling; his first impressions bring him the "rumor of mortality"; and the desolation barely allows him, at the beginning of the second stanza, the conventionally heroic surmise that the dead will enrich the earth, "where these memories grow." From those quoted words to the end of that passage he pauses for a baroque meditation on the ravages of time, concluding with the figure of the "blind crab." This creature has mobility but no direction; energy but, from the human point of view, no purposeful world to use it in: in the entire poem there are only two explicit symbols for the locked-in ego; the crab is the first and less explicit symbol, a mere hint, a planting of the idea that will become overt in its second instance—the jaguar towards the end. The crab is the first intimation of the nature of the moral conflict upon which the drama of the poem develops: the cut-off-ness of the modern "intellectual man" from the world.

The next long passage or "strophe," beginning "You know who have waited by the wall," states the other term of the conflict. It is the theme of heroism, not merely moral heroism, but heroism* in the grand style, elevating even death from mere physical dissolution into a formal ritual: this heroism is a formal ebullience of the human spirit in an entire society, not private, romantic illusion—something better than moral heroism, great as that may be, for moral heroism, being personal and individual, may be achieved by certain men in all ages, even ages of decadence. But the late Hart Crane's commentary, in a letter, is better than any I can make; he described the theme as the "theme of chivalry, a tradition of excess (not literally excess, rather active faith) which cannot be perpetuated in the fragmentary cosmos of today—'those desires which should be yours tomorrow,' but which, you know, will not persist nor find any way into action."

The structure then is the objective frame for the tension between the two themes, "active faith" which has decayed, and the "fragmentary cosmos" which surrounds us. (I must repeat here that this is not a philosophical thesis; it is an analytical statement of a conflict that is concrete within the poem.) In contemplating the heroic theme the man at the gate never quite commits himself to the illusion of its availability to him. The most that he can allow himself is the fancy that the blowing leaves are charging soldiers, but he rigorously returns to the refrain: "Only the wind"—or the "leaves flying." I suppose it is a commentary on our age that the man at the gate never quite achieves the illusion that the leaves are heroic men, so that he may identify himself with them, as Keats and Shelley too easily and too beautifully did with nightingales and west winds. More than this, he cautions himself, reminds himself repeatedly of his subjective prison, his solipsism, by breaking off the half-illusion and coming back to the refrain of wind and leaves—a refrain that, as Hart Crane said, is necessary to the "subjective continuity."

These two themes struggle for mastery up to the passage,

> *We shall say only the leaves whispering*
> *In the improbable mist of nightfall—*

which is near the end. It will be observed that the passage begins with a phrase taken from the wind-leaves refrain— the signal that it has won. The refrain has been fused with the main stream of the man's reflections, dominating them; and he cannot return even to an ironic vision of the heroes. There is nothing but death, the mere naturalism of death at that—spiritual extinction in the decay of the body. Autumn and the leaves are death; the men who exemplified in a grand style an "active faith" are dead; there are only the leaves.

Shall we then worship death . . .

> *. . . set up the grave*
> *In the house? The ravenous grave . . .*

that will take us before our time? The question is not answered, although as a kind of morbid romanticism it might, if answered affirmatively, provide the man with an illusory escape from his solipsism; but he cannot accept it. Nor has he been able to live in his immediate world, the fragmentary cosmos. There is no practical solution, no solution offered for the edification of moralists. (To those who may identify the man at the gate with the author of the poem I would say: He differs from the author in not accepting a "practical solution," for the author's personal dilemma is perhaps not quite so exclusive as that of the meditating man.) The main intention of the poem has been to make dramatically visible the conflict, to concentrate it, to present it, in Mr. R. P. Blackmur's phrase, as "experienced form"—not as a logical dilemma.

The closing image, that of the serpent, is the ancient symbol of time, and I tried to give it the credibility of the commonplace by placing it in a mulberry bush—with the faint hope that the silkworm would somehow be implicit. But time is also death. If that is so, then space, or the Becoming, is life; and I believe there is not a single spatial symbol in the poem. "Sea-space" is allowed the "blind crab"; but the sea, as appears plainly in the passage beginning, "Now that the salt of their blood . . ." is life only in so far as it is the source of the lowest forms of life, the source perhaps of all life, but life undifferentiated, halfway between life and death. This passage is a contrasting inversion of the conventional

> . . . *inexhaustible bodies that are not*
> *Dead, but feed the grass . . .*

the reduction of the earlier, literary conceit to a more naturalistic figure derived from modern biological speculation. These "buried Caesars" will not bloom in the hyacinth but will only make saltier the sea.

The wind-leaves refrain was added to the poem in 1930, nearly five years after the first draft was written. I felt that the danger of adding it was small because, implicit in the long strophes of meditation, the ironic commentary on the vanished heroes was already there, giving the poem such dramatic tension as it had in the earlier version. The refrain makes the commentary more explicit, more visibly dramatic, and renders quite plain, as Hart Crane intimated, the subjective character of the imagery throughout. But there was another reason for it, besides the increased visualization that it imparts to the dramatic conflict. It "times" the poem better, offers the reader frequent pauses in the development of the two themes, allows him occasions of assimilation; and on the whole—this was my hope and intention—the refrain makes the poem seem longer than it is and thus eases the concentration of imagery—without, I hope, sacrificing a possible effect of concentration.

IV

I have been asked why I called the poem an ode. I first called it an elegy. It is an ode only in the sense in which Cowley in the seventeenth century misunderstood the real structure of the Pindaric ode. Not only are the meter and rhyme without fixed pattern, but in another feature the poem is even further removed from Pindar than Abraham Cowley was: a purely subjective meditation would not even in Cowley's age have been called an ode. I suppose in so calling it I intended an irony: the scene of the poem is not a public celebration, it is a lone man by a gate.

The dominant rhythm is "mounting," the dominant meter iambic pentameter varied with six-, four-, and three-stressed lines; but this was not planned in advance for variety. I adapted the meter to the effect desired at the moment. The model for the irregular rhyming was "Lycidas," but other models could have served. The rhymes in a given strophe I tried to adjust to the rhythm and the texture of feeling and image. For example, take this passage in the second strophe:

> *Autumn is desolation in the plot*
> *Of a thousand acres where these memories grow*
> *From the inexhaustible bodies that are not*
> *Dead, but feed the grass row after rich row.*
> *Think of the autumns that have come and gone!—*
> *Ambitious November with the humors of the year,*
> *With a particular zeal for every slab,*
> *Staining the uncomfortable angels that rot*
> *On the slabs, a wing chipped here, an arm there:*
> *The brute curiosity of an angel's stare*
> *Turns you, like them, to stone,*
> *Transforms the heaving air*

Till plunged to a heavier world below
You shift your sea-space blindly
Heaving, turning like the blind crab.

There is rhymed with *year* (to many persons, perhaps, only a half-rhyme), and I hoped the reader would unconsciously assume that he need not expect further use of that sound for some time. So when the line, "The brute curiosity of an angel's stare," comes a moment later, rhyming with *year-there,* I hoped that the violence of image would be further reinforced by the repetition of a sound that was no longer expected. I wanted the shock to be heavy; so I felt that I could not afford to hurry the reader away from it until he had received it in full. The next two lines carry on the image at a lower intensity: the rhyme, "Transforms the heaving *air,*" prolongs the moment of attention upon that passage, while at the same time it ought to begin dissipating the shock, both by the introduction of a new image and by re-duction of the "meaning" to a pattern of sound, the ere-rhymes. I calculated that the third use of that sound (stare) would be a surprise, the fourth (air) a monotony. I purposely made the end words of the third from last and last lines—*below* and *crab*—delayed rhymes for *row* and *slab,* the last being an internal and half-dissonant rhyme for the sake of bewilderment and incompleteness, qualities by which the man at the gate is at the moment possessed.

This is elementary but I cannot vouch for its success. As the dramatic situation of the poem is the tension that I have already described, so the rhythm is an attempt at a series of "modulations" back and forth between a formal regularity, for the heroic emotion, and a broken rhythm, with scattering imagery, for the failure of that emotion. This is "imitative form," which Yvor Winters deems a vice worth castigation. I have pointed out that the passage, "You know who have waited by the wall," presents the heroic theme of "active faith"; it will be observed that the rhythm, increasingly after "You who have waited for the angry resolution," is almost perfectly regular iambic, with only a few initial substitutions and weak endings. The passage is meant to convey a plenary vision, the actual presence, of the exemplars of active faith: the man at the gate at that moment is nearer to realizing them than at any other in the poem; hence the formal rhythm. But the vision breaks down; the wind-leaves refrain supervenes; and the next passage, "Turn your eyes to the immoderate past," is the irony of the preceding realization. With the self-conscious historical sense he turns his eyes into the past. The next passage after this, beginning, "You hear the shout . . ." is the failure of the vision in both phases, the pure realization and the merely historical. He cannot "see" the heroic virtues; there is wind, rain, leaves. But there is sound; for a moment he deceives himself with it. It is the noise of the battles that he has evoked. Then comes the figure of the rising sun of those battles; he is "lost in that orient of the thick and fast," and he curses his own moment, "the setting sun." The "setting sun" I tried to use as a triple image, for the decline of the heroic age and for the actual scene of late afternoon, the latter being not only natural desolation but spiritual desolation as well. Again for a moment he thinks he hears the battle shout, but only for a moment; then the silence reaches him.

Corresponding to the disintegration of the vision just described, there has been a breaking down of the formal rhythm. The complete breakdown comes with the images of the "mummy" and the "hound bitch." (*Hound* bitch because the hound is a hunter, participant of a formal ritual.) The failure of the vision throws the man back upon himself, but upon himself he cannot bring to bear the force of sustained imagination. He sees himself in random images (random to him, deliberate with the author) of something lower than he ought to be: the human image is only that of preserved death; but if he is alive he is an old hunter, dying. The passages about the mummy and the bitch are deliberately brief —slight rhythmic stretches. (These are the only verses I have written for which I thought of the movement first, then cast about for the symbols.)

I believe the term "modulation" denotes in music the uninterrupted shift from one key to another: I do not know the term for change of rhythm without change of measure.

I wish to describe a similar change in verse rhythm; it may
be convenient to think of it as modulation of a certain kind.
At the end of the passage that I have been discussing the
final words are "Hears the wind only." The phrase closes
the first main division of the poem. I have loosely called the
longer passages strophes, and if I were hardy enough to impose the classical organization of the lyric ode upon a baroque
poem, I should say that these words bring to an end the
Strophe, after which must come the next main division, or
Antistrophe, which was often employed to answer the matter
set forth in the Strophe or to present it from another point
of view. And that is precisely the significance of the next
main division, beginning: "Now that the salt of their
blood. . . ." But I wanted this second division of the poem to
arise out of the collapse of the first. It is plain that it would
not have suited my purpose to round off the first section with
some sort of formal rhythm; so I ended it with an unfinished
line. The next division must therefore begin by finishing
that line, not merely in meter but with an integral rhythm.
I will quote the passage:

> The hound bitch
> *Toothless and dying, in a musty cellar*
> Hears the wind only.
>
> Now that the salt of their blood
> *Stiffens the saltier oblivion of the sea,*
> *Seals the malignant purity of the flood. . . .*

The caesura, after *only,* is thus at the middle of the third
foot. (I do not give a full stress to *wind,* but attribute a "hovering stress" to *wind* and the first syllable of *only.*) The
reader expects the foot to be completed by the stress on the
next word, *Now,* as in a sense it is; but the phrase, "Now
that the salt of their blood," is also the beginning of a new
movement; it is two "dactyls" continuing more broadly the
falling rhythm that has prevailed. But with the finishing off
of the line with *blood,* the mounting rhythm is restored; the
whole line from *Hears* to *blood* is actually an iambic pentameter with liberal inversions and substitutions that were

expected to create a counter-rhythm within the line. From the caesura on, the rhythm is new; but it has—or was expected to have—an organic relation to the preceding rhythm; and it signals the rise of a new statement of the theme.

I have gone into this passage in detail—I might have chosen another—not because I think it is successful, but because I labored with it; if it is a failure, or even an uninteresting success, it ought to offer as much technical instruction to other persons as it would were it both successful and interesting. But a word more: the broader movement introduced by the new rhythm was meant to correspond, as a sort of Antistrophe, to the earlier formal movement beginning, "You know who have waited by the wall." It is a new formal movement with new feeling and new imagery. The heroic but precarious illusion of the earlier movement has broken down into the personal symbols of the mummy and the hound; the pathetic fallacy of the leaves as charging soldiers and the conventional "buried Caesar" theme have become rotten leaves and dead bodies wasting in the earth, to return after long erosion to the sea. In the midst of this naturalism, what shall the man say? What shall all humanity say in the presence of decay? The two themes, then, have been struggling for mastery; the structure of the poem thus exhibits the development of two formal passages that contrast the two themes. The two formal passages break down, the first shading into the second ("Now that the salt of their blood . . ."), the second one concluding with the figure of the jaguar, which is presented in a distracted rhythm left suspended from a weak ending—the word *victim*. This figure of the jaguar is the only explicit rendering of the Narcissus motif in the poem, but instead of a youth gazing into a pool, a predatory beast stares at a jungle stream, and leaps to devour himself.

The next passage begins:

> *What shall we say who have knowledge*
> *Carried to the heart?*

This is Pascal's war between heart and head, between *finesse* and *géométrie*. Should the reader care to think of these lines as the gathering up of the two themes, now fused, into a final statement, I should see no objection to calling it the Epode. But upon the meaning of the lines from here to the end there is no need for further commentary. I have talked about the structure of the poem, not its quality. One can no more find the quality of one's own verse than one can find its value, and to try to find either is like looking into a glass for the effect that one's face has upon other persons.

If anybody ever wished to know anything about this poem that he could not interpret for himself, I suspect that he is still in the dark. I cannot believe that I have illuminated the difficulties that some readers have found in the style. But then I cannot, have never been able to, see any difficulties of that order. The poem has been much revised. I still think there is much to be said for the original *barter* instead of *yield* in the second line, and for *Novembers* instead of *November* in line fifteen. The revisions were not undertaken for the convenience of the reader but for the poem's own clarity, so that, word, phrase, line, passage, the poem might at worst come near its best expression.

1938

NOTES

LITERATURE AS KNOWLEDGE

[1] *International Encyclopedia of Unified Science,* Vol. I, No. 2 (Chicago, 1938).

[2] *Denotata* are real things: *designata* may be pointed to, but they are not necessarily real. For example, the Phoenix' "spicy nest." The doctor's call is a *designatum* which is also a *denotatum*—it's "real."

[3] "Esthetics and the Theory of Signs," *The Journal of Unified Science,* VIII, 1-3, pp. 131-150; and "Science, Art, and Technology," *The Kenyon Review,* I, 4, pp. 409-423.

[4] "Foundations for the Theory of Signs," *loc. cit.,* p. 58.

[5] There seems to be evidence in this clause that Mr. Morris is not interested in syntactics.

[6] *Science and Poetry* (New York, 1926), pp. 28-29.

[7] "A Psychologist Looks at Poetry," *The World's Body* (New York, 1938), p. 147. This essay is the most searching examination of Mr. Richards' position—or positions—that I have seen; but it does somewhat less than full justice to Mr. Richards' insights.

[8] *Coleridge on Imagination,* pp. 157-8.

[9] *Ibid.,* p. 163.

[10] *Ibid.,* pp. 171-172.

TENSION IN POETRY

[1] His rejection of Shakespeare's sonnets seems to be a result of deductive necessity in his premises, or of the courage of mere logic; but the essay contains valuable insights into the operation of the metaphysical "conceit."

[2] Mr. F. O. Matthiessen informs me that my interpretation here, which detaches the "yet" from the developing figure, is not the usual one. Mr. Matthiessen refers the phrase to the gold, for which in his view it prepares the way.

THE SYMBOLIC IMAGINATION

[1] Quotations in English from *The Divine Comedy* are from the translation by Carlyle, Okey, and Wicksteed, in the Temple

Classics edition. Here and there I have taken the liberty of neutralizing certain victorian poeticisms, which were already archaic in that period.

[2] It seems scarcely necessary to remind the reader that I have followed in the scene of the Earthly Paradise only one thread of an immense number in a vastly complex pattern.

[3] The difficulties suffered by man as angel were known at least as early as Pascal; but the doctrine of angelism, as a force in the modern mind, has been fully set forth for the first time by Jacques Maritain in *The Dream of Descartes* (New York, 1944).

[4] Charles Williams, *The Figure of Beatrice* (London, 1943), p. 44.

[5] Another way of putting this is to say that the modern poet, like Valéry or Crane, tries to seize directly the anagogical meaning, without going through the three preparatory stages of letter, allegory, and trope.

[6] H. Flanders Dunbar, *Symbolism in Mediaeval Thought and Its Consummation in The Divine Comedy* (New Haven, 1929), p. 347.

[7] By "dramatic" I mean something like *practic,* a possible adjective from *praxis,* a general movement of action as potency which it is the purpose of the poem to actualize. In the Thomist sequence, *potentia:actio:actus,* "dramatic" would roughly correspond to the middle term.

[8] Oedipus does not achieve this, of course, until the end of *Oedipus at Colonus.*

[9] The popular "visual" translation of Aristotle's primary Unmoved Mover producing, *through being loved,* the primary cosmic motion, which is circular. The philosophical source of this idea, Book XII, Chapter 7, of the *Metaphysics,* Dante of course knew.

[10] Only two, placed at unequal distances from the candle, are strictly necessary for the experiment; but three are necessary as pointers towards the anagoge of the Trinity in the Triune Circles.

THE ANGELIC IMAGINATION

[1] *From Poe to Valéry* (New York, 1949).

[2] "Our Cousin, Mr. Poe," pp. 132-45 of this volume.

[3] Jacques et Raïssa Maritain, *Situation de la Poésie* (Paris, 1938), p. 58.

[4] *Cf.* Baudelaire's "Correspondances": "Les parfums, les couleurs, et les sons se répondent."

[5] Paul Valéry, *Variety: Second Series,* trans. from the French by William Aspenwall Bradley (New York, 1938), "The Position of Baudelaire," p. 90.

[6] Jacques Maritain, *The Dream of Descartes* (New York, 1944), Chap. 4, "The Cartesian Heritage," pp. 179-180. My debt to Mr. Maritain is so great that I hardly know how to acknowledge it.

[7] Strictly speaking, an *angelic imagination* is not possible. Angels by definition have unmediated knowledge of essences. See pp. 96-8.

[8] In the Virginia of Poe's time the subjects of conversation and reading were almost exclusively politics and theology. The educated Virginian was a deist by conviction and an Anglican or a Presbyterian by habit.

[9] Pascale's *Pensées,* with an English translation, brief notes and Introduction by H. F. Stewart, D.D. (New York, 1950), Adversaria 16; p. 377.

OUR COUSIN, MR. POE

[1] The theory that Poe was sexually impotent.

[2] I expect to examine Poe's verse on another occasion. It may be remarked that his verse rhythms are for the metronome, not the human ear. Its real defects are so great that it is not necessary to invent others, as Mr. T. S. Eliot seems to do in *From Poe to Valéry* (New York, 1949). Thus Mr. Eliot (and I cite only one of his observations that seem to me wrong) complains that "the saintly days of yore" could not be an appropriate time for the Raven to have lived. Elijah was fed by Ravens, a bird which was almost extinct in America in the 1840's. Ravens frequently fed hermits and saints and were in fact a fairly standard feature of saintly equipment.

THE HOVERING FLY

[1] This essay was read as one of the *Mesures Lectures* at Princeton University, on April 8, 1943. The general subject of the series was "The Imagination and the Actual World."

[2] *Partisan Review,* vol. X, nos. 1-4 (January-February, March-April, May-June, July-August, 1943).

IS LITERARY CRITICISM POSSIBLE?

[1] Analogous to the natural sciences.

[2] I hope it is plain by this time that by "rhetorical analysis" and the "study of rhetoric" I do not mean the prevailing *explication of texts.* If rhetoric is the *full* language of experience, its study must be informed by a peculiar talent, not wholly reducible to method, which I have in the past called the "historical imagination," a power that has little to do with the academic routine of "historical method." For a brilliant recent statement of this difference, see "Art and the Sixth Sense" by Philip Rahv, *Partisan Review,* vol.

IX, no. 2 (March-April, 1952), pp. 225-233. The "sixth sense" is the historical imagination.

LONGINUS AND THE "NEW CRITICISM"

[1] T. R. Henn: *Longinus and English Criticism* (Cambridge, 1934); and Samuel H. Monk: *The Sublime: A Study of Critical Theories in XVIII-Century England* (New York, 1935).

[2] With the exception of a few phrases I quote throughout from the translation by Frank Granger (London, 1935), which seems to me the most perspicuous English version. The exceptions are the result of a collation of the Granger and other versions with what is probably the definitive scholarly translation, by W. Rhys Roberts (Cambridge, 1899). All the modern translations render ὕψος as "sublime," and it has obviously been necessary to keep the word when it occurs in a quoted passage.

[3] I have inserted here W. Rhys Roberts' translation of καθ' ὑπεναντιώσεις because it conveys more accurately the force of the Greek, which means *opposite feelings* rather than "at variance within," as Granger has it.

[4] Roberts has it "a concourse of passions," which is more accurate. The Greek ἵνα μὴ ἕν τι περὶ αὐτὴν πάθος φαίνηται, παθῶν δὲ σύνοδος is literally a "coming together of roads," a crossroads; so better perhaps than either "their whole company" or a "concourse of passions" are the renditions "a clash of feelings," "a crossing of feelings."

[5] Mr. John Crowe Ransom made this observation in "A Poem Nearly Anonymous," *The World's Body* (New York, 1938), pp. 1-28.

A READING OF KEATS

[1] The value of Professor Thorpe's book is somewhat diminished by the instability of his critical terms; but as a rounded descriptive study it is excellent. I have not put Mr. Murry's *Keats and Shakespeare* (New York, 1926) in this list because I find its main argument incomprehensible; though the book is valuable for many brilliant insights.

[2] Quotations from the poems follow Garrod, *The Poetical Works of John Keats* (Oxford, 1939).

[3] Sidney Colvin, *John Keats* (New York, 1917), p. 419.

[4] Brooks, Cleanth, and Robert Penn Warren, *Understanding Poetry* (New York, 1938), pp. 409-415.

[5] Kenneth Burke, "Symbolic Action in a Poem by Keats," *Accent*, vol. IV, No. 1 (Autumn, 1943), p. 42.

[6] *The Well Wrought Urn* (New York, 1947), pp. 139-152.

[7] I am indebted to a note by Colvin (*op. cit.,* p. 549) for the hint which led me to this bitter confession. It appears in *The Complete Works of John Keats,* ed. by H. B. Forman (New York, 1932), iii, p. 268.

[8] Modern readers will find the passage in the edition of Dell and Jordan-Smith, p. 620 (New York, 1927).

YEATS' ROMANTICISM

[1] This paper was written for the special Yeats number of *The Southern Review,* vol. VII, no. 3 (Winter, 1942).

A NOTE ON DONNE

[1] *A Garland for John Donne, 1631-1931,* edited by Theodore Spencer (Cambridge, 1931).

[2] Or the still more recent and more pretentious novelty, Existentialism.

A NOTE ON ELIZABETHAN SATIRE

[1] See T. K. Whipple, *Martial and the English Epigram from Sir Thomas Wyat to Ben Jonson* (Berkeley, 1929); and Evelyn M. Simpson, "Paradoxes and Problems," in *A Garland for John Donne* (Cambridge, 1931).

EZRA POUND AND THE BOLLINGEN PRIZE

[1] The first award of the Bollingen Prize was made in 1949 to Ezra Pound for *The Pisan Cantos,* published in 1948; but the prize was voted to him in November 1948 by the Fellows in American Letters of The Library of Congress, who were then the jury of award. I was a member of the jury. Since 1950 the Bollingen Prize has been given under the auspices of the Library of Yale University.

[2] "Ezra Pound," pp. 257-63 above.

JOHN PEALE BISHOP

[1] Bishop's first book, *Green Fruit,* a collection of undergraduate verse, appeared in 1917. See *The Collected Poems of John Peale*

Bishop (New York, 1948). Bishop was born in 1892 and died in 1944.

[2] "Poets Without Laurels," first published in 1935; reprinted in *The World's Body* (New York, 1938), pp. 55-75.

[3] "Is Verse a Dying Technique?" *The Triple Thinkers* (New York, 1948), pp. 20-41.

EDWIN ARLINGTON ROBINSON

[1] Mr. Robinson died on April 5, 1935.

[2] Edwin Arlington Robinson, *Talifer* (New York, 1932).

HART CRANE

[1] It is now known that this poem is an elaboration of a "sonnet" entitled "Conduct" by Samuel Greenberg. See *Poems* by Samuel Greenberg, edited by Harold Holden and Jack McManis (New York, 1947).

CRANE: THE POET AS HERO

[1] *The Letters of Hart Crane, 1916-1932*, ed. by Brom Weber (New York, 1952).

[2] *Hart Crane, The Life of an American Poet* (New York, 1937).

THE PROFESSION OF LETTERS IN THE SOUTH

[1] John Crowe Ransom, "Modern with a Southern Accent," *The Virginia Quarterly Review*, April, 1935.

THE NEW PROVINCIALISM

[1] The present essay was written for the twentieth anniversary of *The Virginia Quarterly Review*, April, 1945.